Judson Dance Theater

Judson Dance Theater takes a fresh look at the radical, experimental dance presented during the early 1960s at Judson Memorial Church in downtown Manhattan.

Ramsay Burt explores the new artistic agenda set by Trisha Brown, Steve Paxton, Yvonne Rainer, and their fellow dancers, putting it in the context of developments in the visual arts. As well as following their subsequent careers, he traces how the ideas they proposed about the body and performative presence contributed to the development of experimental dance in Europe, for example in the work of Pina Bausch, Anne Teresa De Keersmaeker, and Jérôme Bel.

Informed by recent work in dance studies and art history, this book is, without doubt, the finest assessment of the period so far and will appeal to students of dance history, theory, and practice, as well as anyone interested in the avant-garde arts.

Ramsay Burt is Professor of Dance History at De Montfort University. His publications include *The Male Dancer* (1995), *Alien Bodies* (1997), and, with Professor Susan Foster, he is founder editor of *Discourses in Dance*.

Judson Dance Theater
Performative traces

Ramsay Burt

Routledge
Taylor & Francis Group

LONDON AND NEW YORK

First published 2006
by Routledge
2 Park Square, Milton Park, Abingdon, Oxon OX14 4RN

Simultaneously published in the USA and Canada
by Routledge
270 Madison Avenue, New York, NY 10016

Routledge is an imprint of the Taylor & Francis Group, an informa business

© 2006 Ramsay Burt

Typeset in Baskerville by
Florence Production Ltd, Stoodleigh, Devon
Printed and bound in Great Britain by
Antony Rowe Ltd, Chippenham, Wiltshire

British Library Cataloguing in Publication Data
A catalogue record for this book is available from the British Library

Library of Congress Cataloging in Publication Data
Burt, Ramsay, 1953–
    Judson Dance Theater: performative traces/Ramsay Burt
        p. cm.
    Includes bibliographical references.
    1. Judson Dance Theater – History.   2. Modern dance.   I. Title.
    GV1786.J82 B87
    792.809747'1–dc22   2006003845

ISBN10: 0–415–97573–5 (hbk)
ISBN10: 0–415–97574–3 (pbk)
ISBN10: 0–203–96966–9 (ebk)

ISBN13: 978–0–415–97573–5 (hbk)
ISBN13: 978–0–415–97574–3 (pbk)
ISBN13: 978–0–203–96966–3 (ebk)

For Nicholas Zurbrugg
1947–2001

Contents

Illustrations

Acknowledgements

Institutions have played an important part in enabling me to write this book. It is the second book I have written while I have been Senior Research Fellow at De Montfort University. As a result of this fellowship I have been able to write without the distractions of a normal university lecturer's teaching load. At a crucial stage, I was Visiting Professor and Visiting Scholar at the Department of Performance Studies at New York University, enabling me to spend over half a year in downtown Manhattan meeting many people about whom I was writing, going to libraries, and experiencing for a while living in New York. The end of this stay was made possible with funds from the British Arts and Humanities Research Council. I have relied heavily on the library at De Montfort and on the Dance Collection of the New York Public Library which I have haunted every time I could find an excuse (and the money) for a trip to New York. I have been very grateful for opportunities to speak about Judson Dance Theater, where I have been able to try out material for this book. These include invitations from: University of Copenhagen; University of Stockholm; Collège Internationale de Philosophie; Paris; University of Ljubljana; University of Antwerp; and the University of Rio de Janeiro.

I would particularly like to thank Richard Carlin for his support of this project, and many friends who have helped me in a number of ways with this book over the five years it has taken to write. Valerie Briginshaw deserves special mention for reading every chapter, sometimes in more than one draft and giving me invaluable feedback and encouragement. I would also like to thank friends and colleagues including Michael Huxley, Jayne Stevens, Jo Breslin, Martin Hargreaves, Sally Doughty, Kerry Francksen-Kelly, Theresa Buckland, Sally Luxton, Christy Adair, Dee Reynolds, Bojana Kunst, Karen Vedel, Inge Damsholt, Maaike Bleeker, Luk Van den Dries, Claire Rousier, and Christophe Wavelet, and on the other side of the Atlantic to Susan Foster, Barbara Browning, Richard Schechner, Carol Martin, Peggy Phelan, Diana Taylor, Allen Weiss,

André Lepecki, Douglas Dunn, Deborah Jowitt, Marcia Siegel, Nancy Duncan, Diane Torr, David Vaughan, George Dorris, Don McDonagh, and Vincent Warren. I am also grateful to members of the Corporeality and Choreography working group of the International Federation for Theatre Research (IFTR/FIRT) who have read or heard and discussed various bits of the book at various stages: Ann Cooper Albright, Emilyn Claid, Sarah Cordova, Heili Einasto, Rachel Fensham, Tommy DeFrantz, Isabel Ginot, Lena Hammergren, Jacqueline Shea Murphy, Janet O'Shay, Phillipa Rothfield, Christel Stalpaert, and Myriam Van Imschoot. I should also like to thank artists and writers whose work I have analysed, and who have allowed me to interview them: Trisha Brown, Yvonne Rainer, Steve Paxton, Carolee Schneemann, Jill Johnston, David Behrman, Lea Anderson, Felix Ruckert, and Boris Charmatz.

1 Introduction

Transatlantic crossings

In September 1985 a small incident occurred in Montréal during the first Festival International de Nouvelle Danse which participants have probably long since forgotten. During the same week, Merce Cunningham, Pina Bausch, Trisha Brown, and Anne Teresa de Keersmaeker were all presenting work in the festival and they, together with members of their dance companies, were all staying in the same hotel at the same time. One evening, the dancer Dena Davida, who runs Montréal's experimental dance centre Tangente and was one of the organizers of the festival, was sitting in the hotel coffee shop talking to Trisha Brown and Stephen Petronio (who was still at that time dancing with Brown). Davida commented that Pina Bausch and a few of her dancers were sitting at the next table. When Brown said she knew of Bausch's work but had not met her, Davida introduced them to one another and gradually members of different dance companies started to talk together.[1]

This chance meeting is the starting point for a book about Judson Dance Theater and its legacy because it represents a meeting of innovative dance artists from Europe and the US and raises questions about what they had in common. To anyone outside dance circles, such a meeting of leading international dance company directors might not seem remarkable, but within the English-speaking dance world, Brown and Bausch are almost set up as paradigmatic opposites where innovative dance practice is concerned. Brown, for many scholars and critics in the US, is seen as someone who is constantly refining her search for new, abstract ways of structuring pure, abstract dance. She is, perhaps, the founder member of Judson Dance Theater who appears to have made the most consistent and continuous choreographic development. For many of the same critics and commentators, however, Bausch is a bogey figure who seems to attack the very idea of dance which, in their view, Brown exemplifies. This book argues that innovative dance artists on each side of the Atlantic over the last forty years have had more in common with one another than most existing dance literature about them to date has suggested.

Antipathy towards Bausch's work was evident in press reactions when a few weeks later Bausch's company, Tanztheater Wuppertal, performed at the Brooklyn Academy of Music in New York as part of a festival of new German work. There they performed Bausch's 1984 piece *Auf dem Gebirge hat man ein Geschrei gehört* (*On the Mountain a Cry Was Heard*). One moment in particular upset some audience members. In this, Josephine Ann Endicott repeatedly went down on all fours, pulled up her dress to bare her back; a man then marked a line on her with lipstick so that her back became inexorably crosshatched in red.[2] The festival included a symposium on German *tanztheater* that was held at the New York Goethe Institute in November 1985. During this some American critics expressed incomprehension and condemnation of Bausch's work. Moments such as the one described above provoked criticism that Bausch didn't appear to be obviously critical of violence against women, and one participant complained that Bausch's unrelieved and undeveloping repetitiousness seemed senseless (in Daly 1986).[3] Anna Kisselgoff stated: 'We rarely see pure dance coming out of West Germany [as it was then]. There must be some reason why there are directions being taken in America and Germany that are so opposite.' Turning to Jochen Schmidt, she asked: 'Do you feel that formal concerns are of no interest to German choreographers?' to which Schmidt replied that he thought there was a lot of form in Bausch's work (ibid.: 47–8). As Johannes Birringer observed, when Kisselgoff 'asked Bausch whether she would be interested in working only with "pure form" and without the need to express feelings, the choreographer probably didn't even understand the question' (Birringer 1986: 85). How many of those who criticized Bausch in 1985 for her reportedly un-American-looking work acknowledged that she had trained in New York at the start of the 1960s, performing at the time not only in work by Antony Tudor and Paul Taylor, but also in more experimental pieces by Paul Sanasardo and Donya Feuer?[4] Although Trisha Brown's work was not mentioned in these discussions, the implication of Kisselgoff's position was that whereas choreographers such as Brown, who deal with movement in an abstract way, could fit into a formalist, modernist account of the progressive development of an implicitly American tradition of pure dance, Bausch's supposed expressionism, in comparison, was anachronistic. To many in the symposium her work seemed derivative of issues that had already been addressed by the now old-fashioned American modern dance.[5]

What I believe Bausch and Brown have in common is the way that they both, in effect, offer a similar challenge to the sorts of ideas about 'pure dance' that Kisselgoff articulated in 1985, by framing the materiality of the dancing body in ways that force the spectator to acknowledge the materiality of the bodies of their dancers. In doing so, they contradict conventional aesthetic expectations. Such challenges are a major theme in this book. While Brown can be seen to do this through her deep research into the roots of motor functioning, Bausch uses a more Laban-based approach to space and effort along with mimetic and dramaturgical devices including repetitions of sometimes painful actions; but both use improvisation as a key part of their choreographic process. Each, in different ways, has presented challenges to their audiences to abandon naturalized and automated ways of viewing dance performances. Brown's description of her 1970 piece *Man Walking Down the Side of a Building* exemplifies the way her work has critiqued conventional ideas about what dance is:

> *Man Walking Down the Side of a Building* was exactly like the title – seven stories. A natural activity under the stress of an unnatural setting. Gravity reneged. Vast scale. Clear order. You start at the top, walk straight down, stop at the bottom. All those soupy questions that arise in the process of selecting abstract movement according to the modern dance tradition – what, when, where and how – are solved in collaboration between choreographer and place. If you eliminate all those eccentric possibilities that the choreographic imagination can conjure up and just have a person walk down an aisle, then you see movement as activity.
>
> (in Livet 1978: 51)

An avoidance of the eccentric possibilities and soupy questions inherent in the modern dance aesthetic permits the performer to realize, and the spectator to perceive, the clarity and directness of movement as unembellished activity, and the dancer's actual weight and physicality. Around the time Brown said this in 1978, Pina Bausch expressed a similar distaste for existing dance, and with it a need for new ways of moving, in an interview with Jochen Schmidt: 'I'm always trying. I keep desperately trying to dance. I'm always hoping I'm going to find new ways of relating to movement. I can't go on working in the previous way. It would be like repeating something, something strange' (in Servos 1984: 230). When Schmidt asked her whether she therefore needed to use words in her pieces, Bausch replied:

> It is simply a question of when is it dance, when is it not. Where does it start? When do we call it dance? It does in fact have something to

do with consciousness, with bodily consciousness, and the way we form things. But then it needn't have this kind of aesthetic form. It can have quite a different form and still be dance.

(ibid.)

Bausch's need to find new ways of relating to dance parallels Brown's need to move away from the soupy problems of the modern dance tradition. Both dance artists were articulating the difficulties that came between them and how they wanted to dance, and both, in an avant-garde way, were exercising the right to refuse to comply with existing ways of doing this. Here, then, in their different searches for new movement possibilities, is a point of comparison between Bausch and Brown, whose chance meeting in Montréal is the starting point for this book. It is not my intention here to minimize the evident differences between works by Bausch and Brown, merely to point out that on a conceptual level both were creating work that set comparable challenges to audiences to abandon conventional expectations and develop new structures of perception. Both dance artists identified the body and bodily consciousness as the site at which to try to find something that offers liberation from good old or bad old ways. For Brown they were unequivocally bad old ways and she wanted to move on. Bausch, too, was motivated by a need to move on but the fact that she called her attempt desperate indicates her concern about the loss of what had previously appeared to be certainties.

To create and present work that does not conform to the known and familiar but challenges audiences can have negative consequences. Not only did some audience members walk out of performances by Tanztheater Wuppertal at Brooklyn Academy of Music in 1985, but, as Josephine Ann Endicott (1999) has recalled, some members of the German audience during the first few years at Wuppertal reacted just as negatively. Brown has written about the need to be prepared to make work that challenges audiences:

The result of choreography that goes beyond what the audience is familiar with is that you find out what you can do, and what your own personal limitation edges are. In that arises the possibility of doing that which is not interesting to your audience, not up until now thought of as acceptable to an audience. There is also a question of the tension in the relationship between an audience and a performer.

(Brown 1978: 45–6)

Referring to this tension, Brown has spoken of her feelings of vulnerability and exposure when performing the spare, minimal movements of her choreography during the early 1970s. She has told Marianne Goldberg that, although at that time she was working towards 'objectivity in movement ... I remember feeling emotion and internal commotion while performing those early deductive, systematized, withheld pieces' (Goldberg 1991: 6). Susan Sontag has observed:

> The view that dance should not express emotion does not, of course, mean to be against emotion. Valéry defined the poem as a machine whose function is to create a distinctively poetic feeling: it does not 'express' emotion, it is a method for creating it.
>
> (Sontag 1983: 103)

So, to expand on Birringer's point mentioned earlier, the idea that either Bausch or Brown could separate feeling from form is surely mistaken.

Modernist dance theory and postmodern dance

To find such common ground between European and American dance is to depart radically from the view of postmodern dance developed by Sally Banes. In her view postmodern dance was a 'largely United States phenomenon' (Banes 1987: xxxvi), American choreographers having made their breakthrough by 'reacting against the expressionism of modern dance which anchored movement to a literary idea or a musical form' (Banes 1980: 15). This was something that, in Banes's view, Pina Bausch failed to do. For Banes, Bausch's work was 'expressionist rather than analytical' and seemed 'more influenced by imagistic avant-garde theatre than by either German or American dance traditions' (1987: xxxvi). Either Banes was unaware of the influence of Jooss and Tudor on Bausch's work, and of her time with Taylor, Sanasardo, and Feuer, or she couldn't understand its relevance to Bausch's choreography. In order to trace the development of radical, experimental dance on both sides of the Atlantic, I have to disagree with Banes's assessment of Bausch's work, and challenge beliefs about the separateness and exclusivity of postmodern dance in the United States.

Sally Banes's work on American dance since 1960 is enormously important and has been highly influential. My work in this book would not have been possible without it. Her 1980 book *Terpsichore in Sneakers: Post-Modern Dance*, about Yvonne Rainer, Trisha Brown, Steve Paxton and others associated with Judson Dance Theater, was a key work in the development of dance studies as an academic discipline. Although Banes may not be the only scholar to have written about postmodern dance,[6] she has written at greater length and in more detail than anyone else. Her first book, which defined the terms in which American postmodern dance is still discussed, has been followed by five others. Banes has not only provided invaluable, detailed information about key choreographers of the 1960s and 1970s but shifted discussions of dance history from artist- or company-centred critical studies to discussions of theoretical aspects of contemporary dance practice. Banes developed a framework for discussing theatre dance by drawing on art theory. There were particularly close connections in the 1960s between experimental dance and radical developments in the other arts, particularly the visual arts, and between dancers and visual artists within Judson Dance Theater. In developing her theoretical framework for discussing postmodern dance, Banes drew on the view of modernist painting and sculpture proposed by the extremely influential art critic Clement Greenberg (1909–94) and subsequently developed by the art historian Michael Fried. She was neither the first, nor the only, dance scholar to do this. David Michael Levin (1973), Noël Carroll (1981, 2003), Marshall Cohen (1981), and Roger Copeland (e.g. 1983, 1985) have developed modernist accounts of contemporary dance along similar lines; however, Banes has provided the most thorough and comprehensive account. In doing so, she has introduced many of the issues and themes that inform my discussion in the present book. Because of this, it is necessary to consider her ideas about modernism and postmodernism here in some detail.

In retrospect it is now possible to see that although Greenberg's ideas were dominant during the 1960s, there were a number of other ideas about the nature of modernist art circulating among the visual artists whose work was closest to that of the dancers in Judson Dance Theater. There were, indeed, substantial disagreements with Greenberg's views. Art Historian Jack Flam, writing in the mid-1990s, proposed:

> It now seems clear that Greenberg's definition of modernism was not in fact synonymous with the practices of the artists whom we associate with the greater part of the history of modernist art, but is rather a historically determined response to them – and one that is no longer especially useful.
>
> (Flam 1996: xxv)

This was not, however, as evident when Banes and her peers were writing twenty years earlier. It is from Greenberg's view of the formal purity of the abstract painting produced by members of the New York School that these scholars developed a notion of pure dance. This, I propose, has created an unhelpful barrier to appreciating commonalities and correlations between innovative dance in Europe and the United States during the last forty years.

Clement Greenberg wrote in the 1960s that the task of modernism was to:

> eliminate from the effects of each art any and every effect that might conceivably be borrowed from or by the medium of any other art. Thereby each art would be rendered 'pure', and in its 'purity' find the guarantee of its standards of quality as well as of its independence.
>
> (Greenberg 1982: 5–6)

Banes believed that it was only during the 1960s that innovative American dance artists began to explore these modernist aesthetic concerns but, perhaps confusingly, she called the work they produced postmodern dance. By emphasizing only one aspect, formal radicalism, as though it were driving artistic development, Banes developed a critical model that not only allowed her to analyse modern choreography in detail but also to propose a systematic history of postmodern dance in which developments were internally motivated and entirely independent of any social and historical context. Hence, the initial 'breakthrough' of Judson Dance Theater in the 1960s was followed in the 1970s by 'analytical postmodernism' and 'metaphorical and metaphysical postmodernism', and then in the 1980s by a 'rebirth of content' (Banes 1987: xv–xxiv).

In her new introduction to the 1987 edition of *Terpsichore in Sneakers*, Banes wrote that:

> In the visual-art world and in theatre, a number of critics have used the term [postmodern] to refer to artworks that are copies of or comments on other artworks, challenging values of originality, authenticity, and the masterpiece and provoking Derridean theories of simulacra. This notion fits some post-modern dances but not all.
>
> (Banes 1987: xiv)

To unpack this a little, it was Barthes and Foucault who questioned the role and function of the author. Baudrillard proposed that simulacra – copies without originals – were characteristic of postmodern, media-saturated culture, while Derrida problematized the idea that the author's presence is there in the writing, suggesting that it is undecidably both present and absent or, in his term, 'spectral'.[7] Following Peggy Phelan's essay 'The ontology of performance' (1993), some dance scholars have

discussed the performative presence and absence of dancers within innovative American works from the 1960s as well as dances made by both
American and European choreographers in the 1990s and 2000s.[8] Far
from accepting a poststructuralist theorization of postmodern dance,
Banes backed away from discussions of dance and postmodernism as
such and turned instead to the nature of modernist dance:

> In dance, [she wrote,] the confusion the term 'post-modern' creates
> is further complicated by the fact that historical modern dance was
> never really modernist. Often it has been precisely in the arena of
> post-modern dance that issues of modernism in the other arts
> have arisen: the acknowledgement of the medium's materials, the
> revealing of dance's essential qualities as an art form, the separa-
> tion of external references as subjects. Thus in many respects it is
> post-modern dance that functions as modernist art.
>
> (1987: xiv–xv)

For Banes, dance was progressing through similar aesthetic paradigms
as the other arts but not at the same time. This is to see its development as internally motivated and independent of any social or historical
context.

Susan Manning, in what became known as the 'Terpsichore in combat
boots' debate in *TDR*, argued that in this passage Banes was 'attributing
to only one generation of 20th-century choreographers a set of formal
concerns shared by other generations as well' (Manning 1988: 34).
Manning pointed out that the claims that Banes made for postmodern
dance echoed those made in the 1930s by John Martin and Lincoln
Kirstein. She quoted a statement that Martin made in 1939 about the
modernism of Mary Wigman's dances which closely corresponds to
Banes's definition of modernist dance:

> With Wigman, [Martin wrote] the dance stands for the first time
> fully revealed in its own sphere; it is not story telling or pantomime
> or moving sculpture or design in space or acrobatic virtuosity or
> musical illustration, but dance alone, an autonomous art exempli-
> fying fully the ideals of modernism in its attainment of abstraction
> and in its utilization of the resources of its materials efficiently and
> with authority.
>
> (Martin 1968: 235)

Martin claimed that Wigman revealed these ideals for the first time so
that her work represented a breakthrough and created a new paradigm.

Banes made the same kind of claim for Yvonne Rainer's *Trio A*: 'The history of dance theory,' she wrote, 'has been the repeated conflict between those who value technique and those who value expression. With *Trio A* this cycle is at last broken. It is not simply a new style of dance, but a new meaning and function, a new definition' (Banes 1980: 49). So, for Banes, *Trio A* exemplified the way in which postmodern dance superseded previous ways of thinking about dance by shifting from questions of style to an entirely new conceptual level. But isn't this, in effect, what Martin had suggested back in 1933 in his famous statement that 'The Modern Dance is not a system but a point of view' (Martin 1965: 20)? Wasn't Banes merely arguing that the new, minimalist point of view exemplified in works such as *Trio A* was just a newer point of view than that exemplified by the works Martin was writing about in the 1930s? If we accept that there is a difference between the expressionism of early modern dance and the anti-expressive dances of Rainer, Brown, and their peers, a Greenbergian account of modernism fails to account for it, just as it also fails to recognize any difference between early modern dance and Bausch's *tanztheater*. The root of the problem is the modernist idea of 'pure dance'.

For Martin a breakthrough was achieved by abandoning the external references that characterized the nineteenth-century ballet tradition. I have already noted that, for Banes, postmodern dancers made their breakthrough by reacting against the expressionism of modern dance. Whether or not one accepts these statements, Banes and Martin both believed that formally pure, abstract dance was more sophisticated than the representational types of dance that each believed their chosen dancer was reacting against. But, as the art historian Meyer Shapiro has pointed out, this view of abstraction is based on a mistaken belief 'that representation is a passive mirroring of things and therefore essentially non-artistic; and that abstract art on the other hand is a purely aesthetic activity, unconditioned by objects and based on its own internal laws'. Shapiro, however, argued that 'all art is representational. There is no "pure art" unconditioned by experience' (Shapiro 1978: 196). For the same reasons there is surely no 'pure dance' uncontaminated by its social and political context. Susan Manning observed in her response to the 1987 edition of *Terpsichore in Sneakers* that an exclusive emphasis on the formal aspects of modernist dance has 'deflected attention away from the sociological and ideological dimensions of modernism' (Manning 1988: 37). When she pointed out that issues of 'nationalism, feminism, and male liberation ... rarely appear in the literature on twentieth-century dance' (ibid.), Manning was indicating the principal concerns that would inform her own work on Wigman and more recently on gay and African American dancers in the 1930s and 1940s.[9] The implications of Manning's critique for postmodern rather than modern dance remain largely undeveloped.

Despite advocating a formalist, modernist view of postmodern dance, Banes has sometimes written about representational material; but the works she seems to value most highly, such as Rainer's *Trio A* and Brown's *Accumulation* pieces, were abstract. Banes appeared to believe that the artistic possibilities of representational dance were exhausted and that the most important dancers in the 1960s were moving towards 'pure dance'. Greenberg and Fried argued that artistic progress is independent of social and political factors and artistic value can only be guaranteed when artists are unaffected by, and disengaged from, the social and political context in which they are working. In her early writings Banes subscribed to this view. However, at the start of her later book, *Greenwich Village 1963*, she argued that, in 1963, 'the arts seemed to hold a privileged place in [the American Dream of freedom, equality and abundance] not merely as a reflection of a vibrant, rejuvenated American society, but as an active register of contemporary consciousness – as its product, but also as its catalyst' (Banes 1993: 3). While Banes therefore saw art as a reflection of the spirit of its age, she still subscribed to the modernist paradigm of art's steady progress towards a goal of formally pure abstraction. Progress in the arts, in her view, catalyses social progress, but only through affirmation. She therefore argued that the work of Judson Dance Theater was entirely affirmative in relation to US society in the 1960s:

> the arts suddenly seemed freshly empowered . . . to provide a means for – indeed, to embody – *democracy*. The early Sixties avant-garde artists did not aim to passively mirror the society they lived in; they tried to change it by producing a new culture.
>
> (ibid.: 10, emphasis in original)

The title of Banes's most recent collection *Reinventing Dance in the Sixties: Everything Was Possible* (2003) exemplifies this affirmative view. But if the dancers associated with Judson Dance Theater believed that everything was possible, under what conditions did they believe that these possibilities might be realized? As avant-garde artists, they shared a utopian vision of a more equitable and just society to come. It is, of course, a characteristic of all avant-garde groups that their romantic idealism always seems naive in retrospect. In so far as the reality of the present fails to live up to the promise of a possible future, avant-garde groups naively defend their vision from obstacles to its realization. There is no room in Banes's affirmative account of artists' agency and empowerment for any limitation caused by social or ideological factors. But there is surely always a critical, negative aspect to avant-garde work. Avant-garde attacks on art are an attack on the only institution over which artists have any influence. But in attacking art as an institution, their attitude towards institutions in general is made clear. Whereas Banes believed the new dance of the 1960s embodied democracy, it would be more appropriate to describe the dancers as anarchic. Writing in 1968, Jill Johnston saw the new dance in this way:

> Every underground movement is a revolt against one authority or another. The dance underground of the sixties is more than this natural child–parent affair. The new choreographers are outrageously invalidating the very nature of authority. The thinking behind the work goes beyond democracy into anarchy. No member outstanding. No body necessarily more beautiful than any other body. No movement necessarily more important or more beautiful than any other movement.
>
> (Johnston 1998: 117)

The three No's with which this passage concludes echo the much longer list of No's that Rainer issued in a well-known, polemic statement from 1965 that begins 'NO to spectacle' in which Rainer defined 'an area of concern for me in relation to dance, but existing as a very large NO to many facts in the theatre today' (Rainer 1974: 51). Where these dancers said no to aspects of the mainstream dance of the day, they were not affirming the values of a vibrant, rejuvenated society but criticizing its failures and shortcomings. Rainer, herself, in a panel discussion in 1986, said that she still clung to

> the somewhat romantic ideas of the avant-garde that launched my own creative efforts: ideas about marginality, intervention, an adversative subculture, a confrontation with the complacent past, the art of resistance, etc. Of course, these ideas must be constantly reassessed in terms of class, gender, and race.
>
> (Jayamanne, Kapur, Rainer 1987: 46–7)

The art historians Fred Orton and Griselda Pollock have argued that, where American artists considered themselves to be part of the avant-garde, they constructed 'an identity for themselves that was simultaneously in opposition to, and an extension of, available American and European traditions' (Orton and Pollock 1985: 108).[10] It is this oppositional, critical aspect of the avant-garde dance of the 1960s which, in my view, Banes has underestimated.

The way Banes has used the term avant-garde appears not to carry the adversarial ideas Rainer herself associated with it. Whereas Susan Sontag called the dancers involved with Judson Dance Theater 'neo-Duchampian' and 'Dadaistic' (Sontag 1983: 100, 108), for Banes, postmodern dance was not anti-dance as such. Banes argued that:

> Post-modern dance came after modern dance (hence post-) and, like the post-modernism of the other arts, was anti-modern dance. Since 'modern' in dance did not mean modernist, to be anti-modern dance was not at all to be anti-modernist. In fact it was quite the opposite. The analytical postmodern dance of the seventies in particular displayed these modernist preoccupations and it aligned itself with that consummately modernist visual art, minimalist sculpture.
>
> (Banes 1987: xv)

Not only was Banes wrong in believing that the modern dance of the 1920s and 1930s was not modernist, but she was equally mistaken about minimal art. The minimalist approach to formalist abstraction was more avant-garde than modernist. Greenberg and Fried both therefore saw minimalism as an assault on the values they felt modernist art exemplified. In a well-known essay, Michael Fried argued that minimal sculpture by Robert Morris and Donald Judd represented a deviation from Greenbergian modernist concerns because it positioned its viewers in such a way that they became aware of the presence of the sculpture and of their own embodied, phenomenological relationship to it. This, he argued, was a theatrical situation that was antithetical to the process of aesthetic appreciation as he believed it to be. Minimalist sculpture, in Fried's view, by generating presence makes a demand on the spectator to recognize it as art whereas a true work of art, in his view, is complete in itself. For Fried and Greenberg, aesthetic appreciation of painting and sculpture was an instantaneous process. Fried was particularly critical of Robert Morris's proposition that the experience of perceiving his sculpture was not instantaneous but durational (see Fried 1969: 144). I discuss this further in Chapter 3. Although dance is a time-based art, it is often assumed that aesthetic appreciation of dance as art is also an instantaneous process. Thus Maxine Sheets-Johnstone (1966), following Susanne Langer, argued that one appreciates dance forms in an immediate and pre-reflective way. Doris Humphrey, referring in her checklist for choreographers to the relationship between dance and music, advised that the eye is faster than the ear (Humphrey 1959: 159).

Yvonne Rainer, however, like Morris, stressed duration when discussing her dances. Writing about her 1965 work *Parts of Some Sextets*, she drew attention to 'its length, its relentless repetition, its inconsequential ebb and flow [which] all combine together to produce an effect of nothing happening' (Rainer 1974: 51). Discussing *Trio A*, she pointed out that it was designed to emphasize 'the actual time it takes the actual weight of the body to go through the prescribed motions' (ibid.: 67). It is these demands – that the spectator take time to see a minimalist work and recognize its presence – that Fried called theatrical. This led him to make the much cited assertion that: 'The success, even the survival, of the arts has come increasingly to depend on their ability to defeat theatre' (Fried 1969: 139). The work presented at Judson Memorial Church in the early 1960s, and the 1970s work which Banes called analytical post-modern dance generated a kind of presence that was surely, in Fried's terms, theatrical.

Performance and embodied experience

In Fried's view, the object-like qualities of minimalist sculptures made the spectator aware of their embodied relation to the sculptural object. When the new dance created situations that drew the spectator's attention to the materiality of their dancing bodies, it did so in ways which, in Fried's terms, were 'theatrical'. What Rainer called the problem of performance (Rainer 1974: 67) and dancers' stage presence were topics of discussion among dancers within Judson Dance Theater. Trisha Brown, for example, felt in the early 1960s that modern dancers 'glazed over their eyes, knuckling down behind the gaze to concentrate and deliver their best performance . . . resulting in the robot-look' (Brown 1978: 48). This rigid-ified, performative presence was quite different from the way dancers at Judson, in Brown's view, reconnected with their audience:

> At Judson, the performers looked at each other and the audience, they breathed audibly, ran out of breath, sweated, talked things over. They began behaving more like human beings, revealing what was thought of as deficiencies as well as their skills.
>
> (ibid.)

(The same could be said of Pina Bausch's dancers.) Brown was articu-lating an avant-garde view here, one in which artists attack the elitism of high art in order to reconnect with ordinary people's everyday experi-ence. Calvin Tomkins, writing in 1968 about the work of Duchamp, Cage, Cunningham, Rauschenberg, and Tingley, argued that: 'What they have consistently tried to do is to break down the barriers that exist between art and life and not for art's sake either' (Tomkins 1968: 2). This was surely what Brown, who appeared in many of Rauschenberg's dance pieces during the 1960s, believed she and her fellow dancers were doing during performances at Judson Memorial Church.

The particular kinds of spectatorship produced by innovative dance performances opened up new possibilities for meaningfulness. The way experimental dance performances have positioned spectators by making them actively read works and appreciate them from particular, embodied points of view is a recurring theme throughout this book. For Brown, the practice of improvisation played an important role in the early 1960s in changing the relationship between dancers and spectators.

> There is a performance quality, that appears in improvisation that did not in memorized dance as it was known up to that date. If you are improvising within a structure your senses are heightened; you are using your wits, thinking, everything is working at once to find the best solution to a given problem under pressure of a viewing audience.
>
> (Brown 1978: 48).

In other words, improvisation made the spectator aware of what might be called the performer's bodily intelligence. Many of the dancers who attended composition classes taught by Robert and Judith Dunn used chance, indeterminacy, and task-based methods for creating movement material and structuring choreography. These classes were largely based on the ideas of Merce Cunningham and John Cage, neither of whom used improvisation or valued it. Nevertheless, some of the Judson dancers used improvisation. Brown, Simone Forti, and Rainer, as a result of working with Anna Halprin in San Francisco, improvised together in the early 1960s in New York. Forti and Brown were fortunate in that they started from a position of having less technical training to react against than most of their colleagues, and could therefore use improvisation as a means to find new and unprecedented ways of moving. As Brown herself observed in 1996 during an interview with Charles Reinhart, she was 'eternally grateful to Merce [Cunningham] for not having asked me to join his company. People mould themselves into the body of the person whose company it is. I had to find mine on my own' (Brown 1996). Brown evidently approached improvisation and movement research as positive means through which to rigorously develop her abilities as a professional dancer and dance maker. Brown and Forti were practising during the 1960s what Steve Paxton and others associated with contact improvisation began to practise in the 1970s.

It was during the late 1970s that Pina Bausch began posing questions to her company, to which they responded with short improvisations. Bausch's final pieces were assembled by setting material from these improvisations. Improvisation was, therefore, important at this time for the development of innovative dance in Europe and the US as a means for finding and elaborating new types of movement material and for devising new, more spontaneous kinds of performative presences. But it also led to the performance of work that challenged conventional ideas about the social and cultural meanings of the body and embodied experience. As Bryan S. Turner has observed:

> The Western tradition of the body has been conventionally shaped by Hellenized Christianity, for which the body was the seat of unreason, passion and desire. The contrast in philosophy between the mind and the body is in Christianity the opposition between spirit and flesh.
>
> (Turner 1984: 36)

This dualistic opposition is one that underpins the idea that the dancer has a feeling which the dancing body then expresses. Graham's generation of modern dancers in both Europe and North America had defined the modernity of their practice by saying that it was a living work of art presented through the human body as a means of expression (Wigman 1980: 35), that it worked from the inside out (Humphrey), and that dance movement never lied (Graham 1991: 20). Trisha Brown decisively rejected the dualism implicit in the notion that modern dance works from the inside out when she told Marianne Goldberg that:

> My inside is not a little bird fluttering in my chest – it is chockfull up and down the length of me. My inside comes all the way to the edge of my body, through the columns of my limbs, my neck, my torso, and the bulb of my head.
>
> (Goldberg 1991: 6)

This way of discussing embodied experience repudiated the Cartesian notion of the mind as the ghost in the body's machine. Like the practice of improvisation itself, it suggested that intelligence is not a purely intellectual or mental faculty but an attribute of the body–mind continuum.

Yvonne Rainer also demonstrated a desire to reclaim embodied agency from dualistic ways of thinking that posit a mind/body split when she gave an evening-length piece the title *The Mind is a Muscle*. Her programme note for the first full performance of this in 1968 asserted a materialist view of the dancing body through a characteristically polemical denunci-ation of most of what constituted the mainstream dance culture of the day: 'If my rage at the impoverishment of ideas, narcissism, and disguised sexual exhibitionism of most dancing can be considered puritan moral-izing, it is also true that I love the body – its actual weight, mass, and unenhanced physicality' (Rainer 1974: 69). As I will show in Chapter 3, Rainer's materialist way of thinking about the body was informed by a specifically American philosophical tradition of pragmatism and scepticism in the writings of C.S. Pierce, William James, and American behaviourists. These were also figures who influenced Robert Morris and Donald Judd whose work and writings Fried criticized. Rainer's pragmatic and sceptical critique of dominant, normative discourses of the dancing body can be seen as a starting point for reclaiming the body from traditional, dualistic ways of thinking.

Despite a minimalist reduction of representational elements, the new dance did not render the body neutral. The way in which Rainer's work acknowledged the body's materiality, I suggest, did precisely the oppo-site. In the *Stairs* section of *The Mind is a Body*, there was a moment when each of the three dancers walked up a small set of stairs they brought onto the stage. As each ascended, the other two 'helped'. Thus when Steve Paxton or David Gordon was on the stairs, someone behind inserted a hand between his legs and grabbed his crotch. When Rainer was on the stairs, the other two supported her torso by each placing a hand on one of her breasts (Rainer 1974: 81). In this case, reclaiming the body involved acknowledgement of its biological gender. While I believe it is a mistake to impute feminist aspirations to the work of Rainer, Brown, Childs or their female colleagues during the 1960s, works such as *The Mind is a Muscle*, through reclaiming the body from traditional dualistic ideologies, created the conditions of possibility for a future feminist practice. I will return to this in Chapters 3 and 4.[11] In her description of *Stairs*, Rainer discussed the problem the three performers had in deciding how to respond to being grabbed in this uncomfortable and embarrassing way. Rainer and Gordon decided to show a spontaneous emotional reaction while Paxton hid this by deliberately overreacting. Rather than being solely concerned with formal issues, members of Judson Dance Theater were concerned with the relation between their work and everyday experience.

Key to understanding the difference between the expressionism of early modern dance and the new anti-expressive dances of Rainer and her peers are differing approaches to the signifying properties of the dancing body. In rhetorical terms, expressionist dances presented the body in a metaphorical way while the new dance of the 1960s treated embodied experience metonymically.[12] Peggy Phelan's distinction between metaphor and metonymy is pertinent here:

> Metaphor works by securing a vertical hierarchy of value and is reproductive; it works by erasing dissimilarity and negating difference; it turns two into one. Metonymy is additive and associative; it works to secure a horizontal axis of contiguity and displacement. The kettle is boiling is a sentence which assumes that water is contiguous with the kettle. The point is not that the kettle is *like* water (as in the metaphorical love is like a rose), but rather that the kettle is boiling *because* the water inside the kettle is.
>
> (Phelan 1993: 150, emphasis in the original)

In early modern dance, the dancing body moved in ways which expressed the universality of feeling that transcended individual experience. Thus, for example, Martha Graham's *Lamentation* (1930) was not about an individual's grief at the loss of anyone or anything in particular, but about grief as an experience which everybody, supposedly, could recognize. In Phelan's terms, works such as this secured a vertical hierarchy of humanist values. The new dance of the 1960s eschewed transcendence by asserting the particularity of embodied experience – its actual weight, mass, and unenhanced physicality, as Rainer put it. Another example of a dance that presented the body's materiality in a way that was far from neutral was *Convalescent Dance*, a version of *Trio A* which Rainer performed while convalescing from major surgery. *Convalescent Dance* was presented during *Angry Arts Week* at Hunter College in January 1967, New York, as part of a series of art events protesting against the war in Vietnam. The piece did not express an emotional response to the war, but made an association between Rainer's frailty and the condition of soldiers wounded in action in Vietnam. Rainer did not stop being herself in order to become, metaphorically, a wounded soldier or to express the universal tragedy of war. Instead, *Convalescent Dance* signified metonymically through contiguity and displacement – the weakness of her body emblematizing, in a metonymic way, a soldier's injuries.

An objection could be made that *Convalescent Dance* was not a typical dance of the period because it was 'political'. As Susan Foster has observed, the category of 'political art' is often invented as a way of 'dismissing such art as insufficiently artistic' (Foster 2002: 248). I will return to the problem of 'political art' shortly. However, other dances from the period also presented a debilitated or uncomfortable body that could not be dismissed as merely political and hence insufficiently artistic. These include Rainer's *Stairs*, discussed earlier, and Paxton's *Intravenous Lecture* (1970), during which a doctor friend inserted a medical 'drip' into a vein in Paxton's arm from which salt solution proceeded to flow into his body while he lectured about the nature of performance. In each case the artists did not cease to be themselves in order to express an ideal metaphorically, but their performance troubled such ideals by drawing attention to bodily discomfort. Phelan has argued that:

> In moving from the grammar of words to the grammar of the body, one moves from the realm of metaphor to the realm of metonymy. For performance art itself however, the referent is always the agonizingly relevant body of the performer.
>
> (Phelan 1993: 150)

As in performance art, the referents in *Convalescent Dance*, *Stairs*, and *Intravenous Lecture* were the agonizingly relevant bodies of Gordon, Paxton, and Rainer.

Discursive interventions and unruly dancing bodies

Phelan has written of the grammar of the body and I have suggested, in relation to improvisation, that physical activity is a manifestation of bodily intelligence. To speak about the body in this way is to reclaim it from deeply ingrained beliefs about the opposition between mind and body that underlie ideas about the inferior status of dance as a non-verbal form in relation to the other arts. Aristotle, in his *Poetics*, proposed that dance was inferior to poetry, which for him, and for most Greeks, was the highest form of art. Poetry deals with words that are understood intellectually, while dance, in his view, could not appeal to intellectual understanding because it was a non-verbal form. Dancing nevertheless occurred in his day during performances of plays which also involved music, acting, and poetry. In the eighteenth century, new ideas about aesthetics contributed to the idea of art forms existing in isolation from one another. As the art theorist Craig Owens observed:

> In Germany, Lessing, and in France, Diderot, located poetry and all the discursive arts along a dynamic axis of temporal succession, and painting and sculpture along a static axis of spatial simultaneity. Consequently the visual arts were denied access to discourse, which unfolds in time, except in the form of a literary text which, both exterior and anterior to the work, might supplement it.
>
> (Owens 1992: 45)

Owens argued that the emergence of conceptual art in the 1960s overthrew this division of the arts into discrete disciplinary categories, by reclaiming discourse as a medium of aesthetic activity within the visual arts. 'What I am claiming here,' he wrote, 'is that the eruption of language into the aesthetic field – an eruption signaled by, but by no means limited to, the writings of Smithson, Morris, Andre, Judd, Flavin, Rainer, LeWitt – is coincident with, if not the definitive index of, the emergence of postmodernism' (ibid.). Robert Morris, Carl Andre, and Donald Judd were painters who had turned their attention to sculpture and found the resulting work labelled as minimalist. Robert Smithson, Dan Flavin, and Sol LeWitt were sculptors working with non-traditional materials. The fact that Owens included a dance artist, Rainer, in this list is significant. The way the new dance was reclaiming the body was making an important contribution to the development of art theory at that time. What links all these artists is the way each of them actively engaged in writing as a way of defining the particular, conceptual issues that spectators needed to understand in order to appreciate their work.

One consequence of the adoption by visual artists of writing as a medium was to disrupt the idea that the visual arts were supposedly tied to 'a static axis of spatial simultaneity'. As I have already demonstrated, the new dance and minimalist sculpture stressed the durational nature of spectatorship, thus troubling widely accepted ideas about aesthetic appreciation that had been formed during the Enlightenment. Language and time were thus erupting in an impure, 'theatrical' way (in the sense that Michael Fried used the term) into the field of dance as well as visual art. Where Owens identified visual artists' uses of discourse as an act of reclaiming possibilities that had been 'out of bounds' since the Enlightenment, so, too, dancers have been denied the kind of direct access to discourse that Owens has discussed.

The way in which the new dance of the 1960s engaged in discourse was unruly. Dancers who performed at venues such as Judson Memorial Church in the 1960s not only 'talked things over' as Brown put it (Brown 1978: 48), but addressed the audience and used speech within their dances. During *Ordinary Dance* (1962) Rainer talked about all the places she'd lived in, while performing an unconnected series of mundane and inartistic movements. Brown's own *Skymap* (1969) consisted of a tape recording of a monologue which, as Banes describes it, was 'an attempt to make a dance on the ceiling by verbal instructions to the audience to project words up to its surface' (Banes 1980: 90). The best-known piece in which Brown talked to the audience was *Accumulation with Talking Plus Watermotor* (1979) which I will discuss at length in Chapter 6. Most of Brown's generation of experimental dancers had university degrees and were intellectually well informed. Many have subsequently taught in universities. Not only did Rainer publish statements on her work, but

Steve Paxton, Brown, and Lucinda Childs all published texts in the 1960s and 1970s that were not only informed by current theoretical developments in the visual arts, but steered the reader to take up a particular point of view in relation to their work.[13] In Fried's terms these were 'theatrical' because they made particular demands on their audience rather than presenting works that were self-sufficient aesthetic wholes.

Rainer's *Convalescent Dance* and *Stairs* and Paxton's *Intravenous Lecture* interposed unruly bodies within social and aesthetic discourses. What I am calling here unruly bodies are very different from the effervescent bodies that Sally Banes has suggested were produced in 1960s avant-garde performances. In her view the effervescent body exuded what avant-garde artists saw as the 'amazing grace of fleshly reality' and was part of 'an utopian project of organic unity' that 'created a vision of the "conscious body" in which mind and body were no longer split but harmoniously integrated' (Banes 1993: 191). But *Convalescent Dance, Stairs*, and *Intravenous Lecture*, by placing the performers' vulnerability and mortality at the centre of the privileged space of artistic practice, surely troubled notions of disembodied ideality inherent in Banes's effervescent body. Banes acknowledged that Rainer was 'committed to installing center stage ... the "actual," unidealised body' and by doing so unmasking its human materiality (ibid.). Rainer, she pointed out, championed 'the intelligent body' and saw performance as 'the site where body-consciousness thrived' (ibid.: 242). Banes attributed transcendental qualities to this conscious body of the 1960s, arguing that the avant-garde 'imbued corporeal experience with metaphysical significance' because it was 'through experience of the material body itself that consciousness could be illuminated and expanded' (ibid.: 235). However, the idea of performing work while in an uncomfortable or debilitated physical state surely challenged the kind of affirmative embodied experience that Banes hypothesized. How can an artist who is lacking in vitality and whose attention is divided, being partly directed towards and invested in an awareness of being in pain, express fullness, presence, and totality? Just as I noted earlier that Banes did not believe the work of Judson Dance Theater was anti-dance, she has resisted interpreting the kinds of embodied experiences created by avant-garde dance in anything other than affirmative terms. I am suggesting instead that through avant-garde subversions of conventional aesthetic values, works such as *Convalescent Dance, Stairs*, and *Intravenous Lecture* had a critical potential. Like the scene in Bausch's *Auf dem Gebirge hat man ein Geschrei gehört* when Josephine Ann Endicott's bare back became crosshatched with red lipstick, they presented unruly bodies that, in Phelan's terms, were agonizingly relevant. Through their refusal to conform to normative aesthetic expectations, these unruly bodies of European and American dancers were creating a context in which embodied experience could become a site of resistance against normative ideologies rather than an affirmation of them.

Overlapping European and American contexts

Although dancers associated with Judson Dance Theater created works whose avant-garde radicalism sometimes had a critical potential, individual dancers have never admitted that their work was political. Bausch, Brown, Paxton, Rainer and their fellow dancers grew up during the cold war. They, therefore, became artists at a time when the term 'political art' referred to the aesthetically conservative model of socialist realism that was the official art of the Soviet Union. In the 1960s, Rainer and her peers saw their work as avant-garde rather than political. As members of an avant-garde, they were both 'engaged with, and disengaged from, the current social turmoil and ideological crisis' of the 1960s (Orton and Pollock 1985: 108). This permitted them to present work in the context of protests against the Vietnam war. The failure of these protests, and of the 1960s counterculture as a whole, robbed them of their avant-garde identity and created a situation of political disappointment. This has overshadowed experimental art in the US and Europe since that time. The term avant-garde is rarely used to describe art work created after the mid-1970s. It is under the shadow of political disappointment that Bausch, Brown, and Rainer all refused during the 1970s to accept that their work was feminist.[14]

When Bausch and her generation developed a new experimental modern dance theatre in the late 1960s and 1970s, this involved a re-evaluation of the German tradition of modern dance. In the period of German stabilization following its defeat and partition, modern dance had seemed inappropriate for institutional support because of its strong association with German nationalism. The internationalist focus of West German politicians led to patronage of ballet as an international form. Bausch's teacher and mentor, Kurt Jooss, famously left Germany in 1933 so that he did not to have to make any accommodation with the Nazi Government. The fact that Laban, Wigman, Kreutzberg, and most of the key figures in German modern dance had been involved in preparations for the opening of the Berlin Olympic Games in 1936 meant that dancers of Bausch's generation had to consider the relationship between modern dance and politics. The German debate about the extent to which some of the older dancers had become implicated with Nazi cultural policies[15] needs to be seen in the context of a wider discussion about the basis for post-war stabilization and Germany's subsequent affluence. As Bullivant and Rice (1995) have shown, there were concerns that former Nazis had been too easily re-assimilated within industry and government. I noted earlier Bausch's aspiration to find new ways of relating to movement. When she told Jochen Schmidt that she couldn't go on working in the previous way (in Servos 1984: 230), many Germans of her generation will have understood this in relation to the problem of coming to terms with Germany's recent history.

Dancers in the US have never confronted these kinds of difficult questions about their heritage. Despite, for example, the overt racism of Isadora Duncan's comments about jazz dance and the 'tottering, ape-like convulsions of the Charleston' (Duncan 1983: 265), ideas about the way modern dance expresses freedom have become associated with a particular view of an American tradition which claims Duncan as a founding mother. This view of modern art had its origins during the cold war when, as art historian Serge Guilbaut observes, 'abstract expressionism was for many people an expression of freedom: freedom to create controversial work, freedom symbolized by action and gesture, by the expression of the artist apparently freed from all restraints' (Guilbaut 1985: 163). Scholars in the US have identified this expression of freedom in American modern dance. Thus, for Marcia Siegel, American dancers 'haven't had to please anyone, repeat their past successes, reinforce societal norms, or refrain from shocking people. They have been free to dance as they saw fit' (Siegel 1981: xi). While Duncan's vision of America dancing might have seemed to exemplify abstract, ahistorical ideals of freedom and individualism for a later generation of dance writers, Duncan herself seems not to have recognized the need to extend to all citizens of the US, including African Americans and people of colour, these constitutional rights. While it is widely assumed that the work of Judson Dance Theater exemplified these ideals, it is also the case that the dancers themselves were almost entirely white. African American dancers were not, of course, excluded, but, as I show in Chapter 5, they did not find the artistic aims of Judson Dance Theater particularly appealing. What is at stake is not democratic freedom and individualism as such, but a modernist belief that artistic value can only be assured if artists are unaffected by, and disengaged from, the social and historical context in which they work.

Noting that American art became apolitical in the 1950s as a result of the McCarthy anticommunist witch-hunts, Sally Banes claimed that: 'To some, the detachment of American art from politics was not a measure of freedom but rather of apathy, or even repression' (Banes 1993: 161). In her view the American avant-garde of the 1960s 'sought to give freedom more concrete form, partly through forsaking modernist abstraction and introducing specific political content, and partly through further heightening of the metaphoric emphasis on liberating formal methods' (ibid.: 140). In other words they reacted against the previous generation. Thus pop art replaced abstract expressionism and the work of Judson Dance Theater reacted against 'the abstraction both of Balanchine's modernist ballet and Cunningham's modern dance' (ibid.: 164). One way or another, in Banes's view, artists went on affirming the ideals of democratic freedom. It is, however, sometimes also necessary to refuse to comply with some aspects of the present in order to begin to try and imagine what the world might be like if freedom were realized. There was what may perhaps appear in retrospect a naive idealism about the way dancers engaged in the counterculture of the 1960s. They subsequently had to confront the limitations of these ideals; hence Rainer's comment in 1987 about the romantic ideas of the avant-garde and that any radical cultural practice 'must be constantly reassessed in terms of class, gender, and race' (Jayamanne *et al.* 1987: 46–7). While they subsequently abandoned their romantic idealism, these American dancers, like their European colleagues, have nevertheless continued to exercise the right to say no that is at the heart of the avant-garde's critical project. As I will show, the result has been performances from both sides of the Atlantic which, in sometimes painful and disturbing ways, have signified a sober, legal understanding of bodily freedom that underlies our basic human rights.

The rest of this book

Rather than attempting to narrate a comprehensive historical overview of innovative dance in Europe and the US since 1960, this book covers the period in an intentionally selective and uneven way. Chapter 2 examines the connections between the historical avant-garde of the early 1900s and the new dance of the 1960s, focusing on the precedent and inspiration that Marcel Duchamp and Erik Satie provided Merce Cunningham, John Cage, and the dancers of Judson Dance Theater. As well as tracing personal connections between Duchamp and dancers in the 1960s, it considers the relationship between the theoretical basis of the historical avant-garde and the ideas informing the dances performed by members of Judson Dance Theater. Chapter 3 looks at minimalism, primarily from the point of view of dance and visual art, thus expanding on areas that I have touched on here. Focusing on the work of Trisha Brown, Simone Forti, Robert Morris, and Yvonne Rainer, it therefore examines what dance got from visual art theory and how the insights into the social and experiential construction of embodiment contributed to the theorization of minimal and conceptual art. Chapter 4 sets out to prove that these ideas about embodiment not only informed the work of the more conceptually and theoretically oriented dancers but can also be identified in the work of others working in more dramatic or poetically allusive ways. Looking at work by Lucinda Childs, David Gordon, Fred Herko, Steve Paxton, and Carolee Schneemann, it focuses in particular on the way these artists explored the problem of performance by troubling and undermining conventional notions of presence. Chapter 5 examines the way in which people involved with experimental dance responded to social and political changes in the late 1960s. It reveals cases in which circumstances forced individual dancers or writers involved with dance to confront the limitations of existing value systems. Such confrontations, it argues, represent a turning point in attitudes towards avant-garde dance.

Following this relatively detailed discussion of experimental dance in downtown New York during the 1960s, Chapters 6 and 7 focus in a more selective way on subsequent progressive dance in the US and Europe. Chapter 6 looks at affects generated by uses of repetition in works by Pina Bausch, Trisha Brown, and Anne Teresa de Keersmaeker, created during the late 1970s or early 1980s. Through an analysis of these, it identifies significant absences, missing qualities that the spectator would conventionally expect to be present. These choreographers were building on aesthetic strategies discovered by dancers associated with Judson Dance Theater. What emerges is a process through which an aesthetic that had been informed by a pragmatic, sceptical analysis of the minimalist dancing body turned into a sensibility that was marked by worries and concerns about the social construction of embodied experience. Chapter 7 examines solos by two establish choreographers – Bausch and Brown – and pieces by four younger artists – Lea Anderson, Tim Etchells, Felix Ruckert, and Meg Stuart. It focuses on the way these works troubled distinctions between public and private and subverted conventions surrounding the performer–audience relationship. It argues that, by doing so, these pieces raised questions about the ethics and politics of friendship. The last chapter evaluates the renewed interest in Judson Dance Theater in the 1990s and 2000s, this being the specific context within which this book was written. Just as Chapter 7 brought together older and younger dance makers, Chapter 8 identifies and discusses differences between this revival of interest in Europe and in the US.

To conclude, in their attempt to renew the vitality of dance as art, the generation of Judson Dance Theater critiqued the traditions of ballet and modern dance using strategies and tactics inherited from another tradition, that of the historical avant-garde. In doing so, their sceptical and pragmatic approach to the dancing body led them to discover its sometimes affirmative but sometimes agonizing social and political relevance. Bausch and fellow German *tanztheater* choreographers engaged in a similar critique and, under the shadow of political disappointment, made similar discoveries about the relevance of the dancing body. Judson Dance Theater subsequently became a tradition with which a younger generation of artistic radicals in Europe during the 1990s chose to make contact and explore. Exercising their right to refuse to be limited by the social and political parameters of the time, they too have tried to imagine for themselves what the world might be like if freedom were realized. This is the narrative that I will trace in the rest of this book.

2 Cunningham, Judson, and the historical avant-garde

Reviewing the New York premier of Cunningham's *Walkaround Time* in May 1968, Jill Johnston discussed its similarities with Rainer's *The Mind is a Muscle*, which she had seen the previous month. In particular, she had been surprised by the onstage intermission in *Walkaround Time*:

> The curtains remain drawn, the house lights come up, the performers had been instructed to do what they would as though it were an intermission. Thus the piece continues but with a break in choreographic formality. David Behrman's score shifts from electronic manipulations to South-American tango music, the dancers walk on- and offstage, lounge about in leg warmers, practice their steps, chat with each other, etc. I don't think Cunningham ever presented 'ordinary' movement in this manner before. It was too self consciously casual to be very ordinary but it was a drastic cut from his high-powered dance routine, and it was, after all, presented as valid nondescript movement in the context of a dance piece
>
> (Johnston 1998: 170)

Johnston goes on to say that there had been similar onstage interludes in *The Mind is a Muscle*, some of which had been accompanied by popular music. Curiously, although she had seen Rainer's piece in April, *Walkaround Time* had actually been made before that, receiving its premier upstate in Buffalo on 10 March. Johnston dismissed the idea of accusing either artist of plagiarism: 'That's the game of history. The answer is lost in infinite regress, but we make arbitrary decisions to have something to talk about' (ibid.). She concluded instead with a most interesting observation about the relationship between Cunningham and Rainer's generation of experimental dance artists:

While Cunningham has been unwilling to sacrifice an aesthetic he had become deeply committed to he's been more than sympathetic to a new aesthetic for which he was partly responsible. I think he makes occasional forays into a territory which he completely understands but which remains alien to the sweep of his classical purity
(ibid.: 171)

To put this another way, Johnston was suggesting that Rainer and her peers produced works that were generally more extreme than Cunningham in their break with some of the traditions and conventions of western theatre dance. They were following in an avant-garde tradition that Cunningham and Cage helped reintroduce into the US during the 1940s and 1950s. It is with this re-articulation of avant-garde art-making that the current chapter is concerned.

It is perhaps no coincidence that Cunningham's occasional foray in this case came in the form of an explicit homage to Marcel Duchamp (1887–1968). Duchamp was, in effect, a direct link between the historical avant-garde at the beginning of the twentieth century and what is sometimes called the neo-avant-garde in Greenwich Village in the 1950s and 1960s. *Walkaround Time* was produced by the Merce Cunningham Dance Company in 1968 as a tribute to Marcel Duchamp. *The Bride Stripped Bare by her Bachelors Even* (*La Mariée mise en nu par ses Célibataires, même*, also known as *The Large Glass*), on which Duchamp worked between 1915–23, was used by Jasper Johns with Duchamp's permission, as a basis for its design. Duchamp had been peripherally involved in the ballet, *Relâche* (1924), which was composed by Erik Satie (1866–1925) and designed by Duchamp's friend, the Dadaist Francis Picabia (1879–1953). All three appear in René Clair's (1898–1981) now famous silent film *Entr'acte* which was shown in *Relâche*'s 'interval'.[1] The onstage intermission during *Walkaround Time* referred to the entr'acte in *Relâche* and Cunningham's dance piece contained other references to the ballet. This chapter is about the three-way relationship between Cunningham, Judson Dance Theater, and the historical tradition of avant-garde art within which Duchamp and Satie were central figures. Through a discussion of *Walkaround Time* it considers the debt that Cunningham, Cage, Johns, and Rauschenberg owed to Duchamp. It then locates the avant-garde strategies and tactics adopted by dancers associated with Judson Dance Theater in relation to those of Cunningham and Cage through a discussion of Deborah Hay's *Would They or Wouldn't They?* (1963). It therefore aims to analyse the direct and indirect consequences and implications for dance of the international revival of interest in the historical avant-garde within which Cunningham, Cage, Johns, and Rauschenberg collectively played an important role.

Walkaround Time came at the end of a decade that saw a revival of interest in Duchamp's work, with the publication in book form of Duchamp's *The Green Box* in 1959, and his 1963 retrospective exhibition in Pasadena. John Cage first got to know Duchamp in the 1940s, writing a lyrical, Satie-like piece for prepared piano, *Music for Marcel Duchamp*, in 1947.[2] By the 1960s, Cage and Cunningham were making social visits to Duchamp and his wife Teeny, Cage playing chess with Teeny because he wasn't good enough to play with her husband (or because Cage annoyed Duchamp by not trying to win). Duchamp almost certainly went to dance concerts at Judson Memorial Church, which is only a few blocks from the apartment at 28 West 10th Street in which he lived during the 1960s. He spoke of Robert Morris and Yvonne Rainer as 'terrific people' (Buskirk and Nixon 1996: 47). Most of the dancers associated with Judson must have known who Duchamp was, not just because of Cunningham and Cage's interest in his work but because of the overlaps between dancers and visual artists at Judson.[3] Most of them knew Rauschenberg, who did lighting for some of the dance concerts at Judson Memorial Church and appeared in some of their pieces. When Rauschenberg started creating his own dances, some of them performed in these. Clement Greenberg, as I noted in Chapter 1, wrote that under modernism each art was purifying itself from the effects of any other art (Greenberg 1982: 5–6), and Michael Fried believed that 'the survival of the arts has come increasingly to depend on their ability to defeat theatre' (1969: 139); but at the time they wrote these statements, the ground swell of avant-garde art-making in Greenwich Village was heading in a diametrically opposite direction: first, by refusing to recognize disciplinary boundaries – painters making dances, dancers talking and writing; second, by progressively dismantling traditional links between technical skill and aesthetic value. As I will show, Duchamp had pioneered both of these. When Rainer and her peers spoke of found movement, they appreciated its kinship to the found objects that Duchamp used as Ready-mades.

Duchamp's Ready-mades and the dance work that I am discussing in this chapter raise particular issues concerning the redefinition of the roles of artist, performer, and audience member. It was Duchamp who argued that the audience can have an active role. The creative act, he argued, is not made by the artist alone. The artist's struggle towards the realization of the work of art: 'is a series of efforts, pains, satisfactions, refusals, decisions, which also cannot and must not be fully self-conscious, at least on the aesthetic plane' (Duchamp 1973: 48). Duchamp went on to propose that there is a gap in the chain of reactions accompanying the creative act, and that this gap is completed by the spectator. The work is only completed when the spectator makes an aesthetic judgement about the work's value. The radical implications of this point of view can be seen in Duchamp's celebrated involvement in the exhibition of the Society of Independent Artists in New York in 1916. The Society invited Duchamp to be one of the exhibition's hanging committee. Duchamp agreed to join it and serve as its chair on condition that all works were hung without selection. (This was the policy of the Parisian Société des Artistes Indépendants, founded in 1884, whose Salon des Indépendants showed the work of many of the Impressionist and Post-Impressionist painters.) There are various versions of what happened next. Duchamp submitted his now-famous Ready-made *Fountain*, a urinal signed 'R. Mutt'. Thierry de Duve has suggested that, because the jury democratically decided that they would look fools if they hung the urinal, they rejected it (Duve 1990: 292–4). Following the work's rejection, Duchamp revealed that he had submitted it and resigned from the committee. De Duve argues that 'whether they wanted it or not, the members of the hanging committee were turned into a jury again . . . they were forced to say "this is art" or "that is not art"' (ibid.: 293). Duchamp, de Duve points out, wanted the public to be able to decide this for themselves. Thus, avant-garde art required spectators to become involved in the creative process through active appreciation. This was a significantly different role from that of the detached critic envisaged within accounts of the aesthetic appreciation that derive from eighteenth-century philosophy. Similarly, Duchamp's use of chance procedures and his presentation of Ready-mades undermined the idea that an artist is someone with skilled mastery of their medium, and thus set a precedent for the use of accident and chance procedures by Cage, Cunningham, Johns, and Rauschenberg.

After Duchamp, the other key figure from the early twentieth-century avant-garde to whom Cage and his circle looked back was Erik Satie, who also sought to redefine notions of the composer's authority and expressive genius. As Arnold Whittall has observed, Satie's music

> is reticent in the extreme: it establishes consistency of style by simple repetition, but it is music in which the will, if not the personality of the composer scarcely obtrudes at all . . . It was therefore natural that in the later years of Satie's life his compositions should have aspired, not to the hyper-romantic condition of a philosophy or religion, but to that of furniture.
>
> (Whittall 1977: 196)

Whittall is not particularly sympathetic to Satie, but his description flags up the cool, detached compositional devices that typify Satie's later work.

He is referring to Satie's much-repeated suggestion that 'we must bring about a music which is like furniture – a music, that is, which will be part of the noises of the environment, will take them into consideration' (quoted in Cage 1961: 76). Satie goes on to say he thinks of furniture/furnishing music 'as melodious, softening the noises of the knives and forks, not dominating them, not imposing itself' (ibid.).[4] Satie thus provided Cage and Cunningham with a conceptual framework for redefining the relationship between the arts within the staging of Cunningham's dances from a hierarchical one-to-one of mutual coexistence. The generation of artists who started producing work in the late 1950s and 1960s took this idea further and created, through interdisciplinarity, a blurring of the boundaries between distinct art forms that again troubled traditional notions of the arts as independent, autonomous disciplines. Duchamp, Satie, and the example of the historical avant-garde therefore provided these dance artists with precedents for a libertarian attack on notions of art and of aesthetic judgement.

There is a specifically American dimension to this renewal of interest in Dada and the early twentieth-century avant-garde. Duchamp worked on *The Large Glass* in New York, making it for American patrons and, along with Man Ray and Francis Picabia, was briefly involved in Dada activities in New York around 1916. However, as Andreas Huyssen has suggested:

> New York Dada remained at best a marginal phenomenon in American culture, and neither Dada nor surrealism ever met with much public success in the United States [compared with France and Germany]. Precisely this fact made Pop, happenings, Concept, experimental music, surfiction, and performance art of the 1960s and 1970s look more novel than they really were.
>
> (Huyssen 1988: 167)

Huyssen also suggests that, whereas European scholars have always understood the difference between the avant-garde and modernism, in the US they were often conflated with one another (ibid.: 164–5). He himself defines the difference between them as follows: modernist art has a mission to salvage the purity of high art from the encroachments of urbanization, the impact of technology and industrialization, and from mass culture in general. The avant-garde of the early decades of the twentieth-century however 'attempted to subvert art's autonomy, its artificial separation from life, its institutionalization as "high art" that was perceived to feed right into the legitimation needs of the 19th-century forms of bourgeois society' (ibid.: 163.).

The notion of legitimation is one that occurs in German critical theory, and, in particular, in Peter Bürger's 1984 book *Theory of the Avant-Garde*. Drawing on the work of Theodor Adorno and Walter Benjamin, Bürger proposed that the avant-garde mounted an assault on the false isolation of art and on the ideology of its autonomy. He therefore developed an idea, which I touched on in the first chapter, that the avant-garde aimed to reunite art and everyday life. This is evidently what Cage himself valued about Duchamp's work. He told Joan Retallack that, while visiting an exhibition in Düsseldorf, he found Duchamp's work had a different affect for him than the work of other Dadaists: 'His work acted in such a way that my attention was drawn to the light switch on the wall, away from – not away, but among – the works of art. So that the light switch seemed to be as attention-deserving as the works of art' (Retallack 1996: 101). I will argue later in this chapter that *Walkaround Time* could focus the spectator's attention in a similar way. There is also a curious, passive indifference about Cage's response to Duchamp that also informs his own work. A well-known example of this passivity was Cage's 'Lecture on nothing' which he gave in 1950 to members of an artists' club run by the New York School painter, Robert Motherwell. It was published in his 1961 collection of essays, *Silence*. (Robert Dunn started the course of composition classes that he taught at the Cunningham studio, which Rainer and other future members of Judson Dance Theater attended, by reading a passage from this book.) Cage's lecture was written using the structural procedures he was applying to his music, in this case with four measures per line. It begins:

```
I am here            ,      and there is nothing to say           .
                                             If among you are
      those who wish to get    somewhere    ,      let them leave
at
      any moment        .        What we re-quire     is
      silence            ;       but what silence requires
      is                   that I go on talking     .
```
(Cage 1961: 109)

A few lines below this comes the sentence from this lecture which is most often quoted:

```
                                    I have nothing to say
      and I am saying it
```
(ibid.)

What is striking about this is how little Cage was asking of his audience and how little he was claiming about himself. Moira Roth argues that Cage, Cunningham, Johns, and Rauschenberg were all inspired by Duchamp to develop what she calls an aesthetic of indifference: 'an art characterized by tones of neutrality, passivity, irony and, often, negation' (Roth 1977: 48). I will return to this later in the chapter. While avant-garde art in its subversion of art's autonomy has invariably omitted things up until then considered essential to art practice, negating traditions and conventions, Cage's work invariably accomplished this in a surprisingly generous and undemanding way. Nevertheless, by radically blurring the categories of musical score and written text, the lecture demonstrated that art can be nothingness, thus in effect negating an economy of art works circulating within a market that was supported by a materialist aesthetic.

Yvonne Rainer also negated conventional ideas about aesthetic value in a highly polemical statement which begins 'NO to spectacle' and out-lines an approach to performance that involves a much more confronta-tional and provocative relationship with her audience. This quotation, which is often taken out of context, was written for *The Drama Review*. At the time this newly founded journal was edited by Richard Schechner and included similar essays by artists reflecting theoretically about their work (see Sandford 1995). Rainer's essay discussed her most recent evening-length dance piece, *Parts of Some Sextets* (1965). Towards the end of the essay she defined 'an area of concern for me in relation to dance, but existing as a very large NO to many facts in the theatre today' (Rainer 1974: 51). What she then itemized has been taken by many writing about the period as a manifesto:

> NO to spectacle no to virtuosity no to transformations and magic and make-believe no to glamour and transcendency of the star image no to the heroic no to the anti-heroic no to trash imagery no to involvement of performer or spectator no to style no to camp no to seduction of spectator by the wiles of the performer no to eccen-tricity no to moving or being moved.
>
> (ibid.)

This statement reveals the impact that avant-garde strategies were having on ways of thinking about the dancing body and its relationship to con-temporary culture. As I will demonstrate in the next chapter, when read in relation to the dance pieces that Rainer made in the 1960s, it indicates an avant-garde approach to ways of devising movement vocabularies and choreographic structures which, in turn, prompted Rainer and her fellow dancers to find new ways of performing them. Cunningham's work itself set his dancers problems of interpretation that were a catalyst for the new ways of projecting performative presence explored by Judson Dance Theater, many of whom either danced in the Merce Cunningham Dance Company or took open class at the Cunningham studio.

The way performers in the kind of work Rainer was proposing related to their audience was very different from the way Cage addressed his listeners during his 'Lecture on nothing'. Nevertheless, both acknowledged that negativity and absence were unavoidable aspects of the avant-garde project, and ones that even informed the choices each made about the way their words appeared on the printed page – the blank, white spaces in Cage's lecture, and the breathless lack of punctuation in Rainer's statement.[5] I noted at the beginning of this chapter the subtle, complex interrelationship between *Walkaround Time* and *The Mind is a Muscle* that Johnston so astutely identified. There is clearly also another, equally complex relationship between Cage's ideas and those of Rainer and her generation of experimental dancers. Robert and Judith Dunn's composition classes not only introduced future members of Judson Dance Theater to the ideas informing Cunningham's use of chance and his ideas about the independent coexistence of dancing and music but also to Cage's compositional processes, including the use of innovative musical scores with non-traditional notation to generate indeterminate performances. The composer Steve Reich argued in 1974 that: 'the Judson group was the dance equivalent to the music of John Cage (even more so, curiously, than Merce Cunningham – think of Paxton's *Satisfyin' Lover*, the walking piece, and Cage's *4'33"*, the silent piece)' (Reich 1974: 41). While Cage and Cunningham shared more or less the same aesthetic agenda, there were differences in the way each expected performers to work on the interpretation of pieces for performance. It is also necessary to recognize that, just as Cage and Cunningham developed their own, quite individual readings of Duchamp and Satie's work, so the younger generation of dancers sometimes picked up on tangential and unexpected aspects of Cage and Cunningham's practices. Cage and Cunningham therefore derived a cluster of avant-garde strategies and aesthetic sensibilities from the work of Duchamp, Satie, and other avant-garde artists from the early twentieth century, which were in turn taken up and transformed by the younger generation of dancers associated with Judson Dance Theater.

Walkaround Time

Walkaround Time consisted of two halves each lasting about twenty minutes with a seven-minute intermission during which the performers act on stage as they would normally do if they were off it. It was performed with a commissioned score by David Behrman ... *for nearly an hour* .... The set consisted of seven different-sized boxes of transparent plastic with the elements of Duchamp's *Large Glass* printed onto them; two containing the elements of the upper panel of the painting (containing the 'Bride') were suspended above the stage, while the other boxes (relating to the Bachelor Machines in the painting's lower panel) were spread out across it. At Duchamp's request the various boxes were brought together at the end of the piece to conform approximately to Duchamp's painting, with the dancers slowly walking round in a loop behind them. The piece had, for Cunningham, a large cast of nine dancers who wore primary coloured tights and leotards. It started with them all standing on stage in silence, facing in different directions. After a long pause, Cunningham himself raised his arms above his head to initiate what was, in fact, the opening exercise from their daily class and they all joined in, in unison. They then broke out into a busy variety of different movement activities while gradually, but imperceptibly, leaving the stage free for a long, very slow solo by Valda Setterfield that alternated between small movements in isolated parts of the body, such as an isolated shoulder, and bigger movements while standing still. The piece therefore started with stillness, was briefly very busy and then relapsed into still, slow solos with intermittent moments of quick, precise movement, and brief interruptions as dancers came briefly on stage to perform a short sequence and exit. In the second half of the piece, there was another long slow solo by Carolyn Brown. In many ways *Walkaround Time* is typical of Cunningham's work, and much of what can be said about its choreographic style could equally be said of a number of other pieces by him. Three things are distinctive about *Walkaround Time*: the sort of space made by the presence of the large, transparent boxes and the aural background of Behrman's gentle soundscape; the almost medi- tatively slow, restrained movement material of the few solos and duets interspersed with brief bursts of activity; and finally the way the piece alluded to Duchamp and the historical avant-garde.

There are a number of allusions in *Walkaround Time* both to Duchamp's paintings and his concept of the Ready-made, and to *Relâche* and *Cinésketch*, a live review presented following a performance of *Relâche* on New Year's Eve 1924. In this, Duchamp and Brogna Perlmutter appeared nude, each holding a fig leaf, in a tableau of an early painting of Adam and Eve.[6] Apart from Jill Johnston's review in the *Village Voice*, no one in the late 1960s or early 1970s mentioned these references to Duchamp which remained largely private and hidden.[7] Sally Banes and Noël Carroll mentioned them in a 1983 essay (Banes 1994: 109–18). Cunningham subsequently talked about them with both Jacqueline Lesschaeve (Cunningham 1985) and David Vaughan (1992). The opening group section, he said, used the company's daily class as a 'Ready-made'. In a solo at the beginning of the second half, Cunningham neatly took off his leotard and tights and put on another pair while running on the spot; he even managed to keep up the rhythm of his running by hopping while pulling tights over his foot. The effect was of extreme detachment as Cunningham stood in profile, towards the middle of the stage, half hidden behind the box representing what Duchamp called the nine malic moulds. (In Duchamp's scheme these moulds condensed gas into the nine Bachelor Machines, there being nine dancers in Cunningham's piece.) Cunningham said this solo referred to Duchamp's famous painting, *Nude Descending a Staircase*, and to the painter's naked appearance in *Cinésketch* (Vaughan 1992). Roger Copeland says that Carolyn Brown's long solo 'with its sharp alternation of allegro movement and stillness' also referred to *Nude Descending a Staircase*:

> Her phrases were intended to allude to the way Duchamp conflated the distinctions between cubism and futurism: that is, his nude is both 'still' in the manner of a cubist painting and 'descending' in the manner of a futurist work.
>
> (Copeland 2004: 93)

The year before *Walkaround Time* was created, Robert Rauschenberg had appeared, naked with a fig leaf, as Adam/Duchamp with Elaine Sturtevant, also naked with a fig leaf, as Eve/Perlmutter in Sturtevant's reconstruction of *Relâche*.[8] Banes and Carroll point out that, during *Walkaround Time*, Carolyn Brown, Sandra Neels, and Valda Setterfield each crossed the stage at different moments in extreme slow motion: these, they suggest, 'seem like analogies of the three cinematic blossomings the Bride is said to undergo in *The Large Glass*' (Banes 1994: 116).

Cunningham also said that the 'intermission' in *Walkaround Time* was both a Ready-made and a reference to the entr'acte in *Relâche*. During this 'intermission', David Behrman's score consists of overlaid tracks of the sort of music one might have found on the radio, including Argentine tangos and a Japanese woman shakily singing *Tristesse*, a French popular song, just as Satie's score for *Relâche* used popular music of its day.[9] Behrman's sound score, which is called *. . . for nearly an hour . . .*, also refers to *The Large Glass* and to *Relâche*. At the end of *Relâche*, wearing lavish fur coats and jewels, Picabia and Satie had come on stage to take their curtain call in a tiny five-horsepower motor car. During one section of *. . . for nearly an hour . . .* the musicians manipulate the sounds from a tape recording of Behrman's Volkswagen driving around the streets of Buffalo. Behrman said this referred to the car in *Relâche* and the machines in *The Large Glass*. Another Duchamp allusion was contained in a recording of a walk to the Niagara Falls, which is near Buffalo, as there is a waterfall in *The Large Glass*. Yet another section of Behrman's score overlays recordings of the women dancers in Cunningham's company reading extracts from *The Green Box*. During the performance, these tape recordings were mixed by the musicians according to specifications in Behrman's score and the resulting sounds directed to speakers in all parts of the theatre, creating a surround sound effect.[10]

While all these allusions to the historical avant-garde in *Walkaround Time* provide an interesting excuse for specialist art historical or dance historical research, this should not be taken as an 'explanation' of the dance. They need to be seen in relation to more general strategies which Cage and Cunningham used that were informed by an avant-garde sensibility they derived from their knowledge of the historical avant-garde. One aspect of *Walkaround Time* that utilized an avant-garde strategy was the piece's use of stillness and slow motion. I have noted that during Brown and Setterfield's long, slow solos there were sporadic bursts of activity as other dancers briefly entered the stage. But even within these brief interventions there always seemed to be one or two still dancers, frozen mid-movement. Cunningham himself has said that he deliberately used very, very slow movements in this piece:

> Marcel always gave one the sense of a human being who is ever calm, a person with an extraordinary sense of calmness, as though days could go by, and minutes could go by. And I wanted to see if I could get that – the sense of time.
>
> (Vaughan 1997: 165).

This sense of time is something that Behrman also alluded to in the title of his music ...*for nearly an hour*... . He adapted this from the title of one of Duchamp's glass paintings, *To Be Looked at (from the Other Side of the Glass) with One Eye, Close to, for Almost an Hour*.[11] This suggests a way of looking at pictures in an exhibition that is not only highly unconventional, but also contradicts the eighteenth-century idea, discussed in the first chapter, that aesthetic appreciation of visual art takes place instantaneously. To look at a painting for such a prolonged time would be a physically uncomfortable experience, likely to cause muscle fatigue and cramp. Like Duchamp, Erik Satie was also interested in prolonging the moment of aesthetic appreciation. His *Vexations* (*c*.1920) consisted of a single page of music to be performed 840 times. John Cage organized a performance of this at the Pocket Theater, New York in September

1963, lasting about two-and-a-half hours.[12] The experience of listening to a long, repetitive piece of music or watching an excessively long, slow dance is also one that might cause restlessness and sensations of physical discomfort. Avant-garde works that make the spectator aware of time in this way also make them aware of their own bodies and invite them to recognize what they have in common with the bodies of the performers they are watching. In subsequent chapters I will discuss other long, slow dance pieces that made spectators aware of their own bodies in this way. In Rainer's terms these performances said no to the kind of spectacular virtuosity that was a key component of mainstream ballet and modern dance performances at that time.

Jasper Johns reports that when he asked Duchamp for permission to use *The Large Glass* for *Walkaround Time*, Duchamp asked, 'but who will do the work?' (Vaughan 1992: 67); Johns's reassurance that Duchamp himself need do nothing, can, of course, be read as a typical Duchampian manoeuvre – making art by doing nothing. But Duchamp did in fact do one very important thing in connection with *Walkaround Time*. He took a bow at the end of its first performance on 10 March, in Buffalo.[13] The audience watching *Cinésketch* knew, from their programmes, that the naked man in a false beard representing Adam was the artist Marcel Duchamp.[14] It was this fact that created meaning, rather than any skill with which Duchamp may have performed the role. The physical presence of the artists as themselves on stage served the function of legitimating these performances as art. In both *Relâche* and *Walkaround Time* ordinary, everyday movement was performed in a theatrical time space where an audience would have conventionally expected to watch skilled dance movement. In *Relâche* a fireman wearing the insignia of the Légion d'Honneur wandered around on stage in the first act smoking a cigarette. A female dancer wearing evening dress (Edith Bonsdorff) entered the stage from the auditorium, practised a few steps, sat and smoked. When the music stopped, she danced in silence.[15] The fireman reappeared in the second act to pour water from one bucket into another. No one smoked in *Walkaround Time* but the dancers sat around the set and chatted during the intermission. Wearing dressing gowns or with a jumper or a towel around their waist, some chatted quietly together, or wandered aimlessly around, briefly pausing to exchange a few words, often hiding behind the transparent boxes. Some checked the precise placement of the boxes on the stage.

In both dance pieces everyday movement was presented as a result of conceptual choices made by artists who signified that it was art by taking bows at the premier. Dance performance was thus de-skilled, by which I mean it was produced without any technical skill. Both pieces thus broke with the idea that there was a necessary connection between aesthetic value and the quality of craftsmanship or technical execution. One could describe this as ready-made movement, or as pedestrian, the term sometimes used to describe the use of everyday movement in the work of the artists associated with Judson Dance Theater. As I have already noted, Jill Johnston commented at the time upon similarities between *Walkaround Time* and a contemporary performance by Rainer. In 1968, *Walkaround Time* framed de-skilled everyday behaviour between sections of choreographed material which used, albeit in challenging ways, movement that recognizably derived from the vocabularies of ballet and modern dance. Audience members, attuned to watching what Jill Johnston calls the classical purity of Cunningham's choreography in the first half, must have at least started to watch the 'non-dance' movement during the 'intermission' with the sort of concentrated appreciation with which dance is conventionally evaluated. The effect was to make them see ordinary, everyday behaviour as dance, just as Cage had found at the exhibition in Düsseldorf that the light switch on the wall among Duchamp's pieces became as worthy of attention as the works of art around it.

The feminist art historian Moira Roth, noting that Cage, Cunningham, Johns, and Rauschenberg shared an appreciation of the work of Marcel Duchamp, has suggested ways in which his example allowed them to develop, during the cold-war period, what she calls the aesthetic of indifference. Thus they 'consciously espoused indifference as a virtue, as the correct way to deal with an uncertain world' (Roth 1977: 47). To present de-skilled movement as art involves a degree of detachment and disengagement from the role conventionally associated with artistic production. It involved 'an extreme passivity: a decision not to assert but rather to let happen what may . . . there are no messages, no feelings and no ideas. Only emptiness' (ibid.: 50). Roth has pointed out that this sensibility was dandy-like in contrast to the more macho investments of self that characterized the work of the then dominant abstract expressionist painters of the New York School. While Roth has criticized Cage and fellow artists for the seemingly apolitical stance of their aesthetic sensibility, the gay scholar Jonathan Katz (1998) has pointed out that the 1950s was probably the most homophobic period of American history. He therefore argues that these American artists' aesthetic stance constituted a strategic way of resisting complicity with inimical social and political pressures. At a time when gay men and women were being actively sought out and legally harassed because of their sexual identities,[16] being openly gay was not a realistic option for Cage, Cunningham, Johns, or Rauschenberg. When considered from a queer point of view, the artistic role that Duchamp had assumed might appear as a relatively passive one. Whereas during the 1920s Picasso adopted the persona of the bull to signify his creative powers, Duchamp created the cross-dressing persona of Rrose Sélavy. Cage, Cunningham, Rauschenberg, and Johns saw in Duchamp's oeuvre a precedent for adopting a detached, indifferent aesthetic that could signify their refusal to perform the role of creative genius at a time when modern dancers such as Graham and Limon, and painters such as Pollock and De Kooning incorporated into their work, signs of their existential struggle to express their psychological interiority. As Katz has argued, by troubling and undermining the normative, heterosexual way masculinity was represented within abstract expressionist painting and within expressive ideologies of dance and music, Cage and fellow artists were far from being complicit with hegemonic norms.

Chance, accident, and indeterminacy

I have already noted that Duchamp's Ready-mades exemplify his avant-garde aspiration to reunite art and everyday life by minimizing his own involvement in the process of art creation. Chance was a key strategy through which he attempted to achieve this reunification, one which, as Roger Copeland (2004) has observed directly, influenced Cage and Cunningham.[17] In 1913–14, while planning *The Large Glass*, Duchamp dropped three pieces of thread onto a canvas, fixing each of them where they fell and using the resulting curved shapes to create a piece he called *3 Standard Stops (3 stoppages étalon)*. He then used these three chance shapes in a variety of ways to measure or create lines or shapes in *The Large Glass*. When his magnum opus was broken during its return from an exhibition in 1927, and Duchamp had carefully put the fragments back together again, he noted that some of the resulting cracks resembled the random shapes of the *3 Standard Stops*. His recorded response to the breakage explains the connection between chance procedures and the principal of choosing a Ready-made: he commented on 'a curious intention that I am not responsible for, a Ready-made intention, in other words' (Sanouillet and Peterson 1975: 127). Duchamp's apparent lack of concern here – in Roth's terms, his indifference – about the fate of his work is remarkably similar to Cunningham's expressions of detached interest in the choreographic forms that result from his applications of chance procedures.

When examining the way Cage and Cunningham allowed chance and accident to determine aspects of their work, it is necessary to recognize the difference between using them while composing or choreographing material and specifying their use during performance. When chance operations are used to make a piece, the end result is more or less performed the same each time. With indeterminate structures, certain elements are left unfixed so that the performers can choose how to interpret them each time they perform them. Cunningham has thrown dice, tossed coins or sticks, used the *I Ching*, and, while working on *Canfield* (1969), shuffled a pack of cards and laid them out as if for a game of patience (Cunningham 1985: 115–16). These were all ways in which he allowed chance to intervene while creating movement phrases and taking various kinds of decisions about pieces. Cage and the composers who worked with him to create and perform music for Cunningham's pieces often worked with indeterminacy during the performance itself. This meant that the composer created a score that defined elements within the music but left decisions about some aspects of how these could be played – such as the ordering of sequences, pitch variation, or cues – for the musicians to make themselves during the actual performance itself. The resulting music was not improvised but might vary considerably between one performance and another.

In an essay published three years before he created the score for *Walkaround Time*, David Behrman discussed the way the new kinds of musical scores that Cage and his circle of composers began to use in the 1950s enabled indeterminacy. Behrman pointed to limitations in a situation where a composer tries to control the performer through complicated musical notation that specifies particular qualities and forms of expression:

> the larger the number of elements over which the player must distribute his [*sic*] powers of concentration, and the more conventional will be his execution of individual elements – the more he will be left to technical reflexes built up in the course of his training.
>
> (Behrman: 1965: 59)

Behrman contrasted this very controlling use of scores with new and sometimes unconventional methods of notation that, he said, can

> put the player into a fresh frame of mind, to shock him out of an environment which puts a smoke screen of technique between himself and the experience of playing, to make him feel as though the making of sounds on an instrument were a fresh experience.
>
> (ibid.)

For Behrman, this is achieved by the composer giving up some of the authority over the creative act traditionally ascribed to his or her role, and giving it to the performer. The composers in Cage's circle worked cooperatively, performing each other's works, which were often interpreted with some freedom from the composer's score. Thus, when the

Merce Cunningham Dance Company appeared at the Festival of the Arts Today in Buffalo in March 1968, the music credits in the programme included the following.

> Cage, Gordon Mumma, and David Tudor played Cage's *Variations V*. Tudor and Mumma played Tudor's *Rainforest*. Cage played Satie's *Nocturnes* for Cunningham's piece of the same title, and Behrman, Cage, Tudor, and Mumma played *...for nearly an hour...* for Cunningham's *Walkaround Time*.
>
> (Merce Cunningham Dance Company 1968a)

As Sally Banes has pointed out, Cunningham rarely used indeterminacy during the actual performance of his work, *Story* and *Field Dances* (both 1963) being the main exceptions. Banes suggested Cunningham feared that if he allowed his dancers the kind of freedom to make decisions that Behrman has described, there would be a danger of their accidentally bumping into one another and causing injuries. In *Story* Cunningham therefore attempted to limit his dancers' freedom of choice by prescribed extremely tight conditions around indeterminate elements (Banes 1994: 103–9). Steve Paxton, who danced for Cunningham from 1961 to 1964, wryly observed:

> The thing that surprised me the most about working in the company when I started . . . was that we didn't all sit around and throw coins. I had expected that we would all do that, and what we *did* was come and learn steps.
>
> (Brown *et al.* 1992: 104–5, emphasis in the original)

This suggests that Cunningham carried out chance procedures to determine the content of the movement material before he came into the studio. However, as Carolyn Brown suggested, the dancers in the company brought an unpredictable, chance element into Cunningham's work (ibid.: 105). He put the dancers into situations during the rehearsal process where they, in effect, had to make decisions about how to perform the material he gave them. But whereas Cage and his collaborators knew this was what they were doing, Cunningham was reluctant to offer his dancers any explanations. Valda Setterfield has given an example of this. When she was new to the company she had to take over a role from Viola Farber, who had an injury:

> I was not informed if I was really going to do the part or if I should learn it, so I hovered around in the back, trying to figure out what

to do. Carolyn said to Merce 'Why don't you help her?' He said (she told me later) 'I want to see what she'll do with it'.

(ibid.: 110)

The documentary film *498, 3rd Ave* made in Cunningham's studio in the spring and summer of 1967, shows Cunningham choreographing *Scramble*.[18] At one rehearsal, a number of dancers had come together for the first time to put together the sections that they had learnt in smaller rehearsals. The film reveals that the dancers were not at all happy because they weren't sure what they were supposed to be doing. Sandra Neels was actually crying about it. As the film crew recorded them, they asked Carolyn Brown to go to Cunningham for clarification. She refused and no one else wished to raise it with him. It transpires that the problem was the tempo. At their individual rehearsals, Cunningham had given each of them different tempi. The film makers then interviewed Cunningham himself about it. In a quiet voice, almost as if he didn't want anyone to overhear, he replied that he didn't want to tell them exactly what to do, but was waiting to see what they would make of it on their own. Here, as in the other example, Cunningham was perhaps (to paraphrase Behrman) putting his dancers in a fresh frame of mind, shocking them out of an environment that puts a smoke-screen of technique between themselves and the experience of performing, and making them feel as though dancing in time and space were a fresh experience. It is not clear whether, or to what extent, Cunningham had explained his intentions to his dancers. If Brown understood, this was surely because she had worked it out on her own; Neels must have been in the dark about what was going on. Brown, Paxton, and Setterfield evidently got used to the fact that Cunningham habitually kept to himself what he was doing.

How little these dancers got from Cunningham becomes evident in an interview Steve Paxton gave during the American Dance Festival in 1993. Paxton contrasted the use of masks and of blank faces in Alvin Nikolais's work (which he and his interviewer had just seen at the festival) with the empty faces of Cunningham's dancers. He suggested that the blank face, which Cunningham's dancers adopted in the time he was a member of the company, was not a mask but an empty face (Figure 2.1):

We danced along trying not to add anything to the movement that we didn't know what to do with because we didn't know what context we were performing in. When you're out there in front of an audience you want to do your best and you want to do the movement as well as you can, and it is hard not to want to somehow use that performer's tradition of what the human soul is doing in the body – the recognition of human glances, the expressions, the actual muscles of the face that are actually working while you're dancing.

(Paxton 1996)

Paxton suggested that the lack of these signs in the performance of Cunningham's work left some people emotionally in a void. 'Once you remove the human elements, once you remove the human messages to other humans from a dance work you don't know how to invest it with emotion and there is a great quandary how to perform it' (ibid.). Cage and Cunningham worked with chance and indeterminacy to find previously inconceivable kinds or combinations of material. What Paxton and

Figure 2.1 Merce Cunningham. *Nocturnes*, 1956. Carolyn Brown, William Davies, Shareen Blair, and Steve Paxton in 1964. 'We danced along trying not to add anything to the movement that we didn't know what to do with because we didn't know what context we were performing in.'

Photo: Richard Rutledge. Courtesy of the Dance Collection, The New York Public Library for the Performing Arts, Jerome Robbins Dance Collection.

his fellow dancers, however, discovered through performing their work, or watching or listening to it, were insights into the nature of performance. That, Paxton suggested, was the puzzle about presence and absence which Cunningham set his dancers.

Paxton was describing what was, in effect, an absent performative presence, which was the accidental by-product of Cunningham's secretiveness and reluctance to explain his intentions to his dancers. Here, then, were three distinct stages in the development of what Moira Roth has called the aesthetic of indifference. First there was Duchamp making art by doing almost nothing and signing it with fictitious names; and accepting with seeming equanimity and indifference the accidental damage to *The Large Glass* because it was due to circumstances for which he was not responsible. Then there was Cunningham accepting the accidental qualities that his dancers unintentionally, through lack of direction or information, brought to the development of his choreography during rehearsals, and doing so with a similar indifference to that with which he accepted the result of a throw of his dice. Thus far the choices and accidents that these artists were accepting in an indifferent way concerned those aesthetic aspects of the creative process over which the painter or choreographer as author would conventionally have control. Paxton and his colleagues in Judson Dance Theater, began to pay more attention to the significance of the act of performing rather than considering the choreographic material they created as the repository of their works' value. The aesthetic of indifference now became a factor in the way dancers chose to present themselves to their audience. If Cunningham's dancers found themselves having to adopt an absent mode of performance by default, some of the dancers at Judson Memorial Church deliberately chose to explore the same mode of performance in their own work.

Judson Dance Theater

Robert Ellis Dunn (1928–96) organized the first concert of dance at Judson Memorial Church, 6 July 1962, to show work produced during the classes he had been running with his wife Judith Dunn (1933–83). Sally Banes has given a detailed description of all the pieces performed in this (Banes: 1995: 35–70). From her research, it is evident that most of the pieces in this first concert used chance procedures and indeterminate structures similar to those used by Cage and Cunningham. Of these, Ruth Emerson, Elaine Summers, and William Davis also seem to have used a movement basis that drew on ballet, modern dance, and the kind of movement that Cunningham was teaching at his studio.

Gordon, Hay, Herko, Paxton, and Rainer's works were less obviously Cunningham-derived – Gordon, Hay, Herko, and Rainer also dancing at the time with the choreographer James Waring. Neither Trisha Brown nor Simone Forti, who were more influenced by Anna Halprin's ideas, presented work in this first concert. Nevertheless, Dunn and his wife had a strong influence on the early concerts of dance given at the church.

Dunn was a composer who worked as one of the accompanists at the Cunningham studio. His wife Judith Dunn danced for Cunningham from 1959 to 1963. In their classes the Dunns introduced students to many of Cunningham and Cage's ideas; as I have already noted, the course started with reading a passage from John Cage's book *Silence* defining composition.[19] Two of the pieces performed in the first concert at the church were set to Satie's *Trois Gymnopédies*, which had been made as one of the assignments in the Dunns' class.[20] Following Cunningham's way of using Satie's music in *Septet* (1953) and *Nocturne* (1956), Robert Dunn gave the dancers a numerical time structure of a number of phrases which, although he didn't tell them, came from Satie's piece. The task was to make a dance that would fill out this structure in any form they liked and when they brought it in, he then played Satie's piece on the piano as an accompaniment while they performed their choreography. Dunn also showed them how to use game structures as ways to work collaboratively, and he explained about the use of chance and of scores that specified indeterminate structures. William Davies, Judith Dunn, Barbara Dilley (later Lloyd), Deborah Hay, Steve Paxton, Albert Reid, and Valda Setterfield all performed in work at the church and were members of the Merce Cunningham Dance Company.[21] They would have got to know Cage and Rauschenberg well because, as Carolyn Brown has pointed out, the experience of travelling around the US on tour in Cage's little Volkswagen bus was an intimate one. She later recalled:

> We were very close and John Cage was with us all the time. When I hear discussions now [1987] about the concepts and philosophy of the work – that was simply a part of our diet then. We heard it constantly, we talked about it. Rauschenberg was in the bus with us, he talked about what he was doing.
>
> (Brown *et al.* 1992: 116)

Either through membership of Cunningham's company or through attending the Dunns' classes, the dancers who formed Judson Dance Theater became familiar with many of the avant-garde ideas that I have been discussing in this chapter.

Deborah Hay's *Would They or Wouldn't They?* – sometimes known as *They Will* – exemplifies much of what the Dunns taught in their composition classes. It was made for the thirteenth concert of dance at Judson Memorial Church on 19 and 20 November 1963. For this concert, a young sculptor, Charles Ross, who had worked with Anna Halprin in San Francisco, received a $200 grant to make a sculptural environment, which the choreographers used in various ways (Banes 1995: 169–82). It consisted of a huge, irregular trapezoid made of iron tubes, a see-saw and an eight-foot-high platform made of wood, and smaller items including car tyres, bed springs, and several different types of chairs placed on the platform (Figure 2.2).

The concert, itself, was in the church but, for a few weeks before, the sculpture was set up in the gym for rehearsals. From descriptions and photographs, most dancers seem to have approached it as if it were a big children's play structure. One face of the trapezoid had a horizontal tube just high enough for dancers to hang on with their feet off the ground, while another had a length of rope hanging down. Hay's dance focused on these two parts of the trapezoid and had music by Al Hansen. There were two women and two men in the piece, Deborah Hay and Yvonne

Figure 2.2 Deborah Hay. *Would They or Wouldn't They* at Judson Church, 1963.

Photo by Peter Moore © Estate of Peter Moore/VAGA, New York.

Rainer with Alex Hay and David Lee. A short film shows part of its revival at the First New York Theater Rally in 1965, danced by Deborah Hay and Judith Dunn with Alex Hay and Robert Rauschenberg. This time there was no sculpture, only a suspended scaffolding tube from which to hang. A length of rope dangled from one end of this. From this film and from descriptions (ibid.: 178–9), the choreography appears to have been a series of tasks within a loose, indeterminate structure. Near the beginning the men stood inside the structure, squatted back-to-back with their heads together and pushed against one another until they were standing upright while the women danced around the outside. Female dancers repeatedly gave verbal instructions to the men to lift them up so that they could hang from the tube. The men sometimes jumped up to hang from it, always facing in the opposite direction to the women. No attempt was made to hide the effort of lifting or jumping. A couple of times when all four were hanging, one of the men dropped to the ground and ran on the spot in a leisurely way. The men occasionally also ran while holding the rope. A few times a man caught a woman as she dropped, only for both of them to collapse in an untidy heap on the ground. The overall effect was of ordinary movement performed in an unemphatic, everyday way.

Would They or Wouldn't They? demonstrates the ways members of Judson Dance Theater took up and transformed Cage and Cunningham's practices. It had an indeterminate compositional structure, using a choreographic score in which there were moments when dancers had to make decisions, and these decisions had effects on other dancers, generating chance juxtapositions of unexpected actions. The dance was also free from any conceivable dependence on the Fluxus artist Al Hansen's music, just as the movement Cunningham created and the music that Cage or one of his collaborators composed coexisted independently alongside each other in performance. Deborah Hay has said that when she first came across Merce Cunningham's work at a summer school at Connecticut College in 1961 she was fascinated, sneaking into the auditorium to watch rehearsals (Banes 1995: 50). From Cunningham's open technique class and from seeing his work,[22] Hay was aware of his particular uses of avant-garde strategies in the way he approached the dancing body in time and space. The performers in *Would They or Wouldn't They?* adopted a neutral mode of performance similar to that of the dancers in Cunningham's company.

From this description, Hay's piece might seem to have been a straightforward, formal exploration of abstract movement, yet there were clearly moments of humour in it. A key difference between *Would They or Wouldn't They?* and a performance by Cunningham's company was the casting in

Hay's piece of women who were trained dancers and men who were untrained. Whereas members of Judson Dance Theater who had trained as dancers wanted to unlearn a conventional, habitual manner of presenting themselves to the audience, untrained dancers such as Rauschenberg and Alex Hay had not acquired this habit and therefore didn't have to unlearn it. Having the latter on stage helped Deborah Hay, Yvonne Rainer, and Judith Dunn to see how to behave 'more like human beings, revealing what was thought of as deficiencies as well as their skills' – as Trisha Brown put it in a passage discussed in Chapter 1 (Brown 1978: 48). In some ways the men's interactions with the women parodied moments of partnering in ballet and in Cunningham's work. In the 1965 film, the men seemed endearingly clumsy as they lifted women in a hyperbolically neutral and meaningless manner or caught them in a dysfunctional, comic way. The piece exploited precisely the kind of clumsy accident that Cunningham wanted to avoid. Thus, whereas in Cunningham's work dancers unintentionally brought accidental qualities to the way choreographic material was developed in rehearsal, the men in Hay's piece brought accidental qualities to the performance itself. In *Walkaround Time* the dancers seemed like deliberately unglamorous performers engaged in executing dry, abstruse dance movement, even during the 'intermission' where the dancers, as Johnston observed, were 'too self consciously casual to be very ordinary' (1998: 170). In *Would They or Wouldn't They?* the dancers seemed much more like real people engaged in real actions.

Conclusion

In his 'Theses on the philosophy of history', Walter Benjamin (1892–1940) asserted that 'In every era the attempt must be made anew to wrest tradition away from a conformism that is about to overpower it' (Benjamin 1973: 257). This chapter has outlined a process by which Cage and Cunningham attempted to save the avant-garde tradition of Duchamp, Satie, and Picabia; at a time of social and political reaction they turned it into their aesthetic of indifference, only to have this turned during a less repressive decade into a new, more polemic and disturbing avant-gardism by the dance artists associated with Judson Dance Theater. In doing so I have proposed an account of Cunningham's dance that is not in line with the way his work is usually discussed. While others before me have discussed correlations between Duchamp, Cunningham, and Judson Dance Theater, I have argued that Cunningham's work is more avant-garde, and has more in common with Duchamp's work than is usually accepted. Sally Banes and Noël Carroll have suggested that:

Duchamp strove for an art of ideas, an art that was discursive, an art that was allegorical . . . Duchamp is saying that the spectator brings his own meanings to the work of art. But meanings are precisely the sort of thing that Cunningham's work is designed to deter and deflect.

(1994: 113)

Cunningham's many allusions to Duchamp and to the historical avant-garde in *Walkaround Time* surely open up a wider range of ways in which to approach this work. Nor should this piece be considered an isolated example. Carolyn Brown has talked about private meanings in Cunningham's work (Brown *et al.* 1992); it is surely the way Cunningham has talked about his work rather than the work itself that is designed to deter and deflect people from finding them. Nancy Dalva, noting Cunningham's own admission that 'there are many references, many images' in his work, has observed that at least four of the titles Cunningham has given to his dances derive from James Joyce, leading her to conclude: 'How much more of his imagery and in fact his method are Joycean is a fascinating, and open, question' (Dalva 1992: 181).

Banes and Carroll played down the avant-garde aspects of Cunningham's work, observing 'it is Cunningham's very reliance on dance technique that led the succeeding generation of Judson Dance Theater choreographers to question his practice. Perhaps in this respect they were more Duchampian than their mentor' (1994: 113). The question of technique is undoubtedly a defining difference. However, following Johnston's insightful comments on the relationship between *Walkaround Time* and *The Mind is a Muscle*, I have outlined a more complex relationship between Cunningham and the Judson Dance Theater. Banes and Carroll argued that: 'We don't paraphrase [Cunningham's] dances into propositions about the nature of art as we do Duchamp's Readymades' (ibid.: 10), to which Dalva has responded, 'Maybe not, but there's nothing in the dances that deters this' (Dalva 1992: 182). I suggest that members of Judson Dance Theater experienced Cunningham's dance pieces as open-ended, performative discussions (rather than closed, definitive propositions) about the nature of dance. While recognizing the differences between Cunningham's work and that of the younger generation of experimental choreographers, one must also remember that, compared with the mainstream companies, they were all equally marginalized during the 1960s and that their work was largely ignored. Cunningham's company rarely performed in New York during the 1960s. They had a season in 1960 at the Phoenix Theater on 2nd Avenue between 11th and 12th Streets, and in 1965 appeared at Hunter College Playhouse. In 1967, they appeared for one night at the 92nd Street

YW/YMHA. In 1968 and 1969 they appeared at Brooklyn Academy of Music. This was during a period when the Martha Graham Dance Company appeared on Broadway nearly every year. In 1965 they had a three-week season at the 54th Street Theater. Apart from single pieces presented during two dance festivals, Cunningham's company did not appear in the influential up-town theatres. A 'gentlemen's agreement' between the dance critics of the *New York Times* and the *New York Herald Tribune* meant that dance concerts below 30th Street were not reviewed.[23]

There is no ahistorical yardstick for measuring avant-garde radicalism. As Walter Benjamin pointed out, each generation has to renew its struggle against the particular form that conformism has taken at that time. During a panel discussion in 1986, Yvonne Rainer told Geeta Kapur that her dance work during the 1960s and early 1970s had belonged to a context of 'marginality, intervention, an adversative subculture, a confrontation with the complacent past, the art of resistance' (Jayamanne *et al.*: 1987: 47). She could equally have been describing the context within which Cunningham was working. Considering the 1960s avant-gardes, Andreas Huyssen has pointed out that:

> [like all the] utopian socialists and anarchists up through Dada, surrealism, and the post-revolutionary art of Soviet Russia in the early 1920s, the 1960s fought tradition, and this revolt took place at a time of social and political turmoil. The promise of unlimited abundance, political stability, and the new technological frontiers of the Kennedy years was shattered fast, and social conflict emerged dominant in the civil rights movement, in the urban riots, and in the anti-war movement. It is certainly more than coincidental that the protest culture of the period adopted the label 'counter-culture,' thus projecting an image of the avant-garde leading the way to an alternative kind of society.
>
> (Huyssen 1986: 164)

This is certainly what most of the dancers associated with Judson Dance Theater believed their work was doing. How successful they were in these terms is a question I return to in Chapter 5.

In his *Theory of the Avant-Garde*, Peter Bürger, who had trained as a literary historian and written about French Surrealism, expressed a negative view of more recent avant-garde and postmodern work in the visual arts. The historical avant-garde in his view attacked the autonomous aesthetic of bourgeois art in an attempt to re-establish a connection between art and 'life praxis'. Bürger, however, believed that the neo-avant-garde, to which Cage, Cunningham, Johns, and Rauschenberg belonged, repeated the strategies of the historical avant-garde in such a way as to reinstate and reinscribe the bourgeois autonomy of art by using practices with which earlier avant-garde artists had attempted to attack the institutions that legitimated artistic value. Thus, whereas Dada attacked audiences and the art market, the neo-avant-garde turned their transgressions into marketable, critically acclaimed art works. Andreas Huyssen (1986) and Hal Foster (1994) have both taken issue with Bürger's negative judgement of the post-war avant-gardes. Hal Foster argued that the most advanced work: 'develop[ed] the critique of the conventions of the traditional mediums as performed by Dada, Constructivism, and other historical avant-gardes, into an investigation of the institution of art, its perceptual and cognitive, structural and discursive parameters' (Foster 1994: 20). At its best, Foster argues, post-war avant-garde and postmodern works address the institution of art with a creative analysis at once specific and deconstructive, whereas much early avant-garde work constituted a nihilistic attack on art that was at once abstract and anarchic. Whereas *Relâche* was anarchic and provocative, *Walkaround Time* created conditions in which people were induced to appreciate both 'dance' and 'non-dance' in the same way. *Walkaround Time* and *Would They or Wouldn't They?* both troubled the cognitive, structural, and discursive parameters of theatre dance. Cunningham achieved this through articulating an aesthetic of coolness and indifference that was inspired by the qualities that he, Cage, Johns, and Rauschenberg appreciated in Duchamp and Satie's work. Whether or not audiences perceived Cunningham's work as performative propositions about the nature of dance, I have demonstrated that this is how some of the artists associated with Judson Dance Theater considered Cunningham's work. The next two chapters evaluate the ways in which these artists engaged in their own avant-garde critique of the nature of the dancing body in performance.

3 Minimalism, theory, and the dancing body

For audience members, the only way out of a concert of dance at Judson Memorial Church in the 1960s was across the performance space. Yvonne Rainer told Lyn Blumenthal that, in a concert shared with Steve Paxton and David Gordon[1] at which she first presented *Trio A:* 'People trudged unhappily, disgruntled, disconsolately across the space to get out. You had to be pretty disgusted – pretty unhappy to make a spectacle of yourself in that way' (Rainer 1999: 65). When Blumenthal asked whether she had taken this as a criticism of her work, Rainer replied: 'I was awfully excited about *Trio A*. I felt that I had done something difficult and new' (ibid.). Rainer had confidence in her work that did not just come from supportive reviews by writers such as Jill Johnston. As I shall demonstrate, it came from a process of thinking through, in a theoretical way and writing about the radical consequences of what she was doing in her polemical statement that begins 'NO to spectacle' and in her 1966 essay 'A quasi survey of some "minimalist" tendencies in the quantitatively minimal dance activity amidst the plethora, or an analysis of *Trio A*' (henceforth 'Quasi survey').

When it was first performed in 1966, the full title of Rainer's piece was *The Mind is a Muscle Part One: Trio A.* Rainer published a lengthy statement in the programme for the first full performance of the completed *The Mind is a Muscle* in April 1968. At the beginning of this she wrote: 'If my rage at the impoverishment of ideas, narcissism, and disguised sexual exhibitionism of most dancing can be considered puritan moralizing, it is also true that I love the body – its actual weight, mass, and unenhanced physicality' (Rainer 1974: 71). At the end of it, she described her

> state of mind that reacts with horror and disbelief upon seeing a Vietnamese shot dead on TV – not at the sight of death, however, but at the fact that the TV can be shut off afterwards as after a bad Western. *My body remains the enduring reality.*
>
> (ibid. – my emphasis)

But what exactly did she mean when she said her body remained the enduring reality? Through a discussion of dances by Trisha Brown, Simone Forti, Robert Morris, and Rainer herself, together with a discussion of the theoretical context for Rainer's published essays about dance in the 1960s, this chapter identifies links between Rainer's theoretical writings about dance and minimalism and the growth of a creative anatomical awareness among members of Judson Dance Theater that led to the development in the 1970s of contact improvisation.

Ann Cooper Albright has noted the links between, on the one hand, the area of dance activity comprising contact improvisation and movement research and, on the other, the radicalism of Judson Dance Theater:

> Although it was developed in the seventies, Contact Improvisation has recognizable roots in the social and aesthetic revolutions of the sixties. Contact at once embraces the casual, individualistic, improvisatory ethos of social dancing in addition to the experimentation with pedestrian and task-based movement favored by early postmodern dance groups such as the Judson Church Dance Theater.
>
> (Albright 1997: 84)

I discussed the avant-garde redefinition of theatre dance in the last chapter and look at it further in the present one. This redefinition, as Albright has suggested, led to the creation and performance of movement material that encouraged the dancers to develop focused neuro-skeleto-muscular sensitivities. Such sensitivities would subsequently underpin the development of contact improvisation. The new dance not only prompted performers to develop new kinds of embodied sensitivities, it also made demands on spectators to acknowledge the physical presence of the dancing body in ways that departed radically from spectatorship of mainstream theatre dance. In Chapter 1, I linked Michael Fried's identification of this new kind of presence within minimal sculpture with the way some dancers, associated with Judson Dance Theater, challenged conventional modes of performative presence. Although Fried himself considered theatricality to be a negative quality, ironically it has been adopted as a useful evaluative term by artists, critics, and historians not only for the analysis of minimal and conceptual art of the 1960s and 1970s, but also in discussions of a broad range of late twentieth-century art.[2]

Writing in the early 1980s about Lucinda Childs's work, Susan Sontag was characteristically dismissive about the way the term 'minimalism' had come to be used, calling it a dumb label and noting that, like chewing gum, it had stuck: 'to some painters and sculptors (Sol LeWitt, Robert Morris,

Carl Andre), has spread to architects, composers, even to couturiers – imposing, as such label-mongering invariably does, a specious unity among widely different artists' (Sontag 1983: 105). Being called a minimalist, in Sontag's view, was something of a hindrance: 'Muybridge, Mondrian, Stein and Ozu had the good fortune to pursue careers as virtuosi of obsessive repetition and strong patterning without incurring the label, but not Philip Glass or Lucinda Childs' (ibid.: 108). Sontag was writing at a time when minimalism was not particularly highly regarded, whereas at the end of the 1990s some critics began to claim that it was the first purely American art movement that spanned several art forms (Meyer 2001: 3). Pepe Karmel, in a review of three major exhibitions of minimal art in 2004 observed that: 'Together with Pop art, Minimalism continues to provide the basic language of contemporary art' (Karmel 2004: 90). However, Sontag was surely correct when she complained that the term 'minimalism' has led to misunderstandings about artists' work. There were, nevertheless, connections around shared sets of ideas and concerns between sculptors, composers, and dancers during the early 1960s whose work exemplified an aesthetic sensibility that, for better or for worse, was subsequently labelled minimalist.

One of the few art historians to have looked at the links between minimalism in dance and the visual arts is Anna C. Chave. Her work, which looked at minimal art from an explicitly feminist perspective, has received a mixed reception. Her identification of hidden meanings within minimal painting and sculpture by male artists which she has interpreted in terms of phallic imagery has been widely criticized.[3] More useful to this chapter is her proposal that the impersonality of minimal art became a means through which masculine ascendancy in the art world was maintained. As she has pointed out:

> For a woman to resist the example of Pop and Minimalism by overtly personalizing her art was to risk branding her work as retrogressive and, by the same stroke, to risk reinforcing that tacitly invidious division of labor that presupposes that women will assume 'expressive roles and orientations' while men adopt 'instrumental' ones.
>
> (Chave 2000: 151)

Chave therefore argued that some women artists, such as the sculptors Eva Hesse and Rosemarie Castoro, and the choreographers Simone Forti and Yvonne Rainer, have been unjustly marginalized within the minimalist canon. This is because, as women, their work has been perceived not to be as coolly impersonal or purged of autobiographical references as that of their male colleagues.

Chave pointed out that Morris, as a male artist, has received more scholarly attention than Forti, not only because she was female but also because she was working in the field of dance which, in the modern western world, is perceived as a feminized art. When one examines the dance reviews in the early 1960s that took the new dance seriously, artists such as David Gordon, Fred Herko, and Carolee Schneemann, who included more undisguised, personal material in their work, received less approval; as I shall show in the next chapter, they have been marginalized within canonical accounts of the period. Others, however, such as Lucinda Childs, Steve Paxton, and Yvonne Rainer, who presented work with a minimalist formality that implied a cool impersonality, received more attention and support. Sally Banes has argued that some dances by these three presented 'a criticism of the status quo in terms of gender relations', adding:

> Although they were not presented as feminist polemics, in retrospect it is clear that they challenged gender expectations – in ways that were shocking to contemporary sensibilities – both in the dance tradition (even the avant-garde tradition) and in the larger arena of socio-cultural conventions.
>
> (Banes 1998: 216–17)

While Banes, therefore, ascribed some agency to these dance makers, Chave's point was the extent to which that agency was circumscribed for women choreographers by the institutionalized sexism of the art world. Whereas Banes believed that 'choreographers presented alternatives to what they perceived as the over-emotional female roles in the dance tradition' (ibid.: 219), the implication of Chave's thesis is that female dance artists had to minimize any personal or feminine traits in order to be taken seriously as artists. I shall demonstrate, however, that the impersonal, public nature of minimal art was an integral part of the theoretical position explored by minimal artists and not merely a consequence of the sexist, hierarchical nature of the art world of the 1960s. There is, nevertheless, a complex and somewhat contradictory relationship between the new dance and minimal art. By choosing to explore a minimalist sensibility, some dance artists in the 1960s gained access to a broader cultural milieu. Looking back in 1987, Yvonne Rainer observed:

> On a personal level I could describe my development as a gradual discovery of my own privilege, which I took for granted when I began as a dancer – not realizing that I had automatic entry into

the cultural space of New York's avant-garde milieu, primarily through male artists because I was involved in a 'feminized' art form that posed no threat.

(Jayamanne *et al.* 1987: 47)

While minimalism provided Rainer and others with ways of exploring what Banes has called 'alternatives to what they perceived as the over-emotional female roles', it brought with it a move away from the presentation of personal, autobiographical material. What is interesting, therefore, are the moments when, by adopting a neutral, impersonal role, dancers were by default redefining the significance of the dancing body in the public realm, a point to which I will return at the end of this chapter.

Simone Forti and Robert Morris

There are a number of dancers who attended courses in the San Francisco Bay area with Anna Halprin (or Ann Halprin as she was known professionally until 1972), and subsequently became involved with Judson Dance Theater. It is worth noting that they did so at a comparatively early stage in the development of Halprin's mature work. As Libby Worth and Helen Poynor have pointed out, it was only in 1955, when Halprin seemed on the verge of gaining wide recognition as a Graham-based modern choreographer and performer, that she very deliberately turned her back on mainstream modern dance and began to work with improvisation (Worth and Poynor 2004: 10–12). Halprin's approach to the practice of dance improvisation was one that had developed within dance departments at American universities. Improvisation was central to the work of Halprin's teacher at the University of Wisconsin, Margaret H'Doubler, and Halprin was also influenced by the writings of Mabel Ellsworth Todd. H'Doubler and Todd's pedagogy was underpinned by concerns about fostering somatic and anatomical knowledge.[4] It is with Halprin and Simone Forti that this approach to improvisation made the transition from a practice within dance pedagogy that was underpinned by fairly conventional aesthetic sensibilities to a far more radical, avant-garde performance practice.[5] Forti was a key member of Halprin's group 'The San Francisco Dancers' Workshop' in its early days but left with Morris to live and work in New York in 1959 before Halprin made any of the dance pieces which made her name in the 1960s. Forti, Rainer, Brown, and others thus worked with Halprin at a time when she was looking for new, previously unconsidered possibilities through the use of a strongly kinaesthetic approach.

It was Halprin's facility for setting up pedagogical situations in which a group collectively explored the new and unknown that inspired them.

Rainer initially met Forti through Nancy Mehan, the three of them meeting to improvise together in 1960 (Rainer 1999: 52–3). Through Forti, Rainer heard of Halprin's summer dance workshop which she attended that year, where she first met Trisha Brown. Steve Paxton remembers Rainer, Forti, and Brown improvising in 1961 and 1962 (Teicher 2002: 58). Others who had worked with Halprin and subsequently attended Dunn's classes or became involved in Judson Dance Theater include June Ekman,[6] Ruth Emerson, and Sally Gross who were all, in differing ways, interested in movement research. Ekman became a teacher of the Alexander technique. Gross had worked with Drid Williams who taught alignment and placement based on Todd's kinesiological studies (Banes 1994: 74–5). Elaine Summers, another member of Judson Dance Theater, developed a form of kinetic awareness. Marianne Goldberg (2002: 30) suggests that Brown worked with both Ekman and Summers to develop her physical awareness through these emerging forms. The dance works that Brown, Morris, and, in a slightly different way, Rainer created in the 1960s drew on these new ways of developing bodily awareness, but did so using minimal, conceptual structures and rules, bringing these two approaches together in a way which Forti pioneered.

One of the intriguing aspects of the early pieces that Forti created in 1960 and 1961 was their connection with the visual arts. This is not only because she was at the time married to the visual artist Robert Morris but because she had initially seen herself as an abstract painter before she started work with Halprin. Halprin's dance work, Forti later recalled, seemed to her to be related to painting. When you are painting, she told Agnès Benoit, 'you move a lot, it's a lot about rhythm, putting down paint, it [is] about depth and movement' (Benoit 1997: 155). So, to shift from painting to dance improvisation with Halprin seemed, to Forti, a very natural transition. Her first New York piece *See-Saw* was shown at the Reuben Gallery in December 1960 along with Happenings by Claes Oldenburg and Jim Dine. When Forti and Morris moved to New York, Morris shifted the focus of his work from two-dimensional, expressionist painting to three-dimensional sculpture which, influenced by Duchamp and Johns, gradually evolved towards what became known as minimal sculpture. In 1961 Forti was also interested in sculpture. Her first evening-length concert in May 1961 was part of a series of evenings organized by La Monte Young at Yoko Ono's loft in Chamber Street. Forti's evening was titled 'Five dance constructions and some other things'. She called them 'dance constructions' because: 'The audience could walk around it . . . I saw them existing in space the way sculpture exists in an art gallery space. The audience walked around the pieces. They took place in different spaces in the room' (Forti 1993: 7). Seeing them close up in this way rather than across the conventional divide between seated audience and performance space would have made spectators more directly aware of the relationship between their perception of their own bodies and those of the dancers. This would have been reinforced when, at the end of the evening, the audience were herded three times from one part of the room to another, ending up in the right place to see the last item on the programme, *See-Saw*.

Forti gave descriptions of the dance constructions in her 1974 book *Handbook in Motion*. They included *Platforms*, *Huddle*, and *Slantboard*. *Platforms* used two long, thin, person-sized wooden boxes without bottoms within which a man and a woman lay quietly whistling back and forth to one another on their out-breath. Because of the weight of the boxes, at the start of the piece the man helped the woman under her platform before getting under his own, and at the end let her out. In *Huddle*, six or seven people stood very close together in what in American football is called a huddle, and in English rugby is called a scrum. One performer climbed over the whole group, which collectively has to shift to accommodate the weight and facilitate the climbing. When the dancer had finished, another group member started to climb and so on (see Forti 1974: 59). *Slantboard* used a substantial wooden prop with a 45-degree sloping board to which ropes were attached for dancers to climb up. Forti has described these as 'Conceptual pieces' because:

> You start with an idea, like that you're going to build a ramp and put ropes on it and then you're going to climb up and down. So you don't start by climbing up and down, and then developing movement. You don't start by experiencing the movement and evolving the movement, but you start from an idea that already has the movement pretty prescribed.
>
> (Forti 1993: 11)

This is a very significant shift away from ideas about the aesthetic nature of dance that were current at the time. Forti was saying that she did not use her sensitivity towards aesthetic qualities within movement as a starting point for her creative process. Instead, her approach meant that any aesthetic qualities produced in her 'dance constructions' would only become apparent in the actual moment of their performance. The conceptual nature of these works was undoubtedly inspired by Forti's attendance at Robert and Judith Dunn's composition classes at the Cunningham Studio. But whereas Cunningham worked with a pre-established movement vocabulary and thus within a predetermined range of movement qualities, Forti adopted an approach with the potential for discovering new, previously unknown movement vocabularies and aesthetic qualities. Forti recalled that in Dunn's classes, when they choreographed work using John Cage's new approach to musical notation:

> We would interpret the scores but do it very directly, so there wasn't a lot of . . . it wasn't very plastic, it wasn't very much about movement qualities, which it had been with Ann [Halprin]. She talked a lot about how every movement has its particular quality, so we would look at many things, we would watch each other, being very aware of movement qualities.
>
> (Benoit 1997: 157–9)

What Forti is describing here are improvisations that Halprin had set up for her dancers. There does not appear to have been any room for improvisation in Dunn's classes as Forti recalled them (ibid.). It was while improvising with Halprin that Forti discovered the sensitivity that she wanted dancers and audiences to discover in the kinds of movement qualities she created through these conceptual structures in her dance constructions.

Morris and Rainer have both acknowledged their debt to Forti (Rainer 1999: 52; Morris 1995: 168). In particular, Rainer singles out Forti's first New York piece *See-Saw* (1960) in which she and Morris performed. This piece was perhaps a prototype for many of the pieces subsequently shown at Judson Memorial Church and elsewhere later in the decade. Its central prop was a wooden plank resting on a saw horse or trestle to make a see-saw. Elastic straps at each end of the plank were attached to the wall either side, and a child's toy of the sort that makes a 'moo' sound when lifted or lowered was fixed below one end of the plank. Morris and Rainer, wearing identical shorts and pullovers, sat or lay on opposite ends of the plank to perform movement tasks that caused it to go up and down like a playground see-saw. Forti has described the piece in detail (Forti 1974: 37–43), but Rainer's memories of the piece are particularly interesting. She has pointed out that it consisted of a sequence of largely unrelated events. Some of these used

> the see-saw for its physical properties, like one person lying down, walking back up, tilting it, the other person slides down, walks back up, balancing precariously so the thing is still. It also had some expressionist things in it. At one point Bob Morris read *Art News* to himself, and I had my first screaming fit on the other end. That

came about through Simone flinging a ragged jacket on the floor and saying, 'Improvise that!' and I went to town on my end of the see-saw, screaming and yelling. I couldn't wait.

(Bear and Sharp 1972: 54)

See-Saw ended with Forti singing a country music song, which Forti described as 'a little song I'd heard on some record' (Forti 1993: 8).[7]

Rainer's overall comment on the piece concerns the way its seemingly fragmented components were assembled:

What impressed me structurally about it was that she made no effort to connect the events thematically in any way. I mean the see-saw and the two people, that was the connecting tissue. And one thing followed another. Whenever I am in doubt I think of that. One thing following another.

(Bear and Sharp 1972: 54)

In other words, Forti demonstrated an alternative to the kind of conventional compositional structure that Rainer described in another context, 'wherein elements are connected thematically through variation' and show 'diversity in the use of phrases and space' (Rainer 1974: 68). Rainer told the art historian Lucy Lippard that, in her own work, she was interested in fragmentation but not to the extent of completely exploding material: 'My process is one of accretion and then finding underlying connections' (Lippard 1976: 276). This is surely what she appreciated within *See-Saw*. She has recalled a clash between Forti and Dunn in one of the early composition classes in 1961.[8] In response to a movement assignment he had set, Forti had brought in a poem which Dunn insisted could not be considered dance, but Forti couldn't see why not. Why shouldn't a dance be a poem? Why not have a dance that consists of herding the audience around a loft? Why can't dance involve two performers sitting in wheeled boxes whistling to one another while members of the audience pull on ropes that pull them around the space (*Rollers*)? Why shouldn't one even just put together one thing after another without establishing a thematic connection to justify this? As I will show in this chapter, Forti's refreshingly unconventional approach in these early performances made a significant impact on the way the new dance subsequently developed.

It would be interesting to know what image Forti gave that prompted Morris to read *Art News*. Forti remembered that Morris had a deadpan quality in performance that reminded her of Buster Keaton, and she described Morris and Rainer's relationship in the piece as miserably domestic (Forti 1993: 8). Morris and Rainer were not using any technical skills as actors such as, for example, a Stanlislavskian approach to acting, or the intense, expressionist acting style of the Living Theater, who at the time occupied part of the same building as the Merce Cunningham Dance Company. Although one could say in a loose way that Morris and Rainer were just 'being themselves', it would be more precise to describe what they performed as tasks that signified simple, adopted personae that referred to individual, personal experience in a generalized way. Like *Platforms*, male and female roles in *See-Saw* included references to gender-specific behaviour. It is worth noting, however, that Rainer and Morris wore unisex costumes. Forti, I suggest, was carrying out an early experiment with Morris and Rainer in how to include personal material in a detached, relatively impersonal, minimal way.

Chave compared Forti's piece *Platforms* with another better-known piece devised by Morris for a concert at the Living Theater in 1961 that was also organized by La Monte Young. In this, the curtain opened to reveal a rectangular wooden column, eight feet high with sides two feet wide. After three-and-a-half minutes this fell on its side and after another three-and-a-half minutes the curtain closed. Chave pointed out that whereas Morris's work 'apparently evidenced and addressed a kind of neutral or generically interchangeable viewing subject, Forti's subjects were sometimes marked by gender-coded traits' (Chave 2000: 156). This is true of these two works in isolation but not of Morris and Forti's dance works as a whole. In pieces such as *Huddle*, *Slantboard*, and *Rollers*, Forti used male and female dancers in what could be described as unisex roles. Some of Morris's dances, including *Site*, which I discuss shortly, cast women in roles that included references to gender-specific behaviour although, in the material he himself performed in them, Morris tried to assume a neutral role.

Morris was involved in dance for some time. In the late 1950s, he occasionally accompanied Forti to Halprin's experimental dance workshops in the San Francisco Bay area. Forti remembers that Halprin's

> basic way of working was improvisation following the stream of consciousness. We worked at achieving a state of receptivity in which the stream of consciousness could spill out unhampered. But at the same time a part of the self acted as a witness, watching for movement that was fresh and good, watching the whole of what was evolving between us.
>
> (Forti 1974: 32)

She recalls an incident while Morris was attending one of Halprin's workshops and using this concentrated self-witnessing. This came in a class taught by the painter A.A. Leath, who had set the task of selecting something from the natural environment and taking its movement characteristics. Morris had observed a rock:

> [H]e lay down on the ground. Over a period of about three minutes he became more and more compact until the edges of him were off the ground, and just the point under his center of gravity remained on the ground.
>
> (ibid.: 31)

Morris's embodied response to the rock can be seen with hindsight as a precursor for his later discussion of the spectator's embodied response to the plywood cubes and polyhedrons in his minimalist sculptures to which *Site* clearly referred.

Another lesson that Halprin taught was about the use of objects in performance. This was an approach to performance that Halprin was developing in 1960 when Morris, Forti, Rainer, and Brown attended a summer workshop with her. Forti has written a vivid description of one of Brown's responses to an improvisational task she had been set: this was to take an inanimate object from the environment and find its unique manner of movement. Brown's object was a broom.

> She was holding a broom in her hand. She thrust it out straight ahead, without letting go of the handle. And she thrust it out with such force that the momentum carried her whole body through the air. I still have the image of that broom and Trisha right out in space, traveling in a straight line about three feet off the ground.
>
> (ibid.: 31–2)

That year Halprin's group performed a dance piece called *Birds of America*. As Halprin explained to Rainer, having rehearsed the piece for several months in her studio, she became unhappy about the way it looked on stage in a theatre and:

> just before the performance, I put a bamboo pole in everybody's hands, including me, and we had to do the dance we'd always done, holding these bamboo poles. . . . The poles were very long and they created their own spatial environment. I began to feel that we had paid such strict attention to self-awareness, kinesthetic response, and to each other, that we developed a stifling introspection. So we began to extend our response to adaptive responses in the environment.
>
> (Halprin 1995: 81)

This radical focus on the relationship between somatic experience, spatiality, and modes of performance permeated the new dance of the Judson group, and can be seen very clearly in Morris's *Site* which combined what Morris learnt from Halprin with a knowing, avant-garde intervention within high modernist art theory – Morris was studying for an MA in Art History at Hunter College, New York, at the time.

Site (1964) was first performed at Judson Memorial Church in 1964. It demonstrates the way theory was becoming a factor within dance. As part of a performative riposte to the art historian Clement Greenberg, Morris asserted the kinds of kinaesthetic awareness that he, along with Forti, Rainer, and others, had learnt from working with Halprin. The sensitivity to physical experiences that underpinned *Site* was that which informed Morris's subsequent theorization of minimalism in his three-part essay 'Notes on sculpture' published in 1966 and 1967, and thus written at the same time that his then partner, Rainer, was writing her 'Quasi survey'. I discuss both later in the chapter. *Site* was a twenty-minute piece during which a man (Morris), dressed in white T-shirt and jeans and wearing work gloves, manipulated eight-foot by four-foot sheets of white painted plywood through an increasingly virtuosic sequence of movements. As the piece started, the set consisted of, centre stage, a stack of sheets of plywood leaning in landscape orientation against the back wall of the performance space, and a 'sound cube' in front of this from which came the recorded noise of a pneumatic drill on a building site. The man stood to one side with his back to the audience. In a slow, measured way, he walked to the stack and lifted off the top sheet of plywood, then carried it off stage right. When he faced the audience, he revealed that he was wearing a white mask cast from his own face. He returned at the same, almost ponderous pace and lifted a second sheet and again walked with it to the right, gradually turning it through ninety degrees. When it was upright, he leaned it against the back wall, paused, and then in an unemphatic, neutral manner, slowly ran his right hand a little way along the right-hand edge of the sheet. Returning once more to the stack, he removed a third sheet; but whereas he had lifted the previous ones by gripping them with a hand placed under the middle of the sheet and lifting it straight up, the third sheet was removed with a flourish, tipping it up on one end, to reveal behind it a naked woman, initially Carolee Schneemann,[9] posing on sheets and pillows in front of another eight-by-four sheet of plywood, in a tableau of Manet's famous 1863 painting *Olympia* (Figure 3.1). Schneemann's face and body were whitened with powder and, throughout the performance, she remained motionless while staring in a frank way towards the audience.

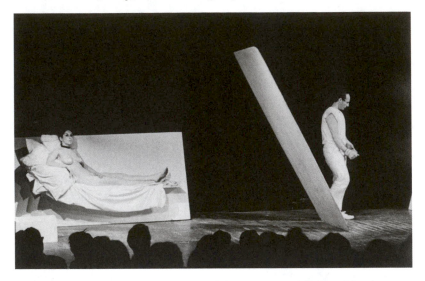

Figure 3.1 Robert Morris. *Site.* Carolee Schneemann and Robert Morris
        performing at Events and Entertainments, Pocket Theater, NYC
        1964.

Photo by Peter Moore © Estate of Peter Moore/VAGA, New York.

For the next quarter-of-an-hour the man continued manipulating the
third sheet of plywood in changing and inventive ways while maintaining
his studiedly neutral manner. Steve Paxton recalled this as 'amazing
. . . bending it and balancing it and twirling it and letting go of it' (Banes
1995: 206). At one moment Morris paused, took off one glove and carefully ran his hand along the jaw line of his mask. This gesture resembled
his earlier action of running his hand down the edge of the second sheet
of plywood. Eventually, he replaced the board in front of 'Olympia',
and, in a recapitulation of the opening sequence, replaced the other
two sheets, returning to his initial standing position with his back to the
audience. Reviewing the piece in *The Village Voice*, Jill Johnston praised
it as a work of 'maximum efficiency with a high-tension charge in [its]
associative potential' (1964: 12):

> Morris is a workman performing a task of balance and control. The
> pneumatic drill corroborates his activity. Both are dramatically
> opposed to the ideal poetic image of the transfixed lady. After the
> initial shock of exposure, the slow revelation of associations sets in.
> Nobody is immune to its cultural significance. The extreme neutrality

– the visual emphasis, the matter-of-fact manipulation, the absence
of contact – is the work of an artist putting different pictures, like
photographs, together on a canvas and letting the audience take it
from there.

(ibid.)

One of the associations which Johnston suggested *Site* brought into play
was an ironic comment on the role Manet's *Olympia* occupied in the
dominant Greenbergian account of modernism. Greenberg had written
in 1960 that: 'Manet's paintings became the first Modernist ones by
virtue of the frankness with which they declared the surfaces on which
they were painted' (Greenberg 1982: 6). For Greenberg, what Manet's
painted surfaces declared was their flatness: 'Flatness, two-dimensionality,
was the only condition painting shared with no other art, so Modernist
painting oriented itself to flatness as it did to nothing else' (ibid.). *Site*
ironically played on the idea of flatness. First, Schneemann as Olympia
was of course not flat but present on stage in all three dimensions.
Second, she appeared from behind a sheet of white plywood as if she
were inhabiting illusionistic pictorial space behind the picture plane.
Third, however, the way Morris himself stroked both the edge of a
plywood sheet and his own jaw, suggests that flat plywood and human
body are, in some way, equivalents for one another.

If *Site* cited Greenberg on Manet, it also referred to the work of other
artists. Morris will have expected many audience members to recognize
references in *Site* to the work of Jasper Johns and Marcel Duchamp.
The mask that Morris wore in the original version of *Site* was cast from
his face by Johns himself. In the mid-1950s, Johns had put plaster casts
of Nan Rosenthal's face in boxes as part of a 'Targets' painting to which
Morris himself seems to refer in his *I Box* (1962). Both Johns and Morris
were interested in the work of Marcel Duchamp, and *Site*'s 'citation' of
Manet's *Olympia* could be seen as a Ready-made. The performance also
referred to Morris's sculptures. The plywood sheets that he was manipulating were the raw material for his plywood cubes and polyhedrons.
On one level, therefore, *Site* located itself ironically within debates about
avant-garde artistic practice; on another level it explored abstract, formal
relationships through movement in the performance space in a way that
performatively challenged Greenberg's theorization of modernism. It
may have done so in an ironic way, but it also anticipated Morris's
serious theoretical challenge in his later 'Notes on sculpture'. In its
spatiality *Site* recalled Halprin's work. Where Halprin's dancers had
manipulated bamboo poles in *Birds of America*, Morris manipulated a
sheet of plywood to explore his response to stage space, drawing on the

same kind of concentrated awareness exemplified in his earlier performance of the movement characteristics of the rock. Morris would later write
about the theoretical implications of this concentrated awareness. While
the sound box in *Site* suggested a building site, the title also punningly
referred to the act of seeing, and to citation – to Greenberg on Manet, to
Johns and Duchamp (of whose work Greenberg disapproved) and to
Schneemann's own work.

Audience members who regularly attended experimental dance
performances and Happenings would have known Schneemann's Judson
dances such as *Newspaper Event* and her naked appearances in works by
Oldenberg and Kaprow. Because of her association with eroticism,
Schneemann's participation in the piece introduced into it a tension
between the conciseness of abstract formalism and the messier complexity
of personal autobiographical reference. Photographs show Schneemann,
as 'Olympia', actively staring in a far from neutral way at her audience.[10] A century earlier, audiences at the Paris Salon had been shocked
by the directness of the prostitute model's gaze in Manet's *Olympia*.
Schneemann was one of the few women involved with Judson Dance
Theater who had any feminist awareness at the time, having written a
dissertation about Simone de Beauvoir's *The Second Sex* as part of her
Master's degree. Her gaze was, therefore, probably fuelled by anger.
She later denounced the undignified ways in which she, as a female
painter, was allowed to join the 'male art team' (Schneemann 1997:
196). She allowed herself to be used as what she calls a 'Cunt Mascot'
(ibid.) to avoid being excluded altogether from the art world to which
she felt she had a right to belong. 'I was permitted to be an image but
not an image-maker creating her own self image' (ibid.: 194), she later
protested. (I discuss Schneemann's work in the next chapter.) Morris,
therefore, gave Schneemann a role that had unavoidable gender connotations while he himself adopted a task-based role that was seemingly
neutral and free of gender connotations. Whether or not the intensity
of Schneemann's stare in *Site* unsettled the neutrality of Morris's role
and drew attention to its tacit masculinity, there was an undeniably
unequal power relation between the roles that Morris and Schneemann
performed in this piece. This had not been the case with the roles
Morris and Rainer performed in *See-Saw*. In Anna C. Chave's terms,
Schneemann was performing an expressive role while Morris was adopting an instrumental one. Comparison of *See-Saw* and *Site* therefore reveals
that the problem of dealing with personal or autobiographical material
related to the difference between expression and the embodiment of
instrumental roles.

Early work by Trisha Brown and Yvonne Rainer

In the dance works they created in the early 1960s Trisha Brown and Yvonne Rainer both initially tried to use expressive material in the way that Forti had used it in *See-Saw*. However, each, in different ways, gradually adopted formal structures through which personal or autobiographical material was rendered more impersonal, leading each to explore ways of minimizing performative presence.

Trillium, which Brown first performed at Maidman Playhouse, New York in March 1962 and went on to show at Judson Memorial Church later that year, was the first piece of choreography that she showed in New York. A trillium is a North American woodland flower. When Brown was a child living in Washington State, she used to try to transplant some trillium to her mother's garden, but it always wilted and faded by the time she got home. Brown saw this as an image for the wildness and transitoriness of movement. She has described *Trillium* as:

> a structured improvisation of very high energy movements involving a curious timing and with dumb silences like stopping dead in your tracks. It was a kinesthetic piece, a serial composition where I involved myself in one movement after another accompanied by a tape by Simone Forti. In thinking of the opening section of *Trillium*, I am reminded of working in a studio on a movement exploration of traversing the three positions sitting, standing, and lying. I broke those actions down to their basic mechanical structure, finding the places of rest, power, momentum and peculiarity. I went over and over the material, eventually accelerating and mixing up to the degree that lying down was done in air.
>
> (Brown 1978: 46)

A photograph by Al Giese of *Trillium* at Judson Memorial Church in 1962 shows Brown just after she has assumed a sitting position upside down in mid-air (Figure 3.2). Sitting, standing, lying down, and doing a handstand are all found movements. Steve Paxton recalled that it was odd at that time to see a handstand in a dance (cited in Banes 1995: 121). (It is also significant that the photograph shows Brown wearing a leotard and tights: in 1962 dancers at downtown events were still dressing in conventional ways while audiences still dressed up smartly to come to see them.) William Davis, who was a member of Judson Dance Theater and danced in Cunningham's company, told Sally Banes that: 'After you watched her for a while, you realized that what might seem quite disturbing or dangerous she had completely under control' (cited in Banes 1995: 121). This improvised execution demonstrated that Brown had a remarkable knowledge of her body which had been developed entirely independently of conventional dance technique.

Speaking in 1998 about the early 1960s, Trisha Brown recalled:

> I had a lot of experience of improvising that brought out very mysterious – it makes my heart race right now – just incredibly magical events. I loved that. I was good at it, and I did not want to be held down in dance technique. I wanted to fly.
>
> (Brown 1998: 16–17)

Writing about Brown's *Lightfall* (1963), a duet with Steve Paxton, Jill Johnston observed:

> Miss Brown has a genius for improvisation, for being ready when the moment calls, for 'being there' when the moment arrives. Such facility is no mere tongue wagging, but the result of an exterior

Figure 3.2 Trisha Brown. *Trillium* at Judson Memorial Church, June 1962.
Photo by Al Giese.

calm and confidence and of highly developed kinesthetic responses. She's really relaxed and beautiful.

(Johnston 1963b: 19)

This was one of the very few reviews of Brown's work in the 1960s. Brown had learnt about improvisation as a student at Mills College and during the summer course she took with Ann Halprin in the San Francisco Bay area in 1960. I have already mentioned Forti's story about Brown flying while exploring the properties of a broom. Through working with Halprin, Brown found a way in which somatic and anatomical knowledge could inform the creation of theatre dance. This not only informed the creation of *Trillium* but became a central preoccupation in her work.

In the late 1990s, Brown told Hendel Teicher about one of her improvisations in the early 1960s that seems to relate to the material she developed for *Trillium*:

> I had had experiences in which I could dispatch my mind where I could do things such as fly. Simone [Forti] mentions this capacity in her book [the broom story]. This is how I found out I could do it – the choreographer Aileen Pasloff happened to come into the studio and just stood there in the doorway watching me. I realized I should stop because she was renting the studio, and I stopped and said 'I'm sorry, I'll get out'. She said 'do you know what you were doing?' And I said 'well, I know what I was instructing myself to do in the improvisations.' And she said 'you were flying'.
>
> (Brown 1998: 16–17)

A preoccupation with flying runs through Brown's work, from *Trillium* through to the opening of *Orfeo* (1998). When Lise Brunel asked Brown in 1986 why she was interested in the idea of flying, she simply replied 'I am a dancer' (Brunel 1987: 70). There was a tension in *Trillium* between improvised movement that led to Brown flying, lying flat out in the air, and the simple, everyday movements that the improvisation framed, and which, as Paxton implies, would subsequently become more familiar within works by artists associated with Judson Dance Theater. At stake was more than just exciting new movement qualities and ideas; underlying it was an intellectual recognition of the redundancy of the conventional compositional device of theme and variation. Just as Rainer was fascinated by Forti's confidence in simply letting one thing follow another, Brown was trying to find something new and interesting by saying no to ways of structuring material that an older generation of modern dancers took for granted.

Trisha Brown has told a story during a videotaped interview about an experience concerning *Trillium* that she had had at the American Dance Festival at Connecticut College in 1962 (Brown 1996). This was not her first visit to the festival; she had gone back especially to attend once more Louis Horst's composition class, having taken Halprin's summer workshop and, more recently, Robert Dunn's composition classes.[11] When there was an audition for students at the festival to perform their own choreography in a concert, Brown offered *Trillium*, which she had first performed earlier that summer. The judges unanimously rejected it but some of the students also taking part in the audition complained and circulated a petition to have it accepted. *Trillium* had a sound score recorded by Simone Forti who sang in multiple pitches with a vacuum cleaner as a background drone. (Forti was at the time singing similar drone music in La Monte Young's music group, 'Theater of Eternal Music'.) When Brown was told she could perform the piece if she removed the music, she refused. Bessie Schönberg was then given the task of explaining to Brown, over a cup of coffee in the college cafeteria, why it was impossible to include the piece in the programme of student work. Brown says Schönberg didn't understand the logic of how *Trillium* was put together and assumed that there was no logic. To make her point Schönberg arranged the salt shaker and sugar bowl randomly on the table in front of them saying you can't just put anything together without any thought just like this, then stopped to remark that actually the arrangement of items on the table did look interesting. Brown remained unconvinced, but *Trillium* wasn't performed.

Brown had a confidence about her work that came from having thought in an intellectual way about the avant-garde nature of what she was doing. This came from belonging to a group of like-minded dancers and visual artists living and working in downtown Manhattan. As Peter Osborne has pointed out:

> The generation of New York artists who came to prominence in the 1960s were the first group of artists to have attended University. Their reaction against the anti-intellectualism of the prevailing ideology of the art world – which was at once a reaction against its social conservatism – was profound.
>
> (Osborne 1999: 50)

Schönberg, like Davis, may have detected the dangerous, improvised energy of *Trillium* and perhaps, as Paxton had done, appreciated its lack of conventional dance movements. If she was unable also to recognize the piece's underlying logic, this was because she lacked knowledge of avant-garde processes and ways of thinking to which Brown had been introduced by Halprin and Dunn. 'My big influence,' she told Hendel Teicher, 'was John Cage because of how he interacted with performance and with conceptual ideas' (Brown 1998: 13).[12] Brown's more avant-garde, intellectual approach to dance brought her an openness to new possibilities that Schönberg, despite her long experience as a dancer and teacher, lacked.

Brown nevertheless subsequently abandoned some aspects that had been central to *Trillium*. As she later told Marianne Goldberg, she had felt too subjective and exposed in *Trillium*.

> I got the picture from everyone around me to tighten up my act.
> I needed to be less exposed. I wanted to fit in with the group. In
> pieces like *Rulegame 5* (1964) and *Man Walking Down the Side of a
> Building* (1970), I created a more systematized framework in which
> to behave.
>
> (Goldberg 1991: 6)

The intellectually backed openness that enabled Brown to recognize and develop her understanding of anatomical and somatic functioning also gave her strategies with which to organize and structure the resulting new movements that she was discovering. Brown's *Homemade* (1965) demonstrates how she, therefore, began to explore personal material in an impersonal, task-based way. In this, Brown performed a series of everyday movements – casting a fishing line, measuring a box, telephoning – while a substantial sixteen-millimetre film projector, strapped to her back, projected a film by Forti's second husband, Robert Whitman, of Brown performing the same movements (Banes 1980: 79). The projected image sometimes showed on a white screen behind her back but also danced all over the walls of the performance space as Brown turned from side to side performing her choreography. The difference between her live performance and her performance in the film demonstrated how much the weight of the projector constrained Brown's freedom of movement. The piece, therefore, demonstrated that dance could be about anti-expressive, everyday movement by conceptually framing the real effort involved in the dance. Underlying her performance of everyday movement, therefore, was a physical awareness informed by Brown's understanding of anatomical and somatic functioning. But the piece was also informed by personal experience. Brown later recalled: 'I gave myself the instruction to enact and distil a series of meaningful memories, preferably those that had an impact on identity. Each "memory-unit" is "lived", not performed, and the series is enacted without transitions' (Brown 2003: 194).[13] The experience for Brown was, therefore, as meaningful personally as that of performing *Trillium*, but it was mediated to the audience through a formal, systematic framework and a conceptual structure which, like those in Forti's 'dance constructions', prescribed the movement quality.

A similar, privately autobiographical reference informed *Ordinary Dance*, the solo that Rainer presented at the first concert of dance presented at Judson Memorial Church in July 1962. While dancing a series of ordinary movements that had no apparent connection with any codified dance vocabulary, Rainer recited a narrative that detailed the addresses of all the buildings in which she had ever lived. Not only were the movements not connected with one another but neither was there any meaningful connection between movements and speech. A similar fragmentation informed Rainer's *Terrain* (1963). Reviewing this, Jill Johnston described Rainer's style as a matter-of-fact combination of:

> 'natural' movements, classical (modern) extensions, hard fast phrases, soft pose changes, limpid or throw-away relaxations, and the spastic distortions, whimsical or grotesque which belong to a class of quirky gestures unique to Miss Rainer. The quirks often look like loony-bin material, although the line between what looks insane and what looks child-like is often pretty thin.
>
> (Johnston 1963c: 11, 18)

Rainer remembered that, in the middle section of her *Three Seascapes* (1963), while she was moving in a diagonal across the performance space, she had looked like 'a goofy, sexy, crippled, possessed, audience-be-damned, nothing-to-lose, shameless, female critter' (cited in Perron and Cameron 1981: 58). This section came after one in which she simply ran around the performance space to the pompous strains of the 'Tuba Mirum' from Berlioz's *Requiem*, and was followed by one in which she threw her winter coat and a big piece of gauzy material on the floor and had one of her screaming fits. As Johnston's comment suggests, Rainer wasn't interested in developing a unified style of choreography, but in juxtaposing different kinds of material. She was letting one thing follow another without any established connection, as Forti had done in *See-Saw*. Rainer took this further in her group works where performers, often both trained and untrained dancers, found their own ways of interpreting these widely divergent types of material from game-like, indeterminate instructions.

A photo by Al Geise shows Rainer in *Three Seascapes* dancing her goofy, sexy solo of slow-motion undulations on a diagonal that brought her right up close to the audience. This was performed to La Monte Young's *Poem for Tables, Chairs, Benches* where these objects were 'played' by pushing them around the floor. A section of *Terrain* called 'Duet', in which Rainer and Brown performed together wearing black tights and black Hollywood Vassarette lace push-up bras, contained a quirky mixture of ballet and erotic movement. While Rainer danced a ballet solo she had learnt in Nina Stroganova's intermediate ballet class, Trisha Brown performed ballet movements in her upper body and burlesque bumps and grinds with her legs and hips. The duet ended with them both performing nineteen 'cheesecake' poses to music from Massenet's opera, *Thais*. Later, in *Terrain*, she performed a duet with William Davis based on poses taken from erotic Indian sculpture, presented in a deadpan manner. Rainer recognized her own attraction to the experience of her power over her audience during the moment of performing. This is evident from her later description of her first experience of dancing her own choreography in public:[14]

> [I]t was as good as orgasm. I knew that was where I lived, that was where I belonged, doing that work and presenting myself physically to an audience. And that, of course, was part of the charisma. That is the urgency, and that pleasure in exhibiting oneself is part of the seduction of an audience. The performer has to experience that in order for the audience to get a sense of this presence or to be taken in by it.
>
> (Rainer 1999: 63)

When in 1965 Rainer said 'no to glamour' and 'no to seduction', she was explicitly rejecting erotic aspects of the act of performing that she had enjoyed performing in her own choreography. She subsequently raged against forms of dancing that she felt were disguised sexual exhibitionism (Rainer 1974: 71), though there had been nothing disguised about the eroticism of parts of *Terrain* or of her later duet with Robert Morris, *Part of a Sextet* (1964). She also later criticized the narcissistic/voyeuristic duality of doer and looker (ibid.: 238). It was all of this that Rainer was therefore consciously renouncing when she adopted a dry, minimalist style of performing.

Rainer has said that she first became aware of the 'problem of performance' (Rainer 1974: 68) through discussions with Steve Paxton.[15] Paxton himself later recalled that he often criticized Rainer for having too strong a stage presence (Banes 1995: 233, fn. 20). Paxton and Rainer's collaboration *Word Words* (1963) is probably the first piece in which she explored the performance of flattened, impersonal material in a cool, neutral manner. Each contributed movement material for *Word Words*, Paxton making complex, Cunningham-like technical moves while Rainer offered 'twisting poses and very tiny, repetitive gestures' (ibid.: 89). The complete sequence was repeated three times in the piece: first Rainer performed it as a solo, it was then danced by Paxton, and this was followed by a unison repeat of the same material by both of them together. The title *Word Words*, like the titles of Paxton's other early pieces – *Proxy* (1962) and *English* (1964) – are, as Lucinda Childs observed, 'intricately Jesuitical': ' "English" ', Childs pointed out, 'is one of those words that is itself and stands for something else' (ibid.: 98). Paxton himself said the title of *Word Words* was one of his self-reflexive titles: 'They do that business like: the first word is a word, the second is the same but pluralized. It doesn't reflect the dance at all; it is a way of using words' (cited in Bear 1975: 26). Paxton then pointed to a photograph of the piece showing Rainer and himself together, almost nude, performing in unison, and explained that: 'It's a singularity and plurality play' (ibid.). This use of language games reflected an awareness of Wittgenstein's philosophy among minimal artists, a point to which I will return later.

Paxton has suggested that a starting point for the piece was a response that he and Rainer had received when they had unsuccessfully auditioned for a concert at the 92nd Street YW/YMHA. They heard that someone at the 'Y' had said 'those Judson people all look alike to me' (ibid.). Rainer remembers that in order to make the two dancers in *Word Words* look the same, they originally thought of wearing gorilla suits, then Santa Claus suits. Then they thought of using make-up to redraw their faces to make them look alike, then finally settled on the idea of dancing in the nude with G-strings and with paper covering Rainer's nipples (ibid.: 89). The idea of using make-up to make dancers look alike was taken up in Paxton's group piece *English* in which skin-coloured greasepaint was used to cover the face, including eyebrows and lips. It is suggestive that a venue that had for so long been associated with modern dance would have rejected choreographers whose work abandoned the angst-ridden expressive individualism of modern dance in favour of a blank, neutral mode of behaving during performance. Paxton and Rainer were not, of course, doing this merely in response to what the programmer at the 92nd St 'Y' may have said. The piece's depersonalization and minimalism were all attributes that it shared with other works created by artists associated with Judson Dance Theater. It didn't therefore just reject existing conventions and traditions but by doing so engaged in a process of performative research into new, simpler, more minimal ways of signifying that corresponded to those that attracted artists to Wittgenstein's theories.

Brown also consciously rejected this kind of expressive individualism. She seems to have had similar thoughts to Paxton and Rainer about how the dancer projects her presence towards the audience, undoubtedly discussing this with them. She explored this in her piece *Inside* (1965). The movement material for this was developed through improvising in a line twelve feet away from the walls of her loft studio. For its performance, Brown arranged the audience's seats into an inward-facing square, recreating the walls of her studio: as she then performed the solo that she had developed in her studio, she moved right up close to her audience as if they were the walls. As she later told Banes:

> Up until that time dancers in dance companies were doing rigorous technical steps and one of the mannerisms was to glaze over the eyes and kick up a storm in there behind your eyes. Many people used that device to hide from their audience; we all knew about it and talked about it. So I decided to confront my audience straight ahead. As I traveled right along the edge of their knees in this dance, I looked at each person. It wasn't dramatic or confrontational; just the way you look when you're riding on a bus and notice everything.
>
> (Banes 1980: 79–80)

Brown's decision to look at each audience member individually was therefore based on a critique of how dancers behave when they perform. Her standpoint was similar to Paxton's observations of his experience dancing with the Merce Cunningham Dance Company. Just as Rainer refused to seduce the audience through projection of her charismatic presence, Brown's look was not dramatic or confrontational. It drew on ordinary modes of contemporary urban behaviour, such as the quality of attention while riding on a bus. Like *Word Words*, *Inside* didn't therefore just say No! to existing conventions and traditions but by doing so engaged in a process of performative research which in this case focused on finding alternative ways of projecting performative presence.

Dance theory and art theory

Yvonne Rainer's *Trio A* brought together all the formal and conceptual concerns and aesthetic sensibilities of the works I have discussed so far in this chapter. Like the material Morris performed in *Site*, *Trio A* consisted of a series of movement tasks and, like Forti's *See-Saw*, there was no attempt to link these tasks thematically in any way. *Trio A* dealt with the problem of performance by doing the opposite of Schneemann in *Site* and Brown in *Inside*. Whereas they looked directly at the audience, Rainer

choreographed the dancer's gaze so that it never met that of the spectator. Like *Trillium*, *Trio A* contained a handstand along with a number of
other, ordinary movements that had no connection with any existing, codified dance vocabulary. Also like *Trillium* it exploited the concentrated
focus on embodied experience that Brown, Forti, Morris, and Rainer had
all learnt from Halprin; Rainer used this to ensure that the moves she had
choreographed contained no logical connection with one another and no
identifiable transitions. Like *Word Words*, the same material was performed in a flattened, uninviting way by deindividualized performers.

There are two solo versions of *Trio A* available on video that are well
known. Sally Banes made a 16 mm film of Rainer dancing it in 1978.
For the Public Service Broadcasting documentary film *Beyond the
Mainstream* (Brockway 1980), first broadcast in 1980, most of *Trio A* was
performed for the camera as a solo by the untrained dancer Frank
Conversano, Bart Cook of the New York City Ballet, and Sara Rudner,
herself a choreographer who had for many years danced with Twyla
Tharp. Their performances were then edited, together with footage from
Banes's film, to create a solo version that alternated between each of
these dancers. I myself was lucky enough to see Rainer's programme
Trio A Pressured at Judson Memorial Church in November 1999. This
included a revival of *Trio A* as it was first performed there in January
1966 with two of the original dancers, Paxton and Rainer, and with
Douglas Dunn taking the absent David Gordon's place. I have also seen
the White Oak Dance Project's version of *Trio A* performed by six
dancers to the musical accompaniment of the Chambers Brothers' *At
the Midnight Hour*. *Trio A* has been performed over the years by a number
of different performers in various different combinations.[16] Rainer gave
tacit permission for anyone to teach *Trio A* to anybody: 'I envisioned
myself,' Rainer later wrote, 'as a post-modern dance evangelist bringing
movement to the masses, watching with Will Rogers-like benignity the
slow, inevitable evisceration of my elitist creation' (Rainer 1974: 77).
Will Rogers was an early film and vaudeville comedian known for his
folksy, 'cracker barrel' philosophy.

The sequence of moves that make up *Trio A* was choreographed in
a conventional, piecemeal way rather than the conceptual way in which
Forti created her dance constructions. As I noted earlier, in these Forti
started with an idea that determined a particular way of moving rather
than evolving a sequence that elaborated an individual aesthetic sensibility. The various ways in which *Trio A* has been cast and staged over
the years, however, has demonstrated that there is no one way of experiencing the movement that can be said to be essential to the aesthetic
identity of the dance. Indeed, its aesthetic identity is so minimal and

neutralized that, in any given performance, it is almost entirely prescribed by the conceptual decisions made by those casting and staging it.

For all the reasons I have just given, *Trio A* is a very difficult dance to watch. In the first version, performed at Judson Memorial Church in 1966, Rainer herself with Steve Paxton and David Gordon, each started at slightly different times rather than in unison. There was no interaction between the dancers, as the label 'trio' might have suggested, because each moved within her or his own lateral strip of the performance space. The dancers started on the far right-hand side of the space (as the spectator looked at it), moved gradually over to the far left and then back again, each in a horizontal plane, one behind the other, none intruding in any of the other's space. As the three dancers, in learning the piece, had to find the movement in their own body, they each developed their own individual pace and therefore, during the performance, occasionally came in and out of time with one another. This was because, in a conventional sense, there was no music with which the dancers could synchronize their moves. Instead the visual artist Alex Hay (whose performance in Deborah Hay's *Would They or Wouldn't They?* I discussed in the last chapter), standing in the church gallery, dropped one by one a series of laths of timber that landed with a regular crash down on the church floor below for the piece's 'music' (Figure 3.3). The piles of fallen timber can be made out on the left of Peter Moore's photograph of *Trio A*, in which all three performers are clearly out of synch with one another. During the 1968 premier at the Anderson Theater of the completed *The Mind is a Muscle*, *Trio A*, was again performed to the sound of crashing timbers, this time dropped from the top of a ladder hidden in the wings. I found when watching the trio version in 1999 that the lack of unison meant that, as a spectator, I started off feeling lost and had to work hard to watch it. The lack of any 'landmark' movements meant that, although I could sometimes recognize that one of the dancers had repeated a movement task I had just seen performed by one of the others, I was afraid I would get even more lost if I switched from watching one to watching another – something that dance audiences have learnt to do from watching work by Cunningham. If one could approach *Trio A* without any knowledge of its history or context, the dance would not seem to make any sense, and indeed it deliberately seems to refuse to make sense in almost all the ways in which theatre dances conventionally signify meanings. It is, however, extremely unlikely that anyone would ever see *Trio A* 'cold' in this way. Almost everyone who has written about it has made some reference to Rainer's 'Quasi survey' or to her statement that begins 'NO to spectacle'. The 'Quasi survey' has become inseparably linked with *Trio A* in the way that Marcel Duchamp's *The Large Glass* has become inseparably linked with *The Green Box*, which contained all the notes and plans he made while working on it (see Chapter 2).

Rainer's 'Quasi survey' reveals the way in which *Trio A* challenged and contradicted the tacit conventions on which mainstream theatre dance – in ballet, modern dance, or Broadway musicals – addressed spectators. But *Trio A* did not just make a normative reliance on conventions explicit, in the way that, for example, her duet with Trisha Brown in *Terrain* had made explicit what was usually tacit. What *Trio A* attempted to articulate were the conditions in which the spectator could perceive the positive values that Rainer wished to substitute for the conventional ones she believed should be eliminated or minimized. The 'Quasi survey' does not tell spectators how to view *Trio A*. However, direct or indirect knowledge of what Rainer wrote in it changes the way a viewer reads the dance by indicating the kind of process through which they can engage with it. Taken together, *Trio A* and the 'Quasi survey' therefore

Figure 3.3 Yvonne Rainer. *The Mind is a Muscle Part One, Trio A*. Judson Memorial Church, January 1966. (From the right) Steve Paxton, David Gordon, and Yvonne Rainer and behind them the pile of wood.

Photo by Peter Moore © Estate of Peter Moore/VAGA, New York.

position the viewer as a self-conscious subject in relation to the experience of viewing and reading the dance. It is this self-consciousness that I described above when I recalled how aware I had been of the effort I was making to watch *Trio A*. As I noted earlier, in Michael Fried's terms, this made it theatrical, because: 'it is concerned with the actual circumstances in which the beholder encounters the literalist [Fried's term for minimalist] work' (Fried 1969: 125). Fried pointed out that Robert Morris, in part one of his 'Notes on sculpture', had said that, whereas in previous art what is to be had from the work is strictly located within it, the experience of minimal art is: 'of an object *in a situation* – and one that, virtually by definition, *includes the beholder*' (ibid., Fried's emphasis). *Trio A*, like *Site*, constituted a performative intervention within the theoretical debates about modernism and minimalism that were taking place at that time. As I argued in Chapter 1, Rainer aligned *Trio A* and the new dance with the theoretical ideas being developed by minimal and conceptual artists, and against the view of the art critics, Greenberg and Fried.

With characteristically blunt candour, Rainer has said that when she wrote her 'Quasi survey' she was 'heavily influenced' by Donald Judd's 1965 essay 'Specific objects', Morris's 'Notes on sculpture' and Barbara Rose's 1965 essay 'ABC art' (Rainer 1999: 103).[17] Taken together, these three essays provide a snapshot of the kinds of intellectual ideas current in New York at the time. Judd, who had a degree in Philosophy from Columbia University, held behaviourist views and was particularly interested in the ideas of the now little-known American philosopher Ralph Barton Perry, who had edited William James's collected works. Morris's 'Notes on sculpture' show his transition from a theoretical framework based on gestalt psychology, to one based on phenomenology, and in particular on Merleau-Ponty's *Phenomenology of Perception*, an English translation of which was published by Routledge & Kegan Paul in 1962. Whereas Judd and Morris were practitioners creating a theoretical context for the reception of their work, Rose was an art critic and historian whose essay took a broad view of minimal art that included dance and was one of the first pieces of art criticism at the time to quote from philosophy, including Wittgenstein, and literary criticism, including essays by Roland Barthes and Alain Robbe-Grillet, all of whose work had recently been published in English (see Meyer 2001: 147).

What these three essays on minimal art had in common was that they were firmly rooted in an Anglo-American, broadly empiricist philosophy. This had a particularly American, pragmatic and sceptical slant, which influenced the early reception of the kinds of French theory that were beginning to interest Americans such as Morris and Rose. (This was before the arrival in the US of poststructuralism and deconstruction at the end of the decade.) As I noted earlier, as a dancer, Rainer was particularly focused on theoretical ideas about the body. This Anglo-American empiricism opposed a continental European rationalism which subscribed to ideas about the dualistic separation of mind and body. Rationalists believe it is possible to arrive at a substantial knowledge of the world through pure reasoning, whereas Empiricists believe that all knowledge is derived from (embodied) experience and that we have no means of acquiring knowledge except through observation of what actually happens. Rationalists tend to doubt the sensory information from embodied perception since, as Descartes argued, it could be an illusion or a dream. Only thinking, he argued, proved indubitably that he existed. In some of his writings Descartes suggested that the body was purely mechanical and the soul was a ghost in the machine (although in his later writings he acknowledged a much more complex union between body and soul). Empiricists reject the rationalist basis for such dualistic thinking. As David Raskin has pointed out, American behaviourists believed that 'inner psychological states are extensions of external behavior, but it is solely the latter that can be objectively observed and investigated'; thus behaviourists held that 'feelings, desires and emotions are actions in the world, not affairs of the mind' (Raskin 2004: 81). As the pieces discussed in this chapter demonstrate, the artists associated with Judson Dance Theater were concerned with external behaviour and actions in the world rather than inner psychological states.

By giving a dance piece the title *The Mind is a Muscle*, Rainer was signalling her opposition to rational, dualistic thinking. Indeed, Rainer's statement from the 1968 programme quoted earlier that 'My body remains the enduring reality' is in direct contradiction to Descartes *cogito* – I think therefore I am. Charles Harrison has pointed out that anti-dualism was a key concern of minimalist artists, who considered the idea of composition as a relationship between parts to be an outmoded, European sensibility informed by Cartesian dualism. For Morris, Judd, and their colleagues, Harrison suggests, wholeness was modern and American (Harrison and Wood 1992: 798). In his essay 'Art and object-hood' Fried used the sculptor Antony Caro's work as an example of what was, in his view, successful high-modernist work. He proposed that a welded modernist sculpture by Caro comprises a number of different elements juxtaposed together, which achieve an artistic wholeness through the 'mutual inflection of one element by another' (Fried 1969: 137). The spectator is able to look at such a sculpture from a detached, objective point of view because of the piece's quality of autonomy and completeness (Figure 3.4). For Morris and Judd, the fact that Caro's sculpture juxtaposed elements was by implication dualistic and European – Caro being an English artist (Harrison and Wood 1992: 798). Where dance was concerned, Rainer found correlations between the spatial qualities of sculpture and the temporal qualities of choreography. She thus observed that:

> The term 'phrase' can . . . serve as a metaphor for a longer or total duration containing beginning, middle, and end. Whatever the implications of a continuity that contains high points or focal climaxes, such an approach now seems to be excessively dramatic and more simply, unnecessary.
>
> (Rainer 1974: 65)

Hence, the dualistic spatial relationship between parts in a modernist sculpture corresponded to the temporal relationship between high points and climaxes in modern dance and ballet. Believing these to be unnecessary, Rainer valued singular actions performed with an unmodulated, unified tone.

Figure 3.4 Anthony Caro. *Early One Morning.* 1962. 'The mutual inflection of one element by another'.

Photograph: The Tate Collections. © The artist, Barford Sculptures Ltd.

Judd famously argued in 'Specific objects' that:

> A work needs only to be interesting. Most works finally have only one quality. [. . .] It isn't necessary for a work to have a lot of things to look at, to compare, to analyze one by one, to contemplate. The thing as a whole, its quality as a whole, is what is interesting.
>
> (Judd 1975: 184, 187)

A key word here is 'interesting'. David Raskin points out that Judd was using this in a specifically behaviourist way. Ralph Barton Perry argued that one can observe from someone's actions that they value something because their actions indicate their interest in it. Raskin has argued that: 'Judd made Perry's interest his main principle, for it reconciled verifiable physical characteristics and private responses, acknowledging that art is both an objective experience and a valuing one' (Raskin 2004: 84). Rainer expressed a similarly behaviourist point of view in the 'Quasi survey' when she stated that: 'The artifice of performance has been reevaluated [by some members of Judson Dance Theater] in that action, or what one does, is more interesting and important than the exhibition of character and attitude' (Rainer 1974: 65).

Whereas Judd's theoretical roots were in Behaviourism, Morris was initially influenced by an American gestalt approach to perception which he subsequently attempted to reconcile with the ideas of Merleau-Ponty.[18] Morris was interested in the gestalt approach to aesthetics, which suggested that individuals perceive wholes at a fundamental level through strong sensations which any complexity or confusion would dilute. In his 'Notes on sculpture', Morris articulates what Charles Harrison has called 'a phenomenologically informed focus upon the conditions of encounters with art works: that is to say, the embodied perception of physical objects and events in time and space' (Harrison and Wood 1992: 799). Observing that art objects have clearly divisible parts which thus create relationships between one another, Morris posed the conceptual problem of getting away from this potentially dualistic situation by creating an object that has only one property. This, he observed, is not wholly achievable because:

> one perceives simultaneously more than one [property] as parts in any given situation: if color, then also dimension; if flatness, then texture, etc. However, certain forms do exist that, if they do not negate the numerous relative sensations of color to texture, scale to mass, etc., they do not present separated parts for these kinds of relations to be established in terms of shapes. Such are the simpler

forms that create strong gestalt sensations. Their parts are bound together in such a way that they offer a maximum resistance to perceptual separation. In terms of solids, or forms applicable to sculpture, these gestalts are the simpler polyhedrons.

(Morris 1993: 6)

Hence, Morris's minimalist sculpture during the mid-1960s largely consists of simple, square, grey boxes and polyhedrons. Simplicity, Morris points out, 'does not necessarily equate with simplicity of experience' (ibid.: 8), but makes the spectator aware of previously unnoticed areas of kinaesthetic and physiological sensations. I suggested earlier that it was Morris's experience of dance improvisation with Ann Halprin that had made him aware of these kinaesthetic and physiological sensations.

In a modular sculpture by Robert Morris, *Untitled (Three 'L' Beams)* (1965), one module lies on the ground, another stands in an 'L' shape, while a third is placed like an upside down 'V' with only two edges touching the ground. The spectator's perception of their mass is in inverse proportion to the amount of the module that is in contact with the ground. Therefore, the upside down 'V' seems much lighter than the lying module. But the spectator is able to recognize the sameness of its three components. Like Morris, Rainer was concerned with the spectator's perception, observing that the point of view of the spectator and that of the dancer do not always correspond, particularly where the real energy used by a dancer and the apparent energy that the spectator perceives in their dancing is concerned. She therefore stated that what is seen in *Trio A* is a sense of unhurried control 'that seems geared to the actual time it takes the actual weight of the body to go through the prescribed motions, rather than an adherence to an imposed ordering of time' (Rainer 1974: 67). She went on to remark on the irony that she had therefore exposed 'a type of effort that is traditionally concealed and [. . .] concealed phrasing where it has been traditionally displayed' (ibid.). Underpinning this is a belief in the morality of only accepting empirically verifiable realities. This is an instance where Rainer was close to Donald Judd's empiricism: as David Raskin has pointed out, Judd ascribed moral agency to the aesthetic qualities that art generated.

Whereas Judd remained consistent throughout his career both in his approach to art theory and in the kind of work he produced, Rainer subsequently abandoned dance for film making and some, but, I shall argue, not all of the theoretical ideas that underpinned minimal art. Rainer's 'Quasi survey' was a tactical intervention that belonged to a specific historical moment in the mid-1960s. As Thomas Crow has observed, the fact that Judd and Morris's minimalist sculpture:

withheld the normal varieties of visual pleasure . . . raised the possibility of critical awareness of institutional power in the art world, but [the sculpture's] residual formal purity allowed them too readily to be drawn into the normal relation of discrete figure against neutral ground that the museum imposes on the objects it contains.

(Crow 1996: 152)

Similarly, the discourse of minimalism in dance has also been reappropriated within the high modernist view of the purity of American postmodern choreography developed by Sally Banes.

'My body remains the enduring reality'

Introducing her 1965 statement that begins 'NO to spectacle', Rainer made the qualification that while she enjoyed many forms of theatre, her statement merely defined more stringently 'the rules and boundaries of my own artistic game of the moment' (Rainer 1974: 51). Compared with Judd, Rainer's rules and boundaries have changed over the years. Self-evidently in the 'Quasi survey' these concerned minimal art. In a 1976 interview with the editors of the journal *Camera Obscura*, Rainer insisted that her films were not feminist, but later acknowledged to Noël Carroll that she was 'grateful to *Camera Obscura* for helping to move things along. They gave me a particular set of tools for thinking about my work at a point at which I had all but used up the ones I had' (Rainer 1999: 179). In a 1981 essay, 'Looking myself in the mouth' (ibid.: 85–97), she developed a critique of John Cage's idea with reference to poststructuralist theory, citing Barthes, Foucault, Kristeva, and Hayden White. The screenplay for her 1985 film *The Man Who Envied Women* included extracts from interviews with Foucault and from an essay by the Australian feminist, Meaghan Morris. As Rainer has wryly observed, she enjoyed having: 'an Australian voice referring obliquely to French feminism that is delivered in English by Jackie Raynal, a French woman and filmmaker in her own right who has a heavy accent. It is the problematized voice of feminist theory itself' (Jayamanne *et al.* 1987: 44). Rainer took up an equally subversive stance when she discussed feminist psychoanalytic film theory in an article 'Some ruminations around cinematic antidotes to the Oedipal net(tles) while playing with de Lauraedipus Mulvey, or, he may be off-screen but . . .' (Rainer 1999: 214–23).

Rainer has thus worked through a succession of different theoretical positions both in her writings and in her work itself. By talking about the rules of her artistic game and about tools for thinking, Rainer was insisting on the public nature of artistic production where the previous generation – of abstract expressionist painters and modern dancers – had made claims about the uniqueness of their individual, internal experience. It is in this context that Jasper Johns and some minimal artists became interested in Wittgenstein's ideas about language. J.O. Urmson has proposed that, in his later thinking, Wittgenstein moved away from the idea of a perfect scientific language, seeing language instead as 'an indefinite set of social activities each serving a different kind of purpose' (Urmson 1989: 329), thus opening up discussions about language games and tools. The problem for Wittgenstein arose where individuals wanted to make language any more than this. In paragraph 23 of *Philosophical Investigations*, Wittgenstein proposed: 'It is interesting to compare the multiplicity of the tools in language and of the ways they are used, the multiplicity of kinds of word and sentence, with what logicians have said about the structure of language' (Wittgenstein 1963: 12). In a famous example Wittgenstein pointed out that although we may think we know what someone means when he says he feels pain, it is not possible to logically verify that the experience which the listener associates with feeling pain is the same as the one to which the speaker refers (ibid.: 89 passim). As Simon Critchley points out, for Wittgenstein: 'Philosophy becomes a practice of leading words from their metaphysical usage to their everyday usage' (Critchley 1997: 118). Minimal dance surely dismantled the metaphysical usage of movement in a comparable way. Rosalind Krauss has explained why some minimalist artists were attracted to Wittgenstein's ideas:

> This question of language and meaning [in Wittgenstein] helps us by analogy to see the positive side of the minimalist endeavor, for in refusing to give the work of art an illusionistic center or interior, minimal artists are simply re-evaluating the logic of a particular *source* of meaning rather than denying meaning to the aesthetic object altogether. They are asking that meaning be seen as arising from – to continue the analogy with language – a public rather than a private space.
>
> (Krauss 1977: 262, emphasis in the original)

Following Krauss, the minimalism of Rainer's dance and of some of her colleagues can therefore be seen as an aspiration to strip dance practice of unverifiable private associations in order to find a dance vocabulary that would be meaningful in this public space.

This provides me with an answer to the question I posed at the beginning of this chapter: what did Rainer mean when, in a discussion of the relationship between *The Mind is a Muscle* and her horror and disbelief at seeing a Vietnamese shot dead on TV, she concluded 'My body remains the enduring reality' (Rainer 1974: 71)? Following Krauss, I contend that in Rainer's view the metaphysical ideals mediated by virtuoso ballet technique and the uniqueness of psychological experience mediated through the expressive vocabulary of mainstream modern dance both posited an illusionistic centre or interiority. In Wittgenstein's terms, the existence of such an interiority could not be verified through formal logic. Only 'the actual weight, mass, and unenhanced physicality' (ibid.) of Rainer's dancing body remained a logically verifiable and therefore enduring reality that could be meaningful within the public sphere. The importance Rainer attached to this conclusion is demonstrated by the fact that she reproduced the 1968 programme note in both her 1974 and 1999 books of collected writings.

Rainer has admitted that: 'I've always had a puritanical streak or a kind of utopian strain that wants to integrate the public citizen with the private person' (Goodeve 1997: 60). This echoes her apology, in the 1968 programme note, for puritan moralizing. However, Rainer has always been too scrupulous to finesse the integration of public and private. In her 1968 programme note, she stated: 'Just as ideological issues have no bearing on the nature of the work, neither does the tenor of current political and social conditions have any bearing on its execution' (Rainer 1974: 71). In other words, *The Mind is a Muscle* was a work of art and not a piece of political propaganda. Donald Judd made a very similar statement: '[Art]'s not a medium for something else, so it's not teaching. It's not a moral thing, it's not an ethical thing, it's not a scientific thing; it's art' (cited in Raskin 2004: 93). David Raskin's commentary on this is pertinent to Rainer's statement as well:

> For with interest as value, morality's address is solely to intuition – exactly as art should be – in that its compass is satisfaction or unease, the feelings that compel us to act and which verify our course every step of the way. Beliefs are constantly tested for their ability to help us live better lives.
>
> (ibid.)

Ideological issues might not therefore have had any bearing on the nature or execution of Rainer's dance work, but her feeling of horror at seeing a Vietnamese shot dead on TV confirmed the rightness of protesting against the war in Vietnam. Furthermore, the same feeling confirmed the rightness of creating and performing work that valued the actual weight, mass, and unenhanced physicality of the minimal dancing body.

If Rainer's programme note spells out the problem of how art and the realm of the social and political relate to one another, the conclusion she drew in 1968 appears only to have offered her a provisional solution, given that within five years she had shifted the focus of her activities from dance to film. The explanation for abandoning dance that she offered to Nan Piene, a critic who wrote for *Art in America*, echoes the terms of her 1968 programme note. Evidently, the fact that her body remained an enduring reality was no longer enough for Rainer. What she now felt was wrong with dance was its limitation as a meaningful public activity because 'the unique nature of my body and movement makes a personal statement' (Rainer 1974: 238), adding: 'Dance ipso facto is about *me*' (ibid., emphasis in original). Because dance was only about 'me' and 'the unique nature of my body and its movement', it could not deal with the kinds of emotional experiences Rainer now wanted to explore. Tellingly, she defined these as something that existed in the public realm, stating that: 'the area of the emotions must necessarily directly concern both of us' (ibid.). This, she believed, was something that dance was ill-equipped to explore because 'the so-called kinaesthetic response of the spectator notwithstanding, it only rarely transcends the narcissistic-voyeuristic duality of doer and looker' (ibid.). I have shown in this chapter that Brown, Paxton, and Rainer produced work during the 1960s that aimed at, and sometimes succeeded in transcending this narcissistic-voyeuristic duality. I will show in subsequent chapters that Brown and Paxton have continued to explore this through dances that drew on a radical approach to movement research that had its origins in the work discussed in this chapter. In retrospect their legacy to subsequent generations of dancers has been a body of work and theory that set a precedent for transcending this narcissistic–voyeuristic duality. But, as I shall show in the last three chapters of this book, the continuation of radical, experimental theatre dance was tempered by an understanding borne out of the disappointments of 1968 that the significance of the dancing body within the public sphere is circumscribed by that body's social and ideological construction.

4   Allegories of the ordinary and particular

Of all the dance work presented at Judson Memorial Church in the 1960s, Yvonne Rainer's *Trio A*, which I discussed at length in the previous chapter, has received the most scholarly attention. In general, works such as *Trio A* which explored issues that were primarily formal and abstract have received more attention than those that contained explicitly representational material. For much of the twentieth century, as I argued in Chapter 1, writers who have adopted formalist, modernist approaches to dance considered that works that included dramatic and representational material were less advanced than ones that were purely abstract or in which any representational elements were abstracted or minimized. This has set up a false dichotomy between abstraction and representation, and between form and content. Don McDonagh, in his 1970 book *The Rise and Fall and Rise of Modern Dance*, divided the dance of the late 1950s and 1960s into work that was concerned with 'the matter of movement' and work concerned with 'the matter of presentation'. He aligned nearly all the artists associated with Judson Dance Theater with the former category, while the section of the book concerning 'the matter of presentation' includes chapters on Alwin Nikolai, Paul Taylor, James Waring, Rudy Perez, Elizabeth Keen, and Art Bauman. With the exception of Waring, none of these had any connection with Judson Dance Theater; however, Fred Herko and David Gordon, who danced in Waring's Company, are included in a round-up chapter at the end of this section. McDonagh described this group of choreographers as 'more romantically skewed' and suggested they sometimes 'brought back to modern dance an interest in the "illusionism" that had been eliminated in the 1930s' (McDonagh 1990: 127–8). Robert Dunn, in an interview with McDonagh published in the book, detected a very similar distinction within the work performed by Judson Dance Theater, which he talked about in terms of architecture and camp: 'I always enjoyed the "camp" element and I never attempted to discourage it but I was interested to get people's minds working on questions of architecture' (ibid.: 51).

This binary distinction is significant because it has been applied to the new dance and has informed the way the dancers themselves thought about their work. But it has also had the effect of hiding what much of the new dance, whether it was concerned with 'matters of presentation' or 'matters of movement', had in common – the fact that it was avant-garde. I demonstrated in Chapter 3 that minimal dance challenged the aesthetic values of Greenbergian modernist theory in an avant-garde way. My aim in the present chapter is to show that the new dance also troubled and subverted the conventions and traditions of mainstream dance in order to explore new kinds of subject matter and experience. By doing so it was substantially changing the ways in which theatre dance functioned as a signifying practice. This chapter focuses on the dramatic and representational aspects of some work by artists associated with Judson Dance Theater. It therefore looks at pieces by David Gordon and Fred Herko who McDonagh considered were concerned with 'matters of presentation', together with work by Lucinda Childs and Steve Paxton whose work, in McDonagh's view, was concerned with 'matters of movement'. Because of the strong links between the new dance and the visual arts, it therefore also looks at the work of Carolee Schneemann who was the first painter to become involved with Judson Dance Theater.

While Chapter 3 examined the close ties between the new dance and minimal sculpture, the present chapter examines similarities between the new dance and pop art, a movement whose sensibility was initially conflated by some writers with camp. Robert Dunn was reticent about calling work at Judson 'camp' and immediately qualified his remark, adding: 'I don't know what to call it. It's not fair to call it camp' (McDonagh 1990: 51). Perhaps he felt uneasy admitting that one or two of the dancers were gay. The term 'camp' entered circulation beyond the confines of the various gay communities in the early 1960s as a result of Susan Sontag's now famous essay 'Notes on camp' published in 1964 in *Partisan Review* (Sontag 1967: 275–82). Several gay scholars have criticized Sontag for taking camp away from gay people (see Gere 2001: 357–62). As Moe Meyer observed, with the publication of Sontag's essay, 'the discourse began to unravel as Camp became confused and conflated with rhetorical and performative strategies such as irony, satire, burlesque, and travesty; and with cultural movements such as Pop' (Meyer 1994: 7). Meyer argued that, by taking camp away from gays, Sontag in effect de-queered and depoliticized it. What she brought to public awareness, he argued, should not properly be called camp at all.

I doubt that Dunn appreciated the fierce disagreements over what the term camp means, nor the extent to which some gay people may have resented Sontag's popularization of it. However, the conflation of a camp sensibility with qualities found in pop art which Meyer identifies may perhaps have contributed to Dunn's uncertainty about using the term.

The art historian Thomas Crow has made some observations about the representational aspects of pop art that are pertinent to the new dance. Crow talked about artists in the 1960s recognizing 'a new symbolic vocabulary, embedded somewhere in the cheap, cast-off furniture of ordinary lives' (Crow 1996: 21). The new dance, too, drew on urban materials and experiences. Pop art's restoration of reference to the world, he argued, 'offered in defiance of the long march of much of advanced art towards abstraction, entailed granting manufactured produce equal or superior status to the human beings who purchased it' (1996: 105). In some of the work discussed in this chapter, dancers manipulated the kinds of ordinary, manufactured objects whose images were appearing at the time on the canvases of pop artists. The way dancers handled these objects contradicted conventional ideas about dancers as superior beings. The new kinds of movement material and subject matter prompted them to develop new, more ordinary modes of performing and less rarefied ways of projecting their presence in performance. Like the minimalist work discussed in Chapter 3, much of this work therefore also challenged and overturned conventional expectations about technical refinement and expressiveness by emphasizing the performer's physicality. Whereas the appeal of the minimal work was partly intellectual, much of the more -dramatic or representational work demonstrated a deliberate lack of depth and trivial emphasis on the ordinary and mundane experiences of city life, or on superficial effects or sensuous experience in ways that sometimes challenged norms of gender and sexuality.

What was happening was not just that the new dance was dealing with new kinds of subject matter and experience, but by doing so it was substantially changing the ways in which theatre dance functioned as a signifying practice. These artists were investigating or discovering new ways of making connections between the kinds of objects and materials they used, the conceptual ideas they came across, and the qualities of movements and modes of performing that they were devising. I noted in the last chapter that, whereas the generation of abstract expressionist painters and modern dancers had made claims about the uniqueness of their individual, internal experience, Rainer was primarily concerned with the public nature of artistic production. I argued that the minimal sensibility in dance was one that sought to strip dance practice of unverifiable private associations in order to find a dance vocabulary that would be meaningful in this public space. What I suggest was problematic about the work of the previous generation of choreographers for Rainer and her generation of dancers were the extravagant claims about the universality of the personal experience they expressed in their pieces. Jill Johnston, for example, grumbled in a review of Ruth Currier's work about the way she was 'hung up with tired ways of moving . . . entrenched in the caving ditch of ideas and emotions which are thought more real and profound than those of dancing itself' (Johnston 1998: 27). It is usually only possible to assert that such profound emotions are universal if they are in accord with conservative social values. Here is Johnston again, this time on Martha Graham's heroines:

> ladies who came and saw and conquered after a bloody mess involving much murder and anguish on a literal or metaphorical journey through the bowels of mind or purgatorial landscape. It's an old Christian story of birth, suffering, redemption, transfiguration.
>
> (Johnston 1968: 10)

The work that I consider in this chapter made different and altogether more anarchic and libertarian claims about the right to express the validity of new kinds of individual, personal experiences. In particular, these were either too mundane or too quirky to be universalized and often, therefore, conflicted with conservative norms, particularly where gender and sexuality were concerned.

The new dance enacted a shift from the universal to the particular, and from the normative mainstream to the sometimes subversive fringes, and this shift not only involved exploration of new kinds of subject matter but also used new modes of representation and signification. The new art exemplified a shift from metaphor to metonymy, and from symbolism to allegory. I discussed the difference between metaphor and metonymy in Chapter 1. In metaphor, a direct, transparent relationship between signifier and signified is evident. Two lines in Coleridge's poem 'Kubla Khan' demonstrate this: 'So twice five miles of fertile ground / with walls and towers is girdled round' (Coleridge: 'Kubla Khan' lines 6–7). Here Kubla Khan's pleasure garden becomes a metaphorical body that is dressed in walls and towers like someone dressed in a cape. Metaphors such as this are the basic medium for an allusive, poetic imagination. Thus, as Martha Graham became each of her heroines, she metaphorically expressed the universal essence that Johnston satirized. Metonymy, however, is a trope that proposes a contiguous or sequential link or substitution. As I noted in Chapter 1, Peggy Phelan has explained that:

> Metaphor works to secure a vertical hierarchy of value and is repro-ductive; it works by erasing dissimilarity and negating difference; it turns two into one [while] metonymy is additive and associative; it works to secure a horizontal axis of contiguity and displacement.
>
> (Phelan 1993: 150)

Metonymy works through allusion and association, often dealing with meanings that are private or for some reason cannot be made explicit except in a coded way. Phelan continues: 'The metaphor I'm most keenly interested in resisting is the metaphor of gender' (ibid.: 151). Gender, she argues, attempts to unify people who have nothing in common except their biological gender. Metonymic signifying codes trouble and disrupt this fictitious unity.

Whereas the metaphorical devices within mainstream modern dances sought powerful but simple ways of resolving universal problems of the human condition, the metonymic and allegorical devices within the new dance sought ways of finding connections within complex and fragmented experiences of contemporary urban life. The art historian Fred Orton, arguing that Jasper Johns used allegorical signifying structures in his work, has summed up the role allegory played in late twentieth-century art:

> Realizing that the modern world is a space wherein things and meanings disengage – that the world is a thing that designates not a single, total, universal meaning but a plurality of distinct and isolated meanings – the allegorist works to restore some semblance of connection between them whilst hanging on to and asserting the distinction between experience and the representation of experience, between signifier and referent.
>
> (Orton 1994: 126)

Where subject matter appeared in the new dance, it often did so in very ordinary ways. As I will show, the distinctly unheroic, sometimes strangely absent ways in which the more experimental dancers projected their presence asserted the distinction between representation and the physicality of the dancing body representing it. Rather than trying to find profound metaphors for supposedly universal truths, many of the Judson generation invented allegories of the ordinary and particular. It is the metonymic and allegorical structures of meaning which underlay the new dance of the 1960s that I discuss in this chapter. It therefore proceeds as follows. First, it examines the work of Fred Herko at some length; this is partly because very little has been written about Herko, but also because his work exemplifies many of the representational strategies employed within the new dance. It also looks at the associative charge generated by the use of objects in Lucinda Childs's *Carnation* and Steve Paxton's *Flat*; and it looks at the early work of David Gordon and Carolee Schneemann who, each in their own ways through the very different kinds of material that each chose to explore, implicitly challenged the boundaries of what could or could not be signified. They thus, in effect, demonstrated the limits of the conditions within which the others were also working. This, I shall argue, demonstrated the efficacy of the allegorical structures and devices that occurred in much of the new dance.

The ultimate fairy tale: Fred Herko

Fred Herko was one of several dancers who were involved with Judson Dance Theater as well as dancing in James Waring's dance company. As Leslie Satin notes, these include Lucinda Childs, David Gordon, Sally Gross, Deborah Hay, Gretchen MacLane, Meredith Monk, Yvonne Rainer, Arlene Rothlein, and Valda Setterfield (Satin 2003: 52). Setterfield recalls that Waring used to give his dancers a complete education: 'He recommended books, films, theater, art shows' (Vaughan 1993: 52). Waring started teaching composition classes before Dunn did and, like Dunn's, these included a version of Cage's use of chance procedures and indeterminate structures. Setterfield remembers that these classes 'were wonderful because of his willingness to talk patiently about dance concepts' (ibid.). In those days 'ballet dancers didn't look at modern dance nor did modern dancers look at ballet, but Jimmy looked at *dancing*, all of it, and he helped me to bring my previous training to bear on everything I was now doing' (ibid.). Waring had links with the poetry scene in Greenwich Village, sometimes helping Diane di Prima print and distribute the low-budget poetry magazine *The Floating Bear* which di Prima and Amiri Baraka, then LeRoi Jones, edited (di Prima 1974). This carried dance reviews, including one by Herko. Waring also directed plays by di Prima and Frank O'Hara. Waring, Jones, di Prima, the composer John Herbert McDowell, and the actor and director Alan Marlowe also ran *The New York Poets Theater* (di Prima 2001: 255–6).[1] In 1962, before the first concert of dance at Judson Memorial Church, several dancers, including Brown, Childs, Herko, and Rainer, presented work at the Maidman Playhouse on 44th Street during the couple of months that it was leased by *The New York Poets Theater*.

Herko was initially very influenced by Waring. Leslie Satin (2003), in her detailed account of Waring's work, has noted that it was often described as 'camp', as articulating a gay sensibility. His work often blurred popular and high culture in an ironic and humorous way – for example through many references to Hollywood stars and films – and he often seemed to encourage a complicitous awareness between audience and performers about the outrageousness of blurring things in this way. Neither John Cage nor Robert Dunn, in comparison, were ever complicitously ironic in the way Waring was. When Rainer subsequently pronounced 'no to camp' in her polemic statement 'NO to spectacle' she was saying no to a quality that had existed in her own work as well as in Waring's work and that of Gordon and Herko (Rainer 1974: 51). Herko and Waring (and also, as I shall show, Gordon, though in a different way) all used imagery in a loose, open-ended, seemingly unstructured way that resembled the work of poets such as Frank O'Hara and underground film makers such as Jack Smith.[2] Where Herko's work differed from Waring's was in his more contemporary, urban sensibility. Satin has described several pieces by Waring that seem to have been almost historical pastiches. Di Prima referred to 'Jimmy's [Waring] baroque Chaplinesque ways, his use of gesture' (di Prima 2001: 280) and his preference for the kind of light-handed references to gay sensibilities found in a Cocteau movie rather than the 'out' gayness of Drag Queens (ibid.: 376–7). Coming from a younger, bolder generation, Herko was more outrageous in his tastes, and also more in touch with the avant-garde. His work was autobiographical and drew on the street-smart energy of the overlapping gay and drug scenes in which he circulated, drug abuse contributing to his untimely, spectacular death.

Reviews suggest his work was an anarchic bricolage of purposely incoherent but evocative images. Di Prima remembers 'Freddie's groping for the allegory, the ultimate fairy tale that could tell his story, could maybe save him' (di Prima 2001: 80). He was probably the most technically accomplished dancer in Judson Dance Theater – the other strong technician being Steve Paxton.[3] Consequently, Herko was mentioned more often in early reviews than other dancers associated with Judson Dance Theater. In Allen Hughes's review of the first concert of dance at Judson Memorial Church, Herko's *Once or Twice a Week I Put on Sneakers to Go Uptown* was the only piece to which he gave more than one sentence, describing it as riveting (Hughes 1962). Subsequently, however, Herko's work and career has received little attention. Along with his friend Billy Name, he was one of a small group of gay men who were involved in Judson Dance Theater, and the entourage at Andy Warhol's 47th Street Factory. Warhol (with his co-writer Pat Hackett), writing in his book *POPism*, suggests that Herko was a failure:

The people I loved were the ones like Freddie, the left overs of show business, turned down at auditions all over town . . . He could do so many things well, but he couldn't support himself on his dancing or any of his other talents. He was brilliant but not disciplined – exactly the sort of person I would become involved with over and over again during the sixties.

(Warhol and Hackett 1996: 56)

Because Warhol (with Hackett) gives more concentrated information about Herko than any other single printed source I have found (ibid.: 55–8), it is necessary to look critically at what he says.[4]

While seeming to write an affectionate memoir of Herko, Warhol nevertheless portrays him in a rather stereotypical manner as the sad, young, homosexual outcast whose inability to cope with life led to a tragic end.[5] Herko was the first of a number of people who became involved with Warhol and frequented the Factory and whose unconventional lifestyles and drug abuse contributed to early deaths. Warhol tells Herko's life story as if it leads inevitably to his death, which he implies was suicide: 'Freddy eventually just burned himself out with amphetamine; his talent was too much for his temperament. At the end of '64 he choreographed his own death and danced out of a window in Cornelia Street' (ibid.: 56). Vincent Warren, who knew Herko well, dancing with him in Waring's company and sharing an apartment with him in the late 1950s, says that in his last years Herko began experimenting with the then new drug, LSD. If Herko had been on LSD at the time, who can tell what his intentions were when, in the middle of dancing naked, he jumped out through an open window of a sixth-floor apartment (di Prima 2001: 398–9). No suicide note was found.

Reading Herko's work in terms of his death can be a distraction from his achievements and from his very interesting and individual qualities as a dance maker. If one ignores its rather mawkish, fatalistic tone, Warhol's memoir of Herko can be read slightly differently. Warhol reveals how little he understood or could remember about the Judson dancers when he wrote: 'I used to wonder how Freddy could be so talented and not be on Broadway or in a big dance company. "Can't they see how incredible he is?" I'd think to myself' (ibid.). Warhol could have mentioned that Herko was the first to define the iconic 'cowboy' figure that recurs in Warhol's films, with his highly erotic performance in *Haircut* (1963) (see Koch 1991: 52–8).[6] Warhol recalled that Herko got work on Sunday morning dance shows on television and then got stage fright when he had an opportunity to appear on the Ed Sullivan show. 'Afterwards he ran out of the theater and back down to the Village, to the security he felt there' (Warhol and Hackett 1996: 56).

Warhol was surely mistaken in assuming that anyone in Judson Dance Theater chiefly aspired to appear on Broadway or become a familiar face on mainstream television, and the ideological distance between Judson and that of the big dance companies doesn't need to be reiterated. Might not what Warhol interprets as Herko's stage fright have been complicated by fear of losing the latter's artistic integrity through increased involvement in commercial entertainment? Warhol seemed to be judging artistic success in purely economic terms, which might have been possible in the art world at the time but not, as Warhol surely found out from experience, in the worlds of underground film or experimental dance in the 1960s and early 1970s. As Annette Michelson observed in 1974, underground films and dances existed in proximity to the art world but were not part of that economy: 'New dance and new film have been, in part and whole, unassimilable to commodity form' (Michelson 1974: 58).

Warhol's opinion of Herko's choreography is equally negative. 'Instead of concentrating on the main idea of his dance pieces,' Warhol complained, 'he'd get all involved with fixing an arrangement of feathers or mirrors or beads on a costume, and was never able to see his choreography jobs through to the finish' (Warhol and Hackett 1996: 57). Yet Herko appears to have completed a number of pieces, showing his first work in 1962 before the first Judson concert in a shared performance with Yvonne Rainer at the Maidman Playhouse (see Telberg 1962). A few months before his death, Herko's evening-length ballet *Palace of the Dragon Prince* was performed by a company of ten dancers on two consecutive evenings at Judson Memorial Church.[7] Rainer was the only other member of the Judson group at the time to have presented an evening-length work with her *Terrain* (1963). Warhol seems to have been criticizing Herko for his attention to the detail of surface effects and for not pulling his pieces together into a conventionally coherent whole, a quality Herko's work surely also shared with other gay artists and writers at the time. One might have expected Warhol to understand an avant-garde, gay-inflected assertion of surface as a refusal to create a fiction of psychological depth, or, as Richard Dyer put it, a camp way of 'prising the form of something away from its content, of reveling in the style while dismissing the content as trivial' (Dyer 1992: 138). Warhol even describes with evident approval an incident in one of Herko's pieces that has exactly this quality:

> Freddy's piece started with a soft note on the organ in the darkened church. A little light appeared in the center of the balcony, and as

the organ note swelled, the light grew till you saw a woman leaning over the light base. She was draped in chiffon and looked more like a mound of light with a face on top of it than a real woman. Slowly, she lifted her arms, picking up a little glitter, and as the crescendo increased, so did the glitter until she became a cloud of glitter in a light. Then she faded away into silence and darkness.

(Warhol and Hackett 1996: 58)

In Warhol's own description, the glitter took on more importance than the woman who became a mere mound of light with a face. Warhol neither recognized the value of Herko's evident skills as a performer nor appreciated the significance and context of simple but startling theatrical images such as this. When he dismissed Herko as someone whose talent was too much for his temperament, he was repeating the same sort of dismissive criticisms that were made of other artists at the time whose work, like Warhol's own, articulated a camp sensibility. As Gavin Butt has pointed out, the painter Larry Rivers and the poet (and art critic) Frank O'Hara, who both undermined 'serious' and 'significant' meanings in their work, were dismissed by many critics in the 1950s and 1960s as phoney, inauthentic, and not genuine artists.[8] Warhol gives us enough information to suggest that Herko's work had similar subversive intentions. Coupled with his failure to acknowledge Herko's formative contribution to his own underground films, the result is a thoroughly distorted assessment of Herko's achievements.

Herko, like Waring, was peripherally involved in the downtown poetry scene. He lived for a while in the Lower East Side in an apartment above Diane di Prima with his then partner Alan Marlowe, who di Prima subsequently married. Di Prima first met Herko in the early 1950s while he was still studying the piano at the Julliard School. She recalled:

He was the first dancer I met who knew the other arts, and knew them well. Gertrude Stein, Matisse, Scriabin, Messiaen, Ionesco, Genet. He was as likely to bring me a new record to listen to as I was to put a new poem into his hands.

(di Prima 2001: 120)

Di Prima seems to have been very fond of Herko and, after his death, dedicated a book of her poems to him.[9] Herko contributed two items to *The Floating Bear*; the second, a review of a concert by Paul Taylor, earned him a waspish rebuke from Edwin Denby.[10] Herko knew Frank O'Hara, both through di Prima and through Vincent Warren whose affair with O'Hara became the subject of twenty love poems, the only ones in which the poet directly acknowledged his homosexuality. Herko also had connections with the emergent Fluxus movement. A photograph by Peter Moore shows him performing George Brecht's *Comb Music* at The Bridge Theater in August 1963 (Figure 4.1). Brecht was a research chemist and painter who started making musical pieces after taking John Cage's celebrated composition course at the New School in the late 1950s. Made while a member of the Fluxus group, *Comb Music* was one of a series of musical compositions in which Brecht either took a musical instrument and used it in a mute way or used a non-instrument to make sounds. In the photograph, Herko appears to be plucking a prong of the comb with his finger nail. As Brecht later observed: 'It was putting them [non-instruments] onto a more equal level with other sound producers. All "instruments", musical or not, became "instruments"' (Nyman 1976: 257). Brecht also had interesting ideas about similarities between objects and performances. From the point of view of quantum mechanics, he observed, an object is not really solid but a fluid event: an atomic structure, for example, is 'described probabilistically as a field of presence of the electron', so an object 'is becoming an event and every event is an object' (ibid.: 258). The simple event of an illuminated woman's head in a cloud of glitter, which Warhol described, blurs the distinctions between sculpture, dance, and theatre, in the way that Brecht describes. This has much in common with the Fluxus attitude which Dick Higgins summed up in the question: 'Why does everything I see that's beautiful like cups and kisses and sloshing feet have to be made into just part of something fancier and bigger, why can't I just use it for its own sake?' (cited in Johnston 1994a: 93).

Di Prima describes an extraordinary concert Herko gave in his loft in 28 Bond Street where the boundaries between dance, concert, and party were blurred. People arrived for the concert to find drinks and dips and no Herko, who at last 'emerged in an odd-looking costume, and did a bunch of stuff, some dances, some playing the hostess' (di Prima 2001: 389). He then disappeared and came back at irregular intervals, each time in a new costume to do 'a handful of anomalous actions. Or dance steps' (ibid.). Di Prima's conclusion is telling:

> No one was asked to pay attention to any of it, but it *was* the concert. This was art or it was not. It was a lifestyle choice or simply madness. This was a boundary, but it moved like a snake.
>
> (ibid.: 290, emphasis in the original)

Herko's group piece *Binghampton Birdie* (1963) began with the lowering of an elaborate chandelier-like construction of self-playing drums, devised

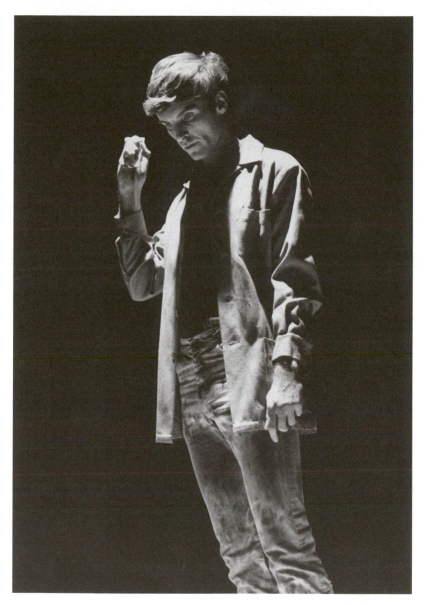

Figure 4.1 Fred Herko performing George Brecht's *Comb Music*. New Music and the Pocket Theater, NYC 1963.

Photo by Peter Moore © Estate of Peter Moore/VAGA, New York.

by Fluxus artist Joe Jones, from the church balcony to the main floor in almost total darkness. Jones made many similar pieces. Here, again, the accepted distinctions between object and event – between sculpture, musical instrument, music, and theatrical performance – become irrelevant. *Binghampton Birdie* was named after a gay friend and fellow amphetamine user who hung around Warhol's Factory and the San Remo Coffee Bar in Bleecker Street. After Jones's construction had finished playing, Herko appeared wearing one roller skate with the other foot bare, and skated around the church taking up various ballet positions and trying to go up on pointe. (This presumably formed the starting point for Warhol's 1963 film *Roller Skate*.) Other parts of *Binghampton Birdie* included a group section of abstract choreography and a moment that Jill Johnston described when Herko appeared walking in a squatting position wearing 'a black cape with a black umbrella for canopy, making a few sweet notes on a flute' (Johnston 1998: 42). The piece, she said, cohered 'with that strange logic of parts that have no business being together, but which go together anyway because anything in life can go with anything else if you know what you're doing' (ibid.: 41). It was Cage and Rauschenberg who had shown that anything can go with anything, while Cunningham and Waring had set a precedent for using ballet movement, stripped of its classical associations. Whereas Cunningham and Cage told the public that there were no symbols in their work, Herko's work evaded the imperative to create conventional, straight meaningfulness. Like Waring's work, and like the downtown poetry and Fluxus scenes in which he participated, it elaborated allusive, evocative imagery. It staged new imaginative possibilities by blurring the boundaries between art forms in ways that resonated with the work of other members of Judson Dance Theater. As I noted earlier, di Prima said Herko groped 'for the allegory, the ultimate fairy tale that could tell his story' (di Prima 2001: 280). Allegory, as Fred Orton noted, asserts the distinction between experience and the representation of experience. The poetic images Herko created had a charming inconsequentiality which, like Brecht's musical performances, took on a life of their own, independent of Herko's actions as choreographer and performer.

Transgressing boundaries: David Gordon

Don McDonagh called David Gordon and Valda Setterfield 'two of the most amiable saboteurs' who used humor as 'a way of pointing out the inadequacies of the tenets of historical modern dance held by a previous generation' (McDonagh 1990: 196). Like Herko, Gordon developed his style of performing and range of theatrical references under the influence of James Waring with whom he first started to dance in 1956. Setterfield, who also danced with Waring and who married Gordon in 1960, recalled that Waring looked at all kinds of dancing and he helped her understand how to use the wide range of her previous training and performance experience – in both ballets and musicals, and performing in traditional English Christmas pantomimes – in experimental dance performance. Although Gordon had less performance experience than Setterfield, he too was interested in a similarly wide range of theatrical dancing and drew on these in his work with her during the early 1960s. Like Waring, Gordon and Setterfield were particularly interested in popular vaudeville and Hollywood musicals.[11] Gordon, himself, seems to have performed in two widely different registers: on the one hand an energetic, hilariously sarcastic entertainer, and on the other a provocative Dadaist trying to make performances while undermining all recognized ways of perform- ing – doing in a dramatic way what others were doing through minimal and conceptual means. 'The only way I knew how to make work,' he told Banes in 1976, 'was if I could sense a discomfort in the people I was making work *for*. If I could sense discomfort, I knew I was doing OK' (Banes 1977: 20, emphasis in the original). As I will show, Gordon discovered that, beyond a certain threshold, discomfort was not OK.

Gordon's *Random Breakfast* (1962), as its name implies, was a loosely connected set of sketches that was performed in slightly varying versions by Gordon and Setterfield. Banes gives a detailed discussion of its sections (Banes 1995: 123–5). These include: a 'Striptease' for Setterfield, dressed in an Edwardian frock loaned by Waring in which she looked like Queen Mary; a 'Pre-fabricated Dance' in which Gordon lambasted and paro- died as many of his fellow choreographers as he could in an outrageous solo improvised lecture demonstration – his equivalent perhaps of Rainer's 'NO to spectacle'; 'The Seasons' consisting of four solos for Setterfield to Vivaldi; 'Girls Don't Cry' in which Setterfield did a parody of typical activities found in artists' Happenings; and two Hollywood- inspired sketches by Gordon: 'Lemon heart dance' in which Gordon, in drag, did an entirely inauthentic Spanish dance somewhat in the manner of Milton Berle's parody of Carmen Miranda; and 'Garlandiana' in which, in top hat and tails, Gordon smiled and looked shy while a Judy Garland record played. In 'Pre-fabricated Dance' Gordon was the hilari- ously sarcastic entertainer; in 'Garlandiana' a provocative Dadaist. Jonas Mekas at the time called some underground film directors Baudelairean because they portrayed 'a world of flowers of evil, of illuminations, of torn and tortured flesh' (Mekas cited in Suàrez 1996: 99). The directors Mekas was referring to included Andy Warhol and Jack Smith, both of whom at the time included drag queens in their work. Following Mekas, one might call Gordon's provocations Baudelairean in their perverse imagery, especially as he, like Warhol and Smith, used drag in his work. Judy Garland and Carmen Miranda were both significant figures within metropolitan gay iconography. It should hardly be surprising that Gordon, who was dancing in a company whose choreographer and some of whose dancers were openly gay, should be well informed about gay subcultural trends. He must also have heard from Setterfield about the cross-dressing dame of the English Christmas pantomime, a role that is usually straight-rather than gay-identified.

What did camp imagery offer Gordon? Like all the dancers of Judson Dance Theater, he rejected the consumerism and conservatism of American life. One way of doing this was to adopt an outlaw image through identifying with socially and culturally marginalized groups. This is what the beat poets and writers did when they immersed themselves in African American culture. Gavin Butt has argued that the painter Larry Rivers, though ostensibly straight, chose to identify with the queer artistic community for similar reasons (Butt 1999: 111) – Rivers being a friend of Waring's who sometimes attended his dance concerts. Waring and his circle shared Gordon's interest in a wide variety of types of dance and theatre, regardless of distinctions between high and low culture. Metropolitan gay culture, and in particular a camp sensibility, offered ways of making sense of the rich diversity of signs and associations within this wide range of theatrical material that Cage, Cunningham, and Dunn, with their abstract and conceptual concerns, did not provide. Gordon's 'Garlandiana' was not a specifically gay piece. Rather, I suggest, it de-queered camp imagery in the way that Sontag did in her 1964 essay. Following Meyer, one might say that Gordon's work was not camp at all.

Dyer has written an exhaustive and much praised close reading of Judy Garland's appeal to gay spectators. This is useful to contextualize Gordon's 'Garlandiana'. Central to Garland's star persona, Dyer proposes, was her comeback after being sacked by the MGM studio in 1950 for drink and drug addictions. Her later performances articulated intense, authentic feelings that, Dyer argues, exemplified 'a combination of strength and suffering, and precisely the one in the face of the other' (Dyer 1987: 149). Knowledge of this allowed a re-reading of Garland's seemingly innocent and 'normal' performances before her break with MGM, finding in them a level of self-reflexive artifice with which many gay men, whose work required them to pass as straight, could identify. The intensity of her performance, Dyer argues, allows the 'real' attitude of the performer to come through. 'The reality of the pretense of illusion' in Garland's star persona, he concludes, is particularly readable within the gay male subcultural discourse of camp (ibid.: 186).

Gordon's description of his performance as Garland, standing still and looking shy, seems to have none of the intensity that Dyer suggests characterized Garland's persona.

> That Garland thing at the end, in top hat and tails . . . with a record of Judy Garland singing *Somewhere over the rainbow* which lasted at least three minutes – in which my only intention was to come out and smile, and I kind of shuffled around and smiled for three minutes.
>
> (Banes 1977: 21)

This very lack of intensity aligned Gordon with Jack Smith's appreciation of the artifice within Hollywood films. Smith wrote for Mekas's magazine *Film Culture* about his appreciation for 'the whole gaudy array of secret-flix' (Smith 1997: 32) and in particular for those of the minor Hollywood star, Maria Montez. Acknowledging that she was 'the World's Worst Actress', Smith nevertheless believed that 'one of her atrocious acting sighs suffused a thousand tons of dead plaster with imaginative life and truth' (ibid.: 25). Like Smith's Montez, Gordon was presenting a performance of disintegration, seemingly unable or refusing to create conventionally coherent material, and thus courting failure by improvising without preparation around ideas that in themselves lacked any vestige of intensity or expression. Gordon's work evoked troubling absences where inspiring genius and metaphysical presence are conventionally sought.

Perhaps the furthest that Gordon went in this direction was his solo *Walks and Digressions* (1966). This was only ever performed at the concert in 1966 that he shared with Steve Paxton and Yvonne Rainer during which the audience booed and shouted, and some walked out. (It was at this performance that *Trio A* was first performed.) I quote Gordon's own description of *Walks and Digressions* at length:

> It had no sound, and the performance space was almost dark. I whistled 'Nothing could be finer than to be in Carolina' while slowly walking back and forth with my torso always turned towards the audience, alternating hands on my crotch – sort of like a smutty typewriter carriage doing a vaudeville turn. I stood on my half-toe while spit drooled out of my mouth and pulled my pants down while balancing on my shoulders, on the floor, with my legs straight up in the air.
>
> (Gordon 1975: 48)

'I remember very clearly as the material came out thinking what the fuck am I doing, this is really grotesque . . . these are ugly things. And I thought all right, I'll keep it, I'll see what happens' (cited in Banes 1980: 101). The concert was reviewed in the *Village Voice* by Robert Morris, who praised Paxton and Rainer's work, but was scathingly critical of Gordon's *Walks and Digressions*.[12] Morris denounced Gordon's 'puerile manipulation of pants and spittle', but said the work was neither shocking nor humorous. Asking 'why this work was as bad as it was', Morris stated that it was childish and derivative, and that 'the performer [was] stranded in his own vacuum of self indulgence' (Morris 1966: 15). Jack Anderson reviewed the concert for *Dance Magazine*. Like Morris, he wrote appreciatively and at some length about both Rainer and Paxton's work but was scathingly brief about Gordon. Here it is in its entirety: 'In David Gordon's older solos and in the smirks and struts of his new *Walks and Digressions* there was a faint hint of comic talent. But it was dwarfed by a narcissism of awesome proportions' (Anderson 1966: 30). It is hardly surprising then that Gordon concluded: 'When the audience and my peers turned on me, I picked up my marbles and went home. I just decided to stop making work' (Gordon 1975: 48). Gordon gave up creating dances for six years.

While some of the audience evidently disliked almost all of the work at this concert, the critics only criticized Gordon, and while Gordon gave up making dances until the 1970s, the other two continued. There was surely more to Morris's attack than critical judgement. Morris, Paxton, and Rainer explored in their work similar minimalist aesthetic sensibilities, which Gordon did not at the time share. As Anna C. Chave has suggested, in an essay to which I referred in Chapter 3: 'Among a generation bent on separating itself from the heroic individualism of Abstract Expressionism, depersonalized visual modalities had come to the fore' (Chave 2000: 151). Gordon was, of course, exemplifying the opposite of the heroic individualism of abstract expressionism or mainstream modern dance but, from Morris's point of view, it was the wrong sort of opposite because it was not depersonalized. Chave continued (in a passage I've already cited) that for a woman to make overtly personal references in her art 'was to risk branding her work as retrogressive and, by the same stroke, to risk reinforcing that tacitly invidious division of labor that presupposes that women will assume "expressive roles and orientations" while men adopt "instrumental" ones' (ibid.). Gordon, working in an already feminized art form and performing expressive roles rather than adopting minimalist, task-like ones, was evidently at risk of the same kind of accusation. His drag roles seem not to have been a problem because they were clearly roles. But when Gordon in *Walks and Digressions* exem-

plified a dandy-like disdain for bourgeois norms including those of masculine behaviour, this seemed to be a personal statement. In Morris's
words, it stranded him 'in his own vacuum of self indulgence' (Morris
1966: 15) and for Anderson it had 'a narcissism of awesome proportions'
(Anderson 1966: 30). Rather than presenting a coherent, self-contained,
'natural' masculinity by expressing fullness, identity, and totality as Morris
had done in *Site* (discussed in Chapter 3), Gordon's display of abject
bodily fluids threatened to overflow the body's discrete boundaries. As
di Prima detected in Herko's concert in his Bond Street loft, Gordon's
attack on conventions marked out a boundary that nevertheless 'moved
like a snake' (di Prima 2001: 290). Indeed, Gordon performed as if lacking any personal boundaries. Like Herko's work, *Walks and Digressions*
seems to have been in danger of disintegrating into incoherence, presenting a body too messy to conform to common sense, supposedly universal norms of masculine behaviour. Herko's weird, poetic allusions and
Fluxus-like deconstructions resulted in work that never directly acknowledged his sexuality but remained in the realm of metonymic association
and allegory; Gordon's 'self-indulgent' and 'narcissistic' performance
in *Walks and Digressions* could too easily be seen as a metaphorical and
symbolic statement about Gordon himself.

Objects and dances: Lucinda Childs and Steve Paxton

While Gordon and Herko's works had affinities with Fluxus, underground film, and the downtown poetry scene, many of those involved
with Judson Dance Theater were, as I have already demonstrated, closer
to advanced practice in the visual arts. I suggested earlier that there
were affinities between some of the objects that dancers used in their
works and the kinds of objects that were appearing in paintings at the
time. One well-known but little-discussed example of this is Merce
Cunningham's *Antic Meet* (1958). There are clear connections between
the kinds of assemblages that Rauschenberg was creating at the time
and the props, costumes, and their unexpected attachments that he
designed for *Antic Meet*. Jill Johnston described one scene in this piece
where the dancers wore sunglasses, another where Cunningham brought
on a small table and laid it. A famous photograph shows Cunningham
dancing with a bentwood chair strapped to his back.[13] Johnston
commented that: 'All these incidents are provocative images. I don't
believe the observer takes time out to analyze or interpret what he sees.
More often he probably notes a novel combination of facts and relaxes
to enjoy the image' (Johnston 1965: 174). It seems to me that Johnston
was acknowledging that while these incidents were not symbolic (in a

metaphorical sense), they nevertheless carried strong, enjoyable associations. She went on to discuss the use of objects in Happenings and in works by Lucinda Childs and Steve Paxton. In *Carnation*, she observed, Childs

> stayed close to the facts of the objects, at the same time making a zany abstraction out of their realistic possibilities. Steve Paxton has done something else with found objects by making dances in which certain actions are taken from photographs of sports and other activities.
>
> (ibid.: 186)

Here, again, while Johnston recognized that these works were not symbolic, she nevertheless seemed to feel that the associations they brought to the performance were significant. Through a discussion of Childs's *Carnation* and Paxton's *Flat*, my aim is to examine these associations.

Lucinda Childs's piece *Carnation*[14] was first performed at Judson Memorial Church on 29 April 1964, made shortly before Childs took Robert Dunn's composition class.[15] It has become one of her best-known early pieces because she continued performing it in the 1980s and allowed Emily Coates to dance it in the White Oak Dance Project's programme of Judson reconstructions (see Chapter 8). Childs has said that it is a piece in which she 'used commonplace materials to explore movement activity outside dance movement' (Childs 2003: 197). She therefore choreographed manipulations of ordinary, household objects that she had bought in Woolworth's and her interactions with them. Cage famously said that everything was music; Childs was demonstrating that anything could become dance. First, sitting astride the corner of a small table with a lettuce shaker, some pink foam rubber hair curlers and small, thin, rectangular sponges, she placed the shaker on her head and made sandwiches with the sponges and curlers. Dismantling these, she inserted a hair curler in each of the shaker's handles and placed all the sponges between her lips. She then inserted the curlers, one by one, between the sponges, turned her head to show the grotesquely comic effect to the audience before spitting them all into a blue plastic sack attached to one leg. In the next section she leaned upside down against a wall with a corner of a bed sheet attached to each of her socks, holding another corner in each hand to stretch the sheet tight and hide herself. Then, having neatly folded up the sheet and put it in the sack, she made a diagonal run across the performance space to jump onto the sack, stare around at her audience and start to cry. Jumping off the sack as if stung, she approached it again a different way, looking round again and then crying again. She repeated this three times and then the piece ended.

Childs has admitted that: 'This was a difficult and perplexing period as I struggled to establish a plausible aesthetic expression in the midst of contradictory influences' (Childs 2003). Leslie Satin has noted that Childs made the decision to stop going to class at the Cunningham studio and only work with James Waring, in whose company she was dancing (Satin 2003: 73). But around this time she also appeared in one of Robert Morris's pieces, *Waterman Switch* (1965) and in some of Andy Warhol's films.[16] Childs has described her aims in the early 1960s as follows:

> Although the dances were composed in a unified idiom of action, I was more interested in a cumulative trend of activity that did not follow along one isolated scheme. I therefore chose to create sections within dances that focused attention on activity from different points of view. *Carnation* (1964) had three sections: first preparation (for the moment); second alternative options; third following through or completion.
>
> (Childs 2003: 197)

This suggests that, although the piece was performed without any music, the structure was musical, following the three movements of classical European sonata form. There was also an extraordinary clarity and precision about everything the performer did. In the first part her hand travelled very slowly and deliberately up and then round the shaker on her head to find a hair curler tucked into a handle. She then plucked this out emphatically, before returning with equal deliberation to insert it among the sponges clenched between her teeth. These were actions designed to be read by an audience, and were thus choreographed with a formalized spatiality that recalls Chinese opera. In the final section, jumping on the sack was similarly directed towards the audience, as Jill Johnston's contemporary description reveals:

> After careful placement of the bag, she runs towards it, jumps on it, stands immobilized, glares in frenetic silence until her face starts to cry, and, at the final moment of wrinkled distortion, returns to deadpan normal and prepares for another attack on the bag.
>
> (Johnston 1964: 12)

Making eye contact with members of the audience invited or seduced them into identifying with the performer, and this was then transformed into sympathy when she cried. The sudden return to deadpan normal disrupted this sympathetic identification, showing that the performer was merely using an acting technique, manipulating the audience as deftly as she had manipulated the sponges and hair curlers. Trisha Brown told Sally Banes that, for an assignment in Robert and Judith Dunn's classes to make a dance for three minutes, Dick Levine had

> taught himself to cry and did so for the full time period while I held a stop watch instructed by him to shout just before the time elapsed, 'Stop it! Stop it! Cut it out!' both of us ending at exactly three minutes.
>
> (cited in Banes 1995: 21)

Childs was using crying as a task in a similar way.

Paxton's *Flat* (1965) was one of the pieces, to which Johnston was referring, that used photos as found objects. Paxton wore a suit (at the time an uncommon costume for dance) and brought on a chair at the start of the piece. He walked in a circle within a limited performance area around the chair, occasionally freezing in a pose that had been taken from the 'score' consisting of photographs of athletes and sportsmen.[17] Gradually, item by item, he took off his jacket, shirt, and trousers and hung each on a hook that had been taped to his skin – on his chest, on his shoulder, and in the middle of his back. He then progressively redressed and exited. The act of sitting down, and the actions of taking off shoes and clothes were repeatedly interrupted as the dancer unexpectedly froze half way through, often pausing long enough to unsettle his audience. It is a piece that both he and Baryshnikov performed in the White Oak Dance Project's programme of Judson reconstructions (see Chapter 8). In the programme for this, Paxton wrote that his inquiry in *Flat*

> was not so much about escaping the legacy of dance as discovering the source of it. Where was something pre-legacy, pre-cultural, pre-artistic? Where was ancient movement? This was the fascinating question for me of those days, and it remains my interest.
>
> (Paxton 2003: 206)

Paxton's ideas here have affinities with a view of time and history proposed by George Kubler, a scholar who specialized in pre-Columbian and colonial American art and architecture, in his book *The Shape of Time* (1962). This was widely read by artists in the 1960s (see Lee 2004). Instead of seeing art history as a line of influence from one artist to another, Kubler argued that it consisted of a succession of discoveries of what he called 'prime forms'. Kubler's idea was that, just as in mathematics all integers can be derived from prime numbers, all artefacts in visual culture could be derived from 'prime forms'. Paxton's project seems to have been to research and identify 'prime movements'. The disturbing interruptions and prolonged pauses in *Flat* can be seen as a process of analysing the ordinary movements that were the subject of the piece and reducing them to irreducible elements.

I mentioned earlier Thomas Crow's observation that in pop art manufactured objects were granted equal or superior status to the human beings who purchased them (Crow 1996: 105). In both Childs's and Paxton's works, the normally hierarchical relationships between humans and objects – the chair, the clothes, the hooks in *Flat*, the sponges, curlers, sheet, and other objects in *Carnation* – were being redefined in a non-hierarchical way. Paxton made his body into an object on which to hang other objects (his clothes). Childs turned her face into a comically grotesque mask, and then hid herself by becoming a frame that stretched the sheet to which she was attached. By troubling and subverting expectations of technical virtuosity and making new sorts of material that were closer to the sorts of movements and behaviour found in everyday life, such works also undermined the hierarchical relationship between dancers and audiences.

It is curious that whereas *Carnation* has been interpreted with reference to Childs's femininity, Paxton's masculinity has not so far been mentioned in relation to *Flat*. Sally Banes has described *Carnation* as an acerbic comment on housework: 'The character's obsession with beauty aids, her compulsive sandwich-making, and her need to fold her linens perfectly – as well as her battle with the garbage bag – constitute a small domestic tragedy' (Banes 1998: 218). Having watched Coates's performance twice and seen videos of Childs performing the piece in the 1980s, my impression of it is that the performer is much cooler and more detached than the words compulsion, obsession, and battle suggest. What struck me was the fierce intensity of the performer's theatrical presence – especially Childs's – which was channelled into the precision with which she manipulated her props. This produced a disturbing disjunction between her intense concentration and the triviality of the objects towards which it was directed. Wearing tight blue jeans with knee length socks over them and with her long, straight hair pulled severely away behind her head, Childs couldn't have looked less like a compulsive, obsessed housewife. Her whole performance seemed to me to create a distance between the performer and the kind of domestic associations that Banes ascribes to it.

Flat articulated qualities that were the opposite of the kinetic excitement of the masculine athletic events to which the photographs referred. In the 1950s, Johns and Rauschenberg both reproduced in their work visual effects that referred ironically to the work of the abstract expressionists without repeating the mythologized, dynamic actions of these moody, volcanic male creators. Rauschenberg, for example, exhibited an erased drawing that had been given to him by Willem de Kooning, rubbing out and thus neutralizing physical signs of de Kooning's expressiveness. Many of Johns's works contain deliberate dribbles that ironically refer to drips in works by Pollock and other abstract expressionists. The paint surfaces of abstract expressionist canvases recorded the expressive energy with which the artist had engaged in the creative process. The surfaces of Johns's paintings said little about his state of mind when he painted them, but referred in a metonymic way to abstract expressionism (see Orton 1994). Jonathan Katz argues that Johns, in his paintings during the 1950s and early 1960s, particularly those containing plaster casts of male body parts, shifted the visual representation of the male body from the position of consonance with authoritative readings that exists in abstract expressionist painting to one of dissonance (Katz 1999). In pieces such as *Flat*, Paxton defamiliarized the male dancer's body through passivity, silences and conceptual deconstructions of representation in ways that both resembled and were indebted to the example of Johns and Rauschenberg's practice as painters, and to the experimental performance strategies of Cage and Cunningham.

In Anna C. Chave's terms, both Childs and Paxton avoided performing 'expressive roles and orientations' by adopting 'instrumental' ones. Thus Childs, as a woman, avoided the risk of having her work branded as retrogressive, while Paxton eluded the kind of punishing criticism that Gordon suffered for his *Walks and Digressions*. Their performances in *Carnation* and *Flat* exemplified a degree of self-conscious detachment that Philip Auslander identified in the later performances of the Wooster Group: 'The multiple, divided consciousness produced by doing something with the knowledge that it is being observed, while simultaneously observing oneself doing it, yields a complex confrontation with self' (Auslander 1997: 42). Performing in this way is, I suggest, allegorical rather than symbolic. Following Orton, it is working 'to restore some semblance of connection between [the disengagement of things and meanings] whilst hanging on to and asserting the distinction between experience and the representation of experience, between signifier and referent' (Orton 1994: 126).

Transgressing boundaries: Carolee Schneemann

Carolee Schneemann was one of the original members of the Judson workshop, and the first visual artist to become involved with this group of dancers. When she first moved to New York with her husband James Tierney, who was a composer, she met the composers Philip Corner and Malcolm Goldstein. Goldstein's partner Arlene Rothlein attended Dunn's composition class and it was through them she first came in contact with the dancers who would form Judson Dance Theater. Corner invited Schneemann to create a piece, *Glass Environment for Sound and Motion*, for a concert he and Dick Higgins were programming at the Living Theater in May 1962 (Schneemann 1997: 21–4). Goldstein, Rothlein, and Rainer all performed in Schneemann's piece, and this seems to have led to the invitation to join the Judson workshop that autumn.[18] Schneemann seems one of the few women in the Greenwich Village avant-garde aware of feminist ideas in the early 1960s. While studying for her Master's degree at the University of Illinois, she wrote about Simone de Beauvoir, despite her philosophy lecturer's recommendation that Sartre was a much more important figure, and received similarly dismissive comments about her interest in Virginia Woolf (ibid.: 193). While a student, she also read Artaud's newly translated writings on the theatre of cruelty, and the work of the sexologist Wilhelm Reich.

Schneemann's first dance piece, *Newspaper Event*, was performed at the third concert by Judson Dance Theater in January 1963. It started with all the performers creating a circular mound of crumpled newspaper by emptying out a number of boxes of this in the middle of the performance area. All the action took place on the newspaper mound. Schneemann, as in all her Judson dances, played 'the free agent' a minor role of timekeeper which left her largely as an outside observer. She says she treated the performance space as her canvas and the dancers as if they were paint or elements with which to compose moving pictures. Each of the performers was given the role of a part or parts of the body. Arlene Rothlein was the spine, Ruth Emerson the legs and face, Deborah Hay the shoulders and arms, Yvonne Rainer the neck and feet, Carol Summers the hands, Elaine Summers the head, and John Worden the fingers. Each had different instructions which they interpreted in a loosely improvised manner. Some of the body parts determined horizontal movement, others vertical. In carrying out these movements, they interacted with one another; and photographs of the performance show piles and groupings of performers within a sea of the crumpled newspaper. The visual effect was to messily blur the boundaries of individual bodies. Put together, the different roles all make one body, and this organic metaphor of messily interconnecting bodies recurred in most of Schneemann's other Judson pieces, including the most famous of all, *Meat Joy* (1964). As Susan Foster has suggested, 'Schneemann celebrated the frictive encounters between bodies as intimate and pleasure-filled' (Foster 2002: 49). By getting involved in the physical, sensual experience of the performance, the dancers seemed to free themselves of inhibitions and make intimate, physical contact with one another in a way that Schneemann interpreted in terms of a Reichian politics of liberation (Schneemann 1997: 194). Schneemann has claimed that works such as *Newspaper Event* (1963) anticipated the development a decade later of contact improvisation.[19]

Schneemann has said that she gave herself an overseeing role as 'Free Agent' in all of these because she didn't feel confident of her abilities as a performer, remaining an outside figure who had planned and appeared to control events. She had appeared naked in some Happenings, including Claes Oldenberg's *Store Days* (1962), but not yet appeared naked in her own. The work in which she began to explore her own position as performer and a liberated female sexuality was the 1963 series of photographic tableaux *Eye Body*. This consists of thirty photographs taken in Schneemann's loft by her friend Erró. She had created an environment out of some of her paintings and constructions and posed in front of these or sometimes looking through holes and gaps within them. She was thus no longer an outside observer and manipulator nor the passive life model for a male artist – the role she played in Morris's *Site* (discussed in Chapter 3) – but was actively using her embodied self to create work that blurred the boundaries between the visual and performing arts. She was naked but had drawn or painted on her face and body – these marks changing in different photographs. In a few she wrapped herself in polythene or in fur or bits of string, linking her face and body with similar materials in her paintings and constructions. In one photograph, she had a horn on her head, in one she bit a sheep's skull, while in another she held it in front of her body. In one she lay back seductively, a dark line running from her hairline down her nose to her chin, while two small snakes curled around her breast and on her abdomen.

Schneemann has said she only later found similar imagery in ancient Minoan art, observing:

> In some sense I made a gift of my body to other women: giving our bodies back to ourselves. The haunting images of the Cretan bull dancers – joyful, free, bare-breasted, skilled women leaping precisely from danger to ascendancy, guided my imagination.
>
> (1975: 25)

There is a parallel here with Martha Graham. Graham felt she had uncovered the archetypal imagery of her work in her own blood memories, and in many of her dances from the 1940s onwards performed the role of women whose desire for their half-clad male partners is undisguised. Where Graham had been interested in Jung's ideas about the collective unconscious, Schneemann was interested in Reich's ideas about the collective sexual energy that he believed was systematically controlled through repressive social institutions. She wrote in 1974:

> I didn't stand naked in front of 300 people because I wanted to be fucked; but because my sex and work were harmoniously experienced I could have the audacity, or courage, to show the body as a source of varying emotional power.
>
> (Schneemann 1997: 194)

Schneemann says that she had never really seen a difference between painting and physical movement. Simone Forti, as I noted in Chapter 3, also found similarities between the physicality of dancing and painting. For as long as Schneemann can remember, she has always done a physical, dance-like warm-up to music before painting or drawing. The dominant painting tradition she encountered as a student had been abstract expressionism, in particular the work of Jackson Pollock. Pollock wrote about 'being in the painting', describing a mental and physical state when dribbling paint on canvas (Pollock in Chipp 1968: 546–8). In her own way in *Eye Body*, Schneemann was, like Pollock, being in the painting. The artists involved in Happenings valued passionate involvement: Allan Kaprow linked Pollock's action painting with the painters' actions in Happenings in an early essay (Kaprow 1958). It is this sensibility that Schneeman brought to Judson Dance Theater. There it brought her into conflict with those who were exploring blank, anti-expressive modes of performance. Schneemann saw these as the result of John Cage's influence, and, knowing Cage's interest in Zen Buddhist philosophy, denounced them as 'fro-zen' (Schneemann 1997: 18).

I noted earlier that David Gordon's reaction against the expressionism of mainstream modern dance went against the dominant minimalist trend by appearing, for its time, too personal. Schneemann's work enacted a critique of abstract expressionism through an attempt to replace its masculine energy with a hyperbolically excessive feminine eroticism. But, as Anna C. Chave has pointed out, for a woman to make overtly personal references in her art 'was to risk branding her work as retrogressive'. Schneemann's attempts to exhibit the photograph from *Eye Body* during the 1960s were rebuffed.[20] She seems to have gone through a personal and artistic crisis in the late 1960s following the way some male anarchist leaders dismissed her piece for the *Congress of the Dialectics of Liberation* in London in 1967. It was after this that she seems to have begun explicitly protesting against male sexism within the art world. 'I was permitted to be an image', she wrote in 1974, 'but not an image-maker creating her own self image' (Schneemann 1997: 194). The abstract expressionist painters dominated the canvas as an object to which they did things, and Schneemann later argued that Kaprow and other makers of Happenings did the same (ibid.: 195–8). Morris had visually and performatively dominated her as an object in *Site*. And of course she, too, in her Judson Dance Theater pieces had been the outside controller.

In *Eye Body* Schneemann was reversing the masculine logic of such objectifying mastery by subjectively merging herself with the paintings and becoming her work. She continued this in later dance works such as *Water Light/Water Needle* (1966) and films such as *Fuses* (1967). This was taking further the way the dancers in *Newspaper Event* became blurred and merged together as parts of an organic whole. These performances, films, and photographic pieces, however, were too easily appropriated into an economy of male-oriented erotic and pornographic imagery.[21] The problem was not just one of imagery but, I suggest, the metaphorical and symbolic way in which this imagery signified. The work in which Schneemann most explicitly confronted the sexism of the art world was her performances in 1975 and 1977 of *Interior Scroll*. In this she stood naked, with paint marks on her skin, and pulled out of her vagina a paper scroll. This was inscribed with a text which she read out. This told of a conversation she had had with a structural film maker, and denounced his sexism and that of the art and experimental film worlds.

Schneemann's artistic philosophy was still the same as it had been when she was a member of the Judson Dance Workshop, but her tactics had changed since the 1960s. Where previously there had been an orgiastic attempt to unify experience, there was now a strategic distance between her body and the text coming out of it. This gave *Interior Scroll* a reflexive self-consciousness. Amelia Jones has argued that *Interior Scroll* 'dynamically enacts the dislocation of the conventional structures of gendered subjectivity' (1998: 3). This kind of dislocation is comparable to the divided consciousness that Auslander identified in the performing style of the Wooster Group, and which I suggested is allegorical in its address. In early seventeenth-century paintings scrolls were often used as a device through which artists could explain their allegorical scheme. Mark Franko has given instances of seventeenth-century burlesque court ballets in which dancers had scrolls or 'cartels' with commentaries on their roles written on them which they threw or shot with a bow into the audience for individuals to read out aloud (Franko 1993: 78). Schneemann's scroll had a similar, allegorical function.

By the 1970s, Schneemann had therefore realized the problems of presenting work whose values clashed with conservative norms. Like Gordon, she had had to learn the hard way. Their experiences demonstrate the limits of the conditions within which the others were working. Some commentators have argued that camp operates as a defence mechanism against a hostile, straight world; Herko, as a gay bohemian in a metropolitan centre, clearly knew all about such mechanisms. Childs and Paxton avoided the hostility that Gordon and Schneemann experienced because their work drew on the kinds of representational strategies prevalent at the time in advanced visual art, particularly in the work of Johns and Rauschenberg. In Chapter 3 I investigated the theoretical basis for the minimalist tactics through which some members of Judson Dance Theater distanced themselves from the claims that an older generation of modern dancers had made about the universal truths expressed in their dances. The present chapter has traced the kinds of alternative signifying practices through which the new dance alluded to individual, personal experiences that were at odds with, and challenged, social norms. Taken together, these two chapters map the emergence of the dancing body as a site of resistance against dominant ideologies.

5   Before and after 1968

Dance, politics, and the avant-garde

The first performance of the complete evening-length version of Yvonne Rainer's *The Mind is a Muscle* at the Anderson Theater in New York on 11 April 1968, took place only a week after Martin Luther King Jr was shot by a sniper in Memphis, Tennessee on 4 April. King had been working on bringing together the Civil Rights and Anti-war movements, and if one looks for dance reviews, listings, and advertisements relating to Rainer and her contemporaries in the pages of the *Village Voice* newspaper during April, they appear near, and sometimes side by side with announcements of a rally that King had been due to attend, as well as meetings to discuss resistance to the war, help for draft dodgers, and other oppositional, anti-war activities. Towards the end of Chapter 3 I briefly discussed Rainer's 1968 programme note for *The Mind is a Muscle*. In this she asserted that 'Just as ideological issues have no bearing on the nature of the work, neither does the tenor of current political and social conditions have any bearing on its execution', adding 'The world disintegrates around me' (Rainer 1974: 71). This was at the beginning of a long summer of mass political action by students and young people in many parts of the world. In the US, King's assassination sparked off riots in Washington, DC and there were riots in Chicago in the August during the Democratic Party's national convention: in Paris, rioting provoked major political crises, while in Prague it brought about an invasion by the combined armies of Warsaw Pact countries. In Chapter 3 I argued that while ideological issues might not therefore have had any bearing on the nature or execution of Rainer's dance work, they were nevertheless connected. Her feeling of horror at seeing a Vietnamese shot dead on TV confirmed the rightness of protesting against the war in Vietnam. Furthermore, the same feeling confirmed the rightness of creating and performing work that valued the actual weight, mass, and unenhanced physicality of the minimal dancing body, leading to her concluding statement that: 'My body remains the enduring reality' (ibid.).

This chapter examines the complex and sometimes problematic relationship between avant-garde art and social and political events during the 1960s. It argues that, by breaking down, blurring, or transgressing artistic conventions and disciplinary boundaries, artists associated with Judson Dance Theater opened up new spaces in which to place dancing bodies side by side with events and thereby generated new social and political meanings. In her 1968 programme statement, Rainer was claiming the freedom to call things into question, a freedom that was central to the turbulent events of 1968. As Julia Kristeva observes:

> There was no nihilism in the contestation that burned up that month of May 1968; instead it was a violent desire to take over the norms that govern the private as well as the public, the intimate as well as the social, a desire to come up with the new, perpetually contestable configurations.
>
> (Kristeva 2002: 12)

While Rainer's work said 'No!' to most aspects of the performance culture at that time, this should not be seen as nihilism but as a violent, revolutionary desire to overturn norms. This is why she wrote in her 1968 programme note that she also loved the body, 'its actual weight, mass, and unenhanced physicality' (Rainer 1974: 71). *The Mind is a Muscle* exemplified the desire for perpetual contestation to which Kristeva refers. If its performance did not therefore attempt to represent or express Rainer's feelings about the world disintegrating around her, this should not be seen as an attempt to deny that her art had any social or political relevance.[1] What it did was open up new sets of parameters through which to rethink the social and political relevance of the dancing body.

The dancers and artists involved with Judson Dance Theater, as part of the bohemian community (or communities) downtown, enjoyed a certain privilege as avant-garde artists while at the same time seeing themselves as marginal outsiders. Within this antagonistic counterculture, radical new ideas about art, social identities and lifestyles, and political activism emerged at around the same time. Rainer and her fellow dancers had grown up in the US during the cold war. Consequently, none of them has ever been happy with the idea that their work might be political. Nevertheless, as Sally Banes has pointed out, some of them became involved in political activism in the late 1960s. She lists dancers' involvement in anti-war protests, and a concert by the Grand Union in support of the Black Panthers' legal defence fund (Banes 1980: 15). They were, therefore, supporting draft dodgers in breaking the law, while the Black Panthers were charged with plotting to assassinate police officers and to blow up a building in New York. Paxton, Rainer, and their fellow dancers were not, therefore, working in a democratic way through existing political institutions to bring about social and political change. Instead, they seem to have favoured civil disobedience and supported those of marginal and outsider status. When Rainer wrote that ideological issues had no bearing on the nature of her work, she was saying that her dance was apolitical. But the fact that she went on to state that the world was disintegrating around her demonstrates that, even though she saw herself as an apolitical choreographer, she could not ignore the urgent social and political problems surrounding her. What she was not denying, however, was a correlation between an avant-garde sensibility and the social and political radicalism of the counterculture.

The uneasy relationship that some dancers had with contemporary radical politics followed a similar trajectory to that which the art historian, Thomas Crow, has identified in the visual arts during the 1960s. Crow argues that the hope during the 1960s that artists could 'provide magical forms of political resistance' rested 'on a mistaken understanding of the position of artists in the most intense years of the Civil Rights and anti-war movements' (Crow 1996: 179). While the conceptual demands of advanced artistic activity required full-time application of artists' resources, 'political activists became similarly absorbed by a total commitment that left next to no time for other pursuits' (ibid.). Crow concludes that in the 1960s 'art was a laboratory of a future politics, but could never be the productive engine' while in the 1970s 'the social and ethical experimentation that had gone on within the culture of the left now set the agenda for advanced art' (ibid.: 170).

In what way, then, did the culture of the left begin to set the agenda for the new dance? Many French theorists rejected Marxism, even before the events of 1968, turning instead to a libertarian politics within which avant-garde art had a significant role.[2] As Tamsin Lorraine points out, the idea was developing, particularly among structuralist and poststructuralist theorists, that avant-garde arts could achieve what Marxism could not, a shift in consciousness that would lead to significant social change (Lorraine 1999: 13). And whereas orthodox Marxists did not consider cultural forms important to class struggle, in the aftermath of 1968, many in the New Left recognized that the arts were an important area in which values are mediated. For the art historian John Berger, 1968 was a moment when: 'hopes, nurtured more or less underground for years, were born in several places in the world and given their names; and in the same year, these hopes were categorically defeated' (1980: 127). He reflected on the impact of the events of 1968 on himself and his generation in an essay on the Renaissance painter Matthias Grünewald's

Isenheim Altarpiece in Colmar, analysing the difference between the way he had responded to this on two visits to see it, first in 1963 and then in 1973. The first time he saw it, he wrote, he had been struck by the devastatingly bleak depiction of pain and suffering in the panel showing the Crucifixion. Returning to Colmar in 1973, however, he found himself fascinated by the quality of inner light in some of its other panels, which seemed to suggest the promise of hope, so that now the work seemed miraculously to offer 'a narrow pass across despair' (ibid.: 133). Before 1968, he had approached Grünewald's work with the hope that revolutionary change was possible, and was on the way. After 1968 he saw it through the need to understand and thus resist underlying processes of social and political reaction that the failures of 1968 had revealed. It was in the aftermath of 1968 that the New Left in Western Europe and North America began to see the kinds of experiences mediated within works of art, including dance, as relevant to an understanding of social and political events. Before and during 1968, therefore, there was a naive idealism that, as philosopher Simon Critchley puts it, the art work can provide 'an image of what the world might be like if freedom were realized [and that] it is through art that we intimate the dimensions of a politically transfigured everyday life' (Critchley 1997: 91). After 1968, however, this naivety was replaced by a realization that individuals had to face what Critchley calls 'the problem of political disappointment in terms of an ethical injunction that might at least permit one to face critically the experience of injustice and domination' (ibid.: 2). In this context, as I proposed at the end of Chapter 4, the dancing body became a site of resistance against dominant ideologies.

In some ways the new dance of the 1960s was in line with more liberal social attitudes than those reflected in more mainstream ballet and modern dance work at the time, but there were, nevertheless, blind spots. The new dance of the 1960s can only partly be seen, following Thomas Crow, as a laboratory of a future politics. Where dancers were working outside existing paradigms and ideological frameworks, they were sometimes only partially successful in imagining or discovering new ones whose logic they did not necessarily recognize or follow through at the time. Retrospectively, however, the fact that some of them eventually did recognize and incorporate new, less naive approaches to art and politics into their embodied practices as dancers and dance makers is, in part, a consequence of these early experiments. It is important, however, to examine the limits of the new artistic imagination implicit in these experiments by investigating its blind spots and considering what was, in some cases, tacitly excluded from them. The sort of shift in consciousness that the dancers and artists produced in their work was correlative to new types of political radicalism. It is both the strengths and blind spots of this radicalism and its naivety, particularly where Asian American and African American issues were concerned, that are the subject of this chapter.

Jill Johnston

Jill Johnston in the 1960s was not a politicized dance writer, and I have not found any reviews she wrote during this time that dealt with either dance by African American artists or of dance used in a context of political protest. In 1969, however, she became deeply involved in the feminist movement, publishing intensely partisan articles advocating lesbian separatist politics. Thus, her 1971 collection of dance reviews, *Marmalade Me*, was followed in 1974 by a collection of her feminist articles, *Lesbian Nation*. It was while writing about dance and performance that Johnston developed the loose, flowing, subjective, and increasingly experimental style of writing (some examples of which I have quoted in previous chapters) that also characterizes the pieces in *Lesbian Nation*. As Liz Kotz points out: 'It is prose to get lost in, but its fracturing of subjectivity and identity is not without purpose; repetition and accumulation become strategies to envision gradual shifts in social realities' (Kotz 1998: 20). Whereas traditional dance critics compartmentalized and classified dance, closing down the possibilities of social and political signification, Johnston broke open the field of dance criticism, allowing new possibilities of meaning to emerge. In her 1965 article, 'Critics' critics', Johnston responded to a recent article by Clive Barnes, dance critic of the *New York Times*, in which he had described his role as dance critic as that of a parasite. In her view criticism is not parasitic but an art in its own right (Johnston 1998: 123–4). Her approach to dance criticism, like the work of the artists she initially discussed, broke and disrupted the conventions and traditions of the medium, exemplifying strategies of breakage, rearticulation, and resistance.

Rather than maintaining a conventional 'critical' distance from the artists of the Greenwich Village scene, Johnston became involved with them. In 1963 she became a programmer of dance events at the Washington Square Art Gallery, across the square from Judson Church, and also started performing herself.[3] In 1964 she reviewed a performance of Stockhausen's *Locale* in which she, herself, was a performer ('Inside *Locale*' Johnston 1998: 77–83). After 1965 her dance column no longer really reviewed dance but largely chronicled what she herself had been doing, which sometimes involved going to dance performances or Happenings or meeting artists at parties. It was fairly common knowledge that Johnston's mental health was not stable. Her article 'Critics' critics' was written and published while she was in a psychiatric ward at Bellevue Hospital. As Kotz observes: 'Up-ended by social and personal cataclysms, intimately involved with major art figures of the day, Johnston would make an ideal subject for anyone working on the entanglements of language, sexuality, madness and subjectivity' (1998: 19).

The wonderfully crazy, subversive energy that flows through Johnston's *Village Voice* dance column allowed her, quite literally, to blur the distinction between writing and performing. First, she showed that she too could perform (if she got drunk enough first), then she wrote about performing in other people's work, and then turned her life into a performance through writing about it. One of the suggestions that Johnston makes in her article 'Critics' critics' is that dancers should write about work themselves, just as many visual artists were already doing. Yvonne Rainer was, in fact, already doing so, and Trisha Brown, Lucinda Childs, David Gordon, and Steve Paxton all subsequently wrote about their work.[4] Indeed, many of the ex-members of Judson Dance Theater have written about their work, often more intelligently and informatively than most of the critics. For these dance artists who had received higher education, intellectual ideas were important in ways that traditional forms of dance criticism could not deal with. Johnston's knowledge of the art world and art theory helped her understand dance work in which theory was increasingly important. Johnston helped generate and legitimate the discourse through which ambitious, experimental dance artists engaged with theory. Johnston herself, in the preface for the 1998 edition of *Marmalade Me*, came to a similar conclusion to Julia Kristeva, writing:

> The social and political revolutions of the decade [1960s] were played out in every medium and field of endeavor. People with either inceptive or developed oppositional identities, finding themselves in a position to make a difference, mobilized to create madness, chaos, and change. Those in limbic states like myself, poised between a repressive past and a promise of fantastic liberties, in love with everything shocking, would be swept into the vortex of revolution, possessed and gripped by it, ultimately becoming synonymous with it.
>
> (Johnston 1998: xii)

Johnston was in a contradictory position within the social discourses of her time. She enjoyed a privileged position as someone who was white, middle class, with higher education, and an established art and dance critic; but, in the notoriously macho New York art world, she was vulnerable and oppressed as a woman who had left her husband,

and as a lesbian in this virulently homophobic social group. In her 1984 autobiography she spells out her awareness of this. In the early 1960s, she says she was tolerated by the men in the art world that she was in contact with

> like a younger sister who had never been broken, a condition toler-able only through the power of my position as a critic. Either to counteract my position and/or express the faith I still had in the system I was attacking (along with my friends), I protected myself by appearing in the degraded form of a drunken fool.
>
> (Johnston 1983: 133)

Then at one drunken party she says she committed the gravest offence against the heterosexual members of her male peer group by picking up the most beautiful young, female dancer who had been the centre of attention, 'usurping their feeling that they had a right to the most desirable women on the scene' (ibid.).

Johnston, by virtue of her contradictory position, was able to say things that other critics would never have dared. In a piece in *Dance Magazine* in 1958, Johnston politely pointed out that the way ballet audi-ences customarily interrupted performances by clapping at any and every display of technical skill was disruptive and dislocating, particularly in the middle of serious, modernist works by Balanchine (Johnston 1958). By 1968 she no longer maintained a façade of politeness when attacking another sacred cow. Martha Graham, she wrote in *Ballet Review*, was clearly 'an inverted homo hetero sado masochistic sodomist . . . who was the lady kidding? She's an incredible ball-breaker. So bloody serious. So hell-bent for leather etc.' (Johnston 1968: 11).[5] If Johnston herself was able to attack the system, it was her intelligent championing of the dancers and artists who did the same for which she will probably be best remembered. What I want to point out, however, is that long before she became aware of sexual politics, her experience as a woman and as a lesbian was a factor in her approach to dismantling conventional crit-ical discourse. In the 1990s, she suggested that subversive critical writing should be called 'Closet Criticism', because:

> It gets into the closets of narrative and surface, undermining, corrupting the words, sounds, gestures, or movement vocabularies, and formalist policies we take for granted. It resonates with the 'closet' of gay and lesbian politics – the only cultural use of the term describing identities hidden from view.
>
> (Alexander 1998: ix–x)

Although this wasn't yet what she was consciously doing in her dance reviews during the 1960s, this is their logical development. Like many of the artists she wrote about, her radical, avant-garde approach generated a practice which, once she became aware of new social and political ideas, enabled her to respond to these in ways that created space for the expression of experiences that, arguably, could not be signified within normative, heterosexual, 'man made' discourse.

16 Millimeter Earrings

Meredith Monk gave the first performance of her early solo piece *16 Millimeter Earrings* at Judson Memorial Church in 1966. Its relationship with countercultural social and political ideas and sensibilities is revealed by the fact that she chose to perform it at Hunter College during 'Angry Arts Week' in 1967 (a series of concerts and events protesting against the war in Vietnam) and by its critical reception in this context.[6] Monk's piece combined dance with live singing and film projection as she had done in previous work, but this was the first piece for which she composed one continuous musical score. Deborah Jowitt (Jowitt 1997: 124) described the stage setting as spare and elegant. It was full of what Monk called 'visual rhymes' (Monk 1998: 72). One such was a series of red items. A trunk with a fan in it blew a series of red streamers up in the air like flames; Monk herself dyed her long, straight, dark hair red for the performance, and at one point wore a red wig. At the end she emerged naked from the trunk as a film of flames were projected over it and her, rhyming with an earlier film of a plastic doll crumpling up and burning in flames. Earlier, the tape-recorded soundtrack included a reading of an extract from Wilhelm Reich's *Function of the Orgasm* which was intercut with a description of a very large, grand ballet leap while Monk herself ironically danced a very small, earthbound movement. One of the black and white film sections showed her first looking through a magnifying glass close up at the camera, then, with clown-like crossed eyes, pulling her hair so that it gradually veiled and obscured her face as her mouth opened to scream. At another moment she put a globe-like frame, like that of a skeletal Japanese lantern, over her head. One side of this was covered in thick white material onto which a colour film of her own face was projected, her projected face being larger than her head inside the sphere. This disjunction between real and filmed was exacerbated when she rubbed her filmed eye with her real hand. When at the end Monk emerged naked from the trunk within filmed flames she danced to a haunting recording of herself singing the old English song 'Greensleeves'. Monk's combinations of images in *16 Millimeter Earrings* refused to make logical or rational sense but all of these visual rhymes opened up possibilities for spectators to build their own allusive and evocative associations.

Monk blurred the boundaries between these different art forms in a way that attempted to achieve an alternative kind of synthesis to that within conventional western theatre practice. Monk told Lisa Bear that, at the time, she was thinking about non-western theatre forms such as Chinese Opera, Kathakali, and Kabuki theatre, 'and trying to get back to a sensory integration that we don't have in the West. A sense of wonder – a triangle that included drama, music, and dance' (Bear 1997: 80). She has said that she used the musical score as the primary structural feature, fitting the visual and dance elements into this. 'I saw that I could make a performance form that had a sense of poetry, nonverbal poetry – a theater of images, sounds, and textures – and by weaving various elements together, a very powerful and multidimensional experience could occur' (Monk 1998: 72). Monk, Kenneth King, and Phoebe Neville have been called the second Judson group (see Poster 1967), because they started to present work at Judson Memorial Church when the original group of the Judson Workshop started to dissolve.[7] Monk said her interdisciplinary way of working had most in common with the way Robert Morris and Simone Forti had taken conceptual ideas or images rather than movement ideas as their starting point; Monk, herself, used images that could equally be explored through music, dance, film, or visual elements in the set. She acknowledged, nevertheless, that her work had little in common with the more minimal work presented at Judson Memorial Church: 'I admired what I saw when I started doing my own work, I wanted it to be more emotionally inclusive in my terms, and I didn't want to deny the magic of theater' (Bear 1997: 83).

Although her work was not minimalist, it challenged conventional ideas about theatre in ways that resonate with the work discussed in Chapter 4. One of the ideas informing her piece *Portable*, a duet she performed with Neville at Judson Memorial Church the same year as *16 Millimeter Earrings*, was the idea of combining formality and informality. In Broadway musicals and at the Metropolitan Opera House, Monk observed, audience and performers were rigidly separated by the formality of the architectural context (Monk 1997: 20). *Portable* mixed this, ending up with the audience inside the piece's set while the performers were on the outside. Some elements in *16 Millimeter Earrings* also mixed up formal and informal audience relations. There was the ironically unspectacular movement performed alongside the taped description of a ballet tour de force. Constance Poster describes Monk's costume as a blue net 'worn over bra and panties with the feet engaged in huge shearing slippers denoting homeliness' (Poster 1967: 19). There was also the intimacy of her live singing, and nudity.

The way in which *16 Millimeter Earrings* negotiated radical social and political ideas can be gauged from Clive Barnes's review in the *New York Times* of this dance concert during the 'Angry Arts Week'. He wrote

> No self-respecting dance protest could be complete without Judson Church, and Meredith Monk gave her Judson solo about a young girl and her difficulties sexual, *16 Millimeter Earrings*. Part witty, the witty part is too small to offset the boredom and particularly when seen a second time this piece does not end a millimeter too soon.
>
> (Barnes 1967)

His appalling comment about 'a young girl's difficulties sexual' must refer to its use of the Willhelm Reich text and Monk's nudity at the end. Barnes missed its relevance: in the context of anti-war protest, it would have been understood by members of the emergent counterculture in relation to the slogan 'Make love not war'. This itself was partly inspired by Reich's equation of fascism with sexual repression and impotence in his then popular work on the mass psychology of fascism.[8]

Monk's piece referred to these ideas in a metonymic rather than a metaphorical way, and was sometimes ironic, sometimes allegorical. Rainer presented her solo version of *Trio A* called *Convalescent Dance* later that week at the same series of concerts. In this, as I discussed in Chapter 1, Rainer's weak body was presented in a metonymic relation with injuries sustained by Vietnam veterans. In *16 Millimeter Earrings* Monk's naked body was situated in a metonymic relation with ideas about sexual and political liberation. Irony and allegory, as Paul de Man (1983) has pointed out, are closely related, both using distanced, multiple viewpoints and allusive, metonymic modes of signification. Irony involves stating one thing in a rhetorical way that implies the opposite, often with humorous effect. In *16 Millimeter Earrings*, Monk performed in an intimate way while simultaneously commenting on herself from a certain distance. Her self-conscious ironizing was exemplified by presenting a small earthbound movement while listening to a description of a grand, balletic leap, and by going cross-eyed when pulling her hair in a strange way. The piece thus created multiple, fragmented viewpoints. The projection of Monk's filmed face as a mask onto the sphere covering her head, which she then wiped intimately with her own hand, also suggested an overlaying of fragmented subjectivities. If Monk had been, as Barnes maliciously suggested, acting out her own 'difficulties sexual', this would have involved the kind of total identification between performer and role that exemplified, for example, the performances of Martha Graham. It was Graham's lack of irony that allowed Johnston to deflate satirically what seemed, in 1968, Graham's pompous seriousness. Monk's use of ironic and allegorical modes in *16 Millimeter Earrings* allowed her to present alternative values that would have been circumscribed through the use of conventionally mainstream theatrical means.

Hand in hand with Monk's rejection of conventionally mainstream theatre was her attraction to the idea of non-western theatre forms, which she knew about intellectually but had not at the time actually experienced. As she told Lisa Bear: 'It's more something in my imagination, what Japanese theatre might be like' (Bear 1997: 83). Yutian Wong has pointed out that some postmodern choreographers in the 1960s troubled choreographic structures and invented new movement techniques using the I Ching, Zen Buddhism, aikido, and t'ai chi (Wong 2002: 76). In her opinion, 'the kinds of American academic Orientalism that the postmodern choreographers created, celebrated forms of ahistoric traditions that are both separate from yet explain the living Asian people in their midst' (ibid.: 80). Where *16 Millimeter Earrings* was concerned, there was nothing in the piece that could be identified as oriental or exoticized, nor, on a formal level, was there any cultural borrowing as such. Indeed the problem, if there is one, lies not so much in this piece in particular but in the naive way Monk subsequently talked about her work in general. The Asian philosophical and aesthetic ideas that Monk and others sincerely respected did not, however, belong to another semi-mythical time and place, as Monk sometimes seemed to imply. Instead they were, as Wong has pointed out, an important contemporary reality for Asian Americans whose cultural authority was in danger of being subsumed and erased by the assumptions that artists such as Monk made about it (ibid.: 81). This was one of the blind spots of the new artistic imagination. In mitigation, many of Monk's works have shown extreme sensitivity towards alterity, which must in some way relate to her own background as a grandchild of Russian Jewish immigrants to the US. Her company, The House, has had an ethnically diverse membership including Ping Chong, Pablo Vela, and Blondell Cummings who Monk has always described as collaborators. I have shown that Monk's avant-garde work during the 1960s bore a strong correlation with socially progressive ideas of their time. As Kotz said of Johnston's writing, repetition and accumulation became strategies to envision gradual shifts in social realities (Kotz 1998: 20). In retrospect, Monk helped generate a practice that subsequently enabled her to respond to alterity in innovative and ethically sensitive ways.

The new dance and African American issues

The blindness of avant-garde dancers towards the cultural needs and aspirations of Asian Americans also extended to African Americans. In her book *Dances that Describe Themselves* (2002), Susan Foster is extremely perceptive in her identification and analysis of appropriations that Richard Bull and some members of Judson Dance Theater made from African American cultural traditions. She observes that when African American choreographers such as Eleo Pomare and Dianne McIntyre used jazz music in their work, they were not breaking with the African American dance and music tradition but reconnecting with it and reassessing its roots. The white dancers associated with Judson Dance Theater, Foster argues, used their radical, boundary-transgressing strategies to break with dominant, mainstream tradition. Foster concludes:

> Unconstrained by the kinds of expectations regarding subject matter or approach that marked choreographers of color, [white experimental choreographers] delved into the improvisatory moment as an opportunity to contest and overthrow prevailing expectations about dance's meaning. Yet their aesthetic choices remained inflected with the power dynamics that had privileged white artists for centuries.
>
> (Foster 2002: 43)

This is undoubtedly true, particularly in the case of white choreographers, such as Richard Bull, who were especially interested in the relationship between jazz and dance improvisation. However, as Foster acknowledges, the kinds of appropriations that she rightly criticizes were not central to the experiments that members of Judson Dance Theater made. The latter were primarily oriented towards European avant-garde ideas.

Very few African Americans were involved with Judson Dance Theater. African Americans were not, of course, excluded. But, as Foster has suggested, they seem to have found the artistic aims of Judson Dance Theater not particularly appealing. Gus Solomons Jr has recently written about his relationship with Judson Dance Theater. He had been, he said, part of the original group from which the Judson group sprang, and hinted that he had been to Robert Dunn's composition workshop.[9] But he concluded that: 'Although I, too, was interested in deconstructing forms and structures, I was too much in love with technical dancing to abandon it in favor of pedestrian, minimalist movement' (Solomons 2003: 108). Looking back in 2005, Brenda Dixon Gottschild, who was one of the performers in Carolee Schneemann's *Meat Joy* at the church in

November 1964, also attested to how little the downtown avant-garde scene offered her as an African American:

> Most of my friends were the dropout generation of hippies or radical civil rights activists, and most were white. We were out to make a brave, new world. We were colorblind, and neither blacks nor whites realized how little we knew about any part of our heritage except the European side. In other words, everything in my immediate world looked/felt basically white, until the winds of African American studies, cultural studies, and race studies blew me off center and helped me see the black at the center of it all.
>
> (Gottschild 2005: 75)

Solomons has also suggested that: 'Because I am African American, critics and historians generally assume I was not of the avant-garde, an almost exclusively Euro-American clique' (Solomons 2003: 108). Evidence of African American involvement in the 1960s avant-garde can be found in Amiri Baraka's writings. Baraka, then LeRoi Jones, was, as I noted in Chapter 4, in touch with the avant-garde dance scene through the New York Poets Theater. Subsequently, he was prominent among the black artists and writers living in downtown Manhattan who, with the rise of the Black Arts Movement in the mid-1960s, made the conscious decision to focus their work on members of the black community and to move up to Harlem. While living downtown, he knew James Waring and members of his company and almost certainly attended dance concerts at Judson Memorial Church.[10] It was while helping Baraka produce the mimeographed newsletter *The Floating Bear* that Fred Herko met the experimental jazz pianist Cecil Taylor, with whom he subsequently collaborated for the piece *Like Most People – For Soren* (1962) performed at the first concert of dance at Judson Memorial Church.[11] The egalitarianism of Judson Dance Theater had much in common with the fluid, inclusive editorial policy of *The Floating Bear*, which Baraka edited jointly with Diane di Prima. Writing in the fifth issue of this, Baraka asked: 'But how to *get in* most constantly . . . and with the most *force*. As the newsletter shd only exist from the point where it is realized and consistently available . . . for all our thot. How to??' (di Prima 1974: 41, emphasis and abbreviation in the original). Baraka's answer was the need to 'attempt to get into the very rhythms of my self', adding:

> I wd say perhaps excerpts, quotes, steals, &c., from some pertinent matter would at least pull in some things that might give at least a de facto existence to all the shit we know & use & reject each minute.
>
> (ibid.)

Baraka was trying to encompass, here, a similar kind of anarchic eclecticism – 'pulling in' ordinary, everyday material into metonymic relationships with aesthetic material. In the last two chapters, I have identified pieces by Brown, Childs, Gordon, Herko, Monk, Paxton, Rainer, and others who have also done this.

In his later autobiography Baraka remembered that he and other African Americans living downtown at the time

> wanted what was new and hip, though we were connected in a lot of ways with some stuff that was old and square. We knew the music was hip and new and out beyond anything anyone downtown was doing, in music, painting, poetry, dance, or whatever the fuck.
>
> (Baraka 1997: 266)

Listening to John Coltrane playing in Greenwich Village jazz clubs, 'we heard our own search and travails, our own reaching for new definition. Trane was our flag' (ibid.: 260). The dancers Baraka knew best were James Waring and Fred Herko. John Coltrane's work was undoubtedly more avant-garde than Waring's. Baraka had drifted away from Greenwich Village by the time Paxton and Rainer were presenting minimal and conceptual works such as *Flat* and *Trio A*. For Baraka, the libertarian aspects of avant-garde artistic practice seemed to enable the breaching of restrictive mechanisms that maintained boundaries in terms of race. In his 1963 book *Blues People*, he wrote that the new hard bebop music of musicians such as John Coltrane and Cecil Taylor placed itself outside any mainstream consideration.

> I cannot think that the music is any more radical, or any more illogical extension of the kinetic philosophy that has informed Negro music since its inception in America. Negro music is *always* radical in the context of formal American culture.
>
> (Baraka 1995: 235, emphasis in the original)

The Judson dancers showed no signs of the hipster's desire to become 'white Negroes' who, as Kobena Mercer puts it, went into black culture in search of sex, speed, and psychosis (Mercer 1994: 304).[12] It was the Beats who had been fascinated by bebop musicians, such as John Coltrane and Cecil Taylor. There are clear parallels between improvised jazz and the freewheeling, stream-of-consciousness outpourings of Beat poetry and prose. There was, however, a clear distinction between the coolness of avant-garde jazz and the cool indifference of minimal art. Steve Paxton, asked in 2001, didn't remember Fred Herko and

Cecil Taylor's performance, saying that he must have been backstage at the time. He said he wasn't listening to improvised music in the mid-1960s, but listening to indeterminacy: 'I was listening live to Morton Feldman, Christian Wolff and John Cage. Cecil seemed a little brash and unconsidered' (Paxton 2001). The harsh, disruptive nature of both bebop and the new indeterminate music of Cage constituted breaks with mainstream western aesthetic norms. As I have already indicated, Baraka believed that the way bebop music broke with these norms signified radical changes within social and emotional attitudes. Judson Dance Theater might have been new and hip, but there was little sign in the early 1960s that its members were making the connections Baraka was making between avant-gardism and the politics of race, nor recognizing the need to oppose mechanisms that maintained boundaries in terms of race.

Simone Forti and Bill T. Jones at Woodstock

Not only did Simone Forti and Bill T. Jones both attend the most famous pop festival of the 1960s at Woodstock in 1969, but both have subsequently written about their experiences there. Reading their two accounts together reveals the distance between black and white avant-garde points of view.

What Forti wrote about the festival in her 1974 book *Handbook in Motion*, exemplifies many of the issues and problems surrounding the relationship between an avant-garde blurring and transgressing of limits and non-western performance traditions. When writing her book, Forti was retrospectively aware of many of the contradictions that had surrounded Woodstock. While she was there, she believed that she 'had forever abandoned the sheath of surface tension that seemed to separate my identity from the rest of the universe of flux in time and space' (Forti 1974: 102). She therefore seems to have believed she had blurred the limits between herself and others, but, as I shall show, a naive lack of awareness of black politics, in effect, blocked her from the kind of openness she aspired to achieve. Subsequently, she realized how much her ability to experience a sense of oneness with the universe had been based on conditions of economic privilege:

> We were flowing through channels of national, economic surplus. Riding on checks from home, on gifts, scavenging and finding a wealth of refuse. It was beautiful, and it left us free to explore in many ways. But it wasn't the messianic vision I took it for.
>
> (ibid.)

By 1974 Forti had therefore become aware of the problem of political disappointment.

Forti seemed to have sensed the centrality of African American dance and music to the Woodstock phenomenon, though she did not seem aware of any problems surrounding its appropriation. From the auto-biographical parts of *Handbook in Motion*, it appears that Woodstock was a turning point for Forti, coming at a time of crisis in her relation to avant-garde practice.[13] She seems to have spent the whole festival high on drugs, dancing with different groups of people. 'And as I danced, my body was enough on some kind of automatic pilot that all these musics came together, somehow merged into a pattern that included them all in a dynamic, rolling kind of falling together' (ibid.: 15). She remembered dancing with a group of naked people in the middle of the night to drums around a fire. Among them she remembered one black man in particular:

> The drums kept going, and he was doing a bouncing kind of stomping, left, right, left, right, left, right, his spine tilting from side to side. It seemed like a tuning, a finding of certain forces, an over-lapping of the body into a certain bounciness which matter can get into. Sometimes I think back on him in terms of laser light, which is so powerful not because there's so much light involved but because the light is bounced back and forth until it is tuned. As sound can be tuned.
>
> (ibid.: 15–16)

All her experiences while dancing at Woodstock clarified in Forti's mind the idea that there is a dance state:

> Like there's a sleeping state or a state of shivering ... When I'm in a dance state, the movement that comes out through me enchants me. It can be very simple movement, but it always comes with a sense of wonder, and as one of life's more delicious moments.
>
> (ibid.: 108–9)

It is this insight that has underpinned much of her subsequent teach-ing and performing in Europe and the US. Forti associates this state, within the book, with an appreciation of music from the Third World, and with non-western philosophies, including the beliefs of the Hopi Indians (ibid.: 103–6) and movement forms such as t'ai chi (ibid.: 107–8). Like Monk, she naively believed these came from an ahistorical, pre-modern past. It is as if this black man dancing naked to drumming around a fire at night was returning to some mythical, 'primitive', magical African context. There is no hint in her account that she might have been sensitive to what the experience of dancing like this might have meant to this African American – either of what his diasporic memory or retention of African expressive culture might have meant to him, or of what his experience of participating in the Woodstock festival might have been.

In his autobiography *Last Night on Earth* (1995), Bill T. Jones wrote about going to Woodstock with his elder brother Azel. On the last morning he recalls being with a group who were bathing in a pond. The situation he describes presents an uncanny parallel with the scene of dancing around the fire that was so important for Forti. I quote Jones at length:

> Around me were topless blonde girls with pink flowers painted on their breasts, and an old beatnik wearing an Australian infantryman's hat and nothing else. A pregnant woman hummed softly to herself as she carefully picked her way through the reeds into the water. I wasn't naked, but Azel was. I watched him – my magnificent brother with his athlete's body – as he waded into the pool. He carried himself formally, almost as though in uniform. Everyone watched him. Something brushed past him and he flinched. I saw my brother at that moment as a beautiful object. As an icon. I think that even those who have no notion of what the auction block was can still feel it, as if the memory of it is handed down to us through our mother's milk. It was there with Azel as he moved through the water. It is there with me when I dance before you on stage. My eroticism, my sensuality is often coupled with wild anger and belligerence. I know that I can be food for fantasy, but at the same time I am a person with a history – and that history is in part the history of exploitation. We all carry this history inside and it costs us.
>
> (Jones 1995: 73–4)

Forti's mythical, 'primitive' Africa, however sensitive and insightful she was in her movement description, seems naive when contrasted with Jones's traumatic memory of a slave auction. Jones's complex and conflictual feelings about his brother's dancing indicate a point of view that is both personal and political, but none of this had occurred to Forti.

Kobena Mercer (1994) has proposed that the Woodstock phenomenon represented both an appropriation of African American political radicalism and a somewhat ambiguous appropriation of the aesthetics of black music and dance by the white middle-class counterculture. He points out that the black political notion of brotherhood and community inspired other sorts of communities, such as the solidarity of sisterhood within the women's movement or the sense of community – of being a nation within a nation, the Woodstock Nation – among the hippies. What Forti admired about the naked black dancer was the way his cool movement offered not just an alternative to white western ways of dancing but one that was oppositional. Mercer argues that the performance by The Jimi Hendrix Experience, who were the headline group at Woodstock, crystallizes the problem of countercultural appropriations. Because the festival programme overran, Hendrix didn't actually perform until Monday morning after most of the audience had dispersed. Nevertheless, it is film of him playing his guitar version of 'The Star Spangled Banner' – with interruptions of amplifier feedback that some have likened to the sounds of war and rioting – that has become the iconic moment of the festival. Hendrix's piece had provoked threats to the group from both the police and white racists when it was played on a tour of the southern states earlier in the year. Mercer has suggested that Hendrix's 'sublime deconstruction of this hymn to national identity gave voice to an antagonism that questioned its own conditions of representability' (Mercer 1994: 304). The attraction that members of the white, middle-class counterculture felt towards Hendrix's oppositional stance was, for Mercer, an ambiguous appropriation because of the lack of appreciation of ways in which Hendrix's music drew on a long history and tradition of the use of music and dance as a resistance to racism.

Just as Hendrix was disrupting and shattering western conventions of melodic coherence, Forti wanted to break with existing western conventions concerning dance. In her search for ways to do this, she clearly greatly admired the black dancer round the fire. Her enthusiasm is remarkably similar to that with which members of the historical avant-garde earlier in the century had greeted, for example, African masks or the dancing of Josephine Baker.[14] Like them, Forti seems to have seen African otherness, to use Jones's phrase, as food for fantasy: as a screen on which to project a nostalgically fantasized, aestheticized, mythical past that had more to do with perceived shortcomings in contemporary white western subjectivity than in contemporary African or African American realities. This was the limit of Forti's imagination, but, in mitigation, it was not one that had any direct impact on her practice as a dancer and teacher. Forti's approach to improvisation had its roots in things she had begun to learn over a decade earlier with Anna Halprin (see Chapter 3) and owed little to African American dance and music traditions. As with Monk's *16 Millimeter Earrings*, Forti did not engage in cultural borrowing from non-western dance and music traditions in either her teaching or performing, but was merely naive in the way she wrote about the black dancer round the fire. Furthermore, she was an important contributor to the development of an avant-garde dance tradition to which Bill T. Jones, Ishmael Houston Jones, and other African American dance artists subsequently also made distinguished contributions. Forti's lack of awareness of African American issues was part of a more widespread blindness that this chapter maps.

Trio A at The People's Flag Show

About fifteen months after Hendrix played the 'Star Spangled Banner' at Woodstock, *Trio A* was performed by dancers who were naked but for American flags tied around their necks. In November 1970 David Gordon, Nancy Green, Barbara Lloyd, Steve Paxton, Yvonne Rainer, and Lincoln Scott performed a version of *Trio A* naked but for three-foot by five-foot US flags tied like bibs round their necks during 'The People's Flag Show' at Judson Memorial Church (Figure 5.1). In Clarinda Mac Low's 1999 revival, which I assume bore a reasonable resemblance to the 1970 performance, the dancers entered the performance space clothed; each undressed in a corner and tied a flag round their neck before coming out and beginning to dance *Trio A*. They therefore each began in their own time. They danced the piece through twice and then returned to their clothes to dress again and neatly fold their flag. When everyone was dressed they all came out as a group to bow. Although I had seen Peter Moore's photographs of this performance, it wasn't until the summer of 2002 when I watched a video at the New York Public Library of this 1999 revival that I became aware of how subversive Hendrix and Rainer's pieces must have seemed in their time. The Stars and Stripes has always seemed much more prominent in the US than national flags are in most European countries – US public institutions and private companies often flying it over their buildings. Following the attack on the World Trade Center in September 2001, many New York citizens displayed the Stars and Stripes in the windows of their apartments, and on balconies and fire escapes. In Manhattan in June 2002, these were still there, mostly somewhat degraded by the effects of their long exposure to sunlight and weather. I was conscious of this as I watched the video at the library and worried that some still traumatized New Yorker might challenge me about the piece's challenging alternative to patriotic flag-waving. And as I walked past Judson Memorial Church that evening I was handed a flyer for a meeting about to be held there by the 'Not in my name' anti-war movement protesting against the build-up to the war in Iraq. I was therefore reminded both about the sensitivities surrounding the US flag and about the radical tradition underlying the mission of Judson Memorial Church.

'The People's Flag Show' in 1970 was a response to the arrest of a New York City Art Dealer, Steven Radich, on charges of violating *The Desecration of the Flag* law for having exhibited an anti-war sculpture by Marc Morell. A number of artists, including John Hendricks, Jean Toche, and Faith Ringgold of the Art Workers Coalition, organized an exhibition of works based on the Stars and Stripes as a protest, and Rainer was invited to participate. Rainer has said she feels it was all right to tinker with *Trio A* because she had already been performing it for a long time. Using flags metonymically in this way made it a political dance by placing its aesthetic structure side by side with a political cause. Through making this gift to the cause, it suggested common ground between the radical, iconoclastic nature of the generic work *Trio A* and the radical nature of libertarian protest. In claiming their right to use the flag in this way they were, in effect, asserting their pluralist, inclusive vision of what kind of democracy the US should be. The US

Figure 5.1 Trio A at The People's Flag Show at Judson Memorial Church, November 1970. Barbara Lloyd, David Gordon, Nancy Green, Steve Paxton, Yvonne Rainer, and Lincoln Scott with works from the exhibition behind them.

was founded through revolution and *Trio A* was a revolutionary piece. The sight of naked bodies juxtaposed with the Stars and Stripes disrupted in a conceptually violent way the kind of conservative behaviour one might otherwise associate with the handling of a national flag, though the dancers' actual handling of it – the neat folding – was sincerely respectful and patriotic. The conceptual violence of this performance of *Trio A* paralleled the acoustic violence of Hendrix's performance of 'The Star Spangled Banner'. I suggest that each constituted a moment of breakage and rearticulation that, in Mercer's terms, 'gave voice to an antagonism that questioned its own conditions of representability' (Mercer 1994: 304).

'The Peoples Flag Show' brought together a number of black and white artists, including many women artists, in a kind of rainbow coalition. One if its organizers, Faith Ringgold, had been involved in a guerrilla art action earlier that year against 'Art Strike'. As Ringgold's daughter, Michele Wallace, who also took part in this, has explained:

> A group of famous white male artists led by Robert Morris decided to withdraw their work from the Venice Biennale, a prestigious international exhibition, in order to protest US military involvement in Vietnam. Although the protest was supposed to be against 'racism, sexism, and repression', Art Strike then expected to mount a counter-Biennale in New York without altering the all-white male composition of the show. This seems to be the key to understanding the intrinsic limits of Western cultural avant-gardism: while it can no longer deny its own white male supremacist presuppositions, it cannot be rid of them either.
>
> (Wallace 1989: 107)

'The Peoples Flag Show' and the guerrilla actions against 'Art Strike' were instances where social and ethical initiatives that had developed within the Civil Rights Movement were being applied critically to art practice and were setting the agenda for advanced art. Yvonne Rainer and others were able to respond to this agenda because their involvement in minimalism had provided them with conceptual tools that prepared them for a subsequent politicization of their art. Their understanding of allegorical and metonymic signifying strategies helped them recognize that establishing chains of equivalence between individual political struggles could be the basis for new micro-political coalitions.

Years later, in a panel discussion in 1986, Rainer said that she still clung to 'the somewhat romantic ideas of the avant-garde that launched my own creative efforts: ideas about marginality, intervention, an adversative subculture, a confrontation with the complacent past, the art of resistance, etc. Of course, these ideas must be constantly reassessed in terms of class, gender, and race' (Jayamanne *et al.*: 1986: 46–7).[15] This exemplifies the shift from the naive idealism of the 1960s to attempts to deal in aesthetic terms with the problem of political disappointment that I trace in the rest of this book. The Judson Flag Show performance of *Trio A* nevertheless marked the moment when the naive idealism I have been criticizing in this chapter began to face the consequences of political disappointment. Rainer's 1968 statement that her dancing body remained an enduring reality had not been an attempt to disengage from the world that appeared to be disintegrating around her, but should be seen as part of a countercultural attempt to disengage from reactionary forces.

What Julia Kristeva has identified as a violent, revolutionary desire to overturn norms that characterized the revolts of 1968 entangled an avant-garde sensibility with a desire for radical social and political change. What the failures of 1968 revealed, however, was the need to understand and resist underlying processes of social and political reaction, including the way issues of class, gender, sexuality, ethnicity, and alterity are mediated through mainstream cultural forms. The new dance, by bringing to the surface issues concerning embodiment, enabled dancers to recognize that the dancing body was not, in fact, value-free or an enduring reality but a site of contestation and resistance against dominant ideologies. But just as countercultural values seemed in danger of reappropriation, of 'selling out', so the avant-garde seemed in danger of becoming institutionalized. Although a sense of political disappointment therefore suggested that the avant-garde had failed, the desire and, indeed, the need to go on making work that is radical and critical remained. Samuel Beckett gave the title *Imagination Dead Imagine* to a short, minimal piece of prose published in 1966. As Simon Critchley points out, the title suggests an imagination that 'goes on imagining in the knowledge that imagination has come to an end' (Critchley 1997: 28). The rest of this book looks at ways in which, under the shadow of political disappointment, dancers have gone on producing radical, critical work despite the knowledge that the time of the avant-garde seemed to have come to an end.

6 Repetition
Brown, Bausch, and De Keersmaeker

A recurring choreographic motif in much new dance in Europe and the US during the late 1970s and early 1980s was serial repetition. This chapter looks at three key works of this time – Pina Bausch's *Café Müller* (1978), Trisha Brown's *Accumulation with Talking plus Watermotor* (1979), and Anne Teresa De Keersmaeker's *Rosas Danst Rosas* (1983) – which each used serial repetition, though in different ways and with different effects. Through a discussion of these three works my aim is to show that, while there are obvious differences between the way that advanced theatre dance developed on either side of the Atlantic during the 1970s and 1980s, there were nevertheless some similarities in the way each of these pieces asserted the materiality of the dancing body in order to distance itself from older, expressive modes of choreography. This, I propose, is a central legacy of Judson Dance Theater to ambitious, experimental dance on both sides of the Atlantic during the last decades of the twentieth century. In choosing Bausch and Brown, I am revisiting the discussion initiated in the first chapter about the relationship between new dance on either side of the Atlantic; I have chosen *Rosas Danst Rosas* because De Keersmaeker shared Brown's concern for rigorous formal and conceptual structures but also adopted a deconstructive approach to dramaturgy and theatrical representations that can be usefully compared with Bausch's work.

Accumulation with Talking plus Watermotor was a solo that cut back and forth between material from two earlier pieces. The first of these was Brown's 1971 piece *Accumulation*, which consisted of repeated, simple rotations of the body's joints that produced angular movements, including almost mechanical turning of the thumb, forearm, and leg. As its title suggests, these modular units of movement accumulated in an almost reductively simple, clear way. The other piece was her 1978 solo *Watermotor* whose movements had a radically different quality that was soft, silky, flowing and seemed to explode out of her body in an unpredictable, eccentric, and exciting way. In addition to cutting abruptly from one dance to the other, Brown also alternated between telling two stories, each with a simple, linear narrative about making the piece and previous performances of it. Brown was unable to talk while performing the more strenuous material from *Watermotor* but resumes narrating, sometimes out of breath, when changing back to the *Accumulation* material. One story was about a concert that went disastrously wrong, while the other was about dancing the piece when she had been invited to go back to her high school to accept an award. Both Brown and Lucinda Childs used accumulation as a choreographic device during the 1970s. Some commentators have called the resulting pieces mathematical, which has the perhaps unintentional effect of suggesting that their performance presented the result of complex, deductive, mathematical reasoning, whereas the formal structures of their pieces were actually extremely simple. Roselee Goldberg points out that the process of choreographic accumulation can be compared with some nursery rhymes and fairy stories and cites 'The House that Jack Built'. 'Each verse', Goldberg points out, 'begins with the house, and no matter how many are added, we always return to the first, second, third verses, and so on. So with the movement phrases' (Goldberg 1976: 57).[1] As the rhyme gets longer, the first few lines become so well known that they gradually lose their explicit meaning, becoming instead a familiar, regular, rhythmic pattern. As philosopher Gilles Deleuze observed: 'Repetition changes nothing in the object repeated, only in the mind which contemplates it' (Deleuze 1994: 70). It is the way serial repetition makes explicit meanings disappear that is a key feature which these three pieces have in common.

Café Müller explored the absurd and apparently dysfunctional interactions of three men and three women, including Bausch herself, in a stage set representing a fairly large café, complete with small, round café tables and wooden chairs. Two of the dancers, originally Dominic Mercy and Malou Airaudo, had a series of intimate encounters during the piece and appeared to be moving with their eyes closed. A third dancer, Bausch, also had her eyes closed and seemed to be entirely self-absorbed. One large, suited man, Jan Minarik, played a powerful figure who often dominated or interfered with other dancers. Another man, who also wore a suit, was a 'chair mover' whose task was simply to move the furniture out of the way of the other dancers but not engage in any way with them; originally this task was carried out by the piece's designer, Rolf Borzik, who found that his role of 'making space for the dancing' necessitated, in this case, his presence on stage. The last role was a woman with a red wig and loose overcoat, originally Meryl Tankard, who wandered around tottering on high heels in a mindless-looking way, ineffectually hovering around the other dancers, trying to get their attention. At the end she swapped roles with Bausch to whom she gave her wig and coat, perhaps suggesting that their roles were interchangeable and that the piece as a whole was circular, repeating itself interminably. Initially the dancers who had their eyes shut picked their way nervously through the chairs and tables, their arms held out in front, palms forwards to feel for invisible obstacles with which they inevitably collided. When music played – arias from Purcell oratorios – they danced movement sequences that were made up of expressive reaching, circling and bending phrases. Bausch trained with Kurt Jooss, a pupil and close collaborator of Rudolf Laban. In Laban's terms these movements were gathering and scattering and they made use of the full range of space around the body that Laban had explored in his movement scales. These gathering and scattering movements were repeated in loosely varying sequences, sometimes picked up for brief unison passages by a second performer, or repeated later in the piece more or less unchanged, and certainly without any sense of development. A few sequences were made up of ordinary, unembellished actions, albeit sometimes of an extreme and painful nature – as when Mercy and Airaudo took turns in swinging one another crashing into a side wall. These, however, were choreographed into sequences of serial repetition so that what might initially have appeared to be naturalistic acting became ritualized through repetition. The art historian Craig Owens, discussing repetition in minimal and conceptual art, described them as a game-like play of substitutions, classifications, reversals and repetitions. These, he suggested, 'suspend any reference outside the series itself, as well as any subjective relation between artist and viewer . . . each mutually absent to the other' (Owens 1992: 118). Repetition in Bausch's work creates the same effect.

Rosas Danst Rosas had something in common with both of these two pieces. It was a work for four women, initially including De Keersmaeker herself, and consisted of five sections, which explored in turn lying, sitting, standing, and walking (the basic 'pedestrian' movements that some of the Judson choreographers had explored). Much of De Keersmaeker's material, as in *Café Müller*, was taken from everyday, social behaviour, but it was without the heavy, emotional associations of Bausch's work, suggesting instead the slightly self-conscious mannerisms of young women in their late teens or very early twenties. Mostly, these mannerisms were broken down into a number of short, simple elements, each taking one or two beats of the piece's minimalist musical score to perform. These were combined into the precise, rigorously systematic movement sequences that the performers danced in an unrelenting, repetitive way. Again, as in *Café Müller*, the choreography appeared to contain no development. Within the unvarying energy level of each section, however, De Keersmaeker created subtle shifts and changes over time within the overall pattern of the movement. The piece as a whole exhibited a tightly defined, grid-like structure, which also resembled the kind of game-like, inwardly focusing repetitions Craig Owens has discussed.

Not only did these three pieces all use serial repetition in comparable ways, but, as I will show, they also all built on ideas, qualities, and choreographic strategies that had been discovered in the 1960s by artists associated with Judson Dance Theater. Furthermore these pieces did so in ways that are exemplary of the majority of ambitious, experimental dance of the late 1970s and early 1980s. As I noted in Chapter 1, Sally Banes proposed a teleological view of postmodern dance as a succession of distinct phases. First, there was an initial breakaway phase (1961–8), followed by a transitional period (1968–73). This was followed by a period of consolidation with three distinct approaches – analytical, metaphorical, and metaphysical: postmodern dance in her view was a purely American phenomenon. Then in the 1980s, Banes said, a truly postmodernist postmodern dance emerged.[2] *Accumulation with Talking plus Watermotor* was an instance of what Banes has called 'analytical' postmodern dance. *Café Müller* exemplified many of the qualities that Banes attributed to 'metaphorical and metaphysical' postmodern dance, while *Rosas Danst Rosas* would fit either category, if one ignores the fact that neither was created in the US. Metaphoric and metaphysical postmodern work, in Banes's account, emphasized 'images of private and communal devotion' (Banes 1987: xxiii) typified by the circle dances of Deborah Hay and the dance theatre of Meredith Monk. By 1966, Monk, Kenneth King, and Phoebe Neville had, in fact, presented work at Judson Memorial Church exemplifying many of the qualities of the 1970s work that Banes termed 'metaphorical and metaphysical', just as works from the 1960s such as Rainer's *Trio A* and Paxton's *Flat* exemplified qualities Banes associated with the later analytical postmodern dance. The discoveries that artists made through Judson Dance Theater surely, therefore, established new traditions and conventions which many experimental dance artists on both sides of the Atlantic (and elsewhere) subsequently explored in more explicit and detailed ways.

The uses of repetition in *Accumulation with Talking plus Watermotor, Café Müller,* and *Rosas Danst Rosas* were a continuation of the minimalist sensibility that I discussed in Chapter 3. There I pointed out that many minimal artists during the 1960s were interested in the work of Samuel Beckett and Alain Robbe-Grillet.[3] As the art historian Rosalind Krauss has pointed out, the repetitive, self-generating systems in these writers' books and plays solve 'problems' that are, in themselves, not particularly interesting but, simply, pretexts for a display of skill. The same, she suggests, is true of some of the systems within minimal art:

> It is the ironic presence of the false 'problem' [in minimal art] that gives to this outburst of skill its special emotional tenor, its sense of purpose and necessity, its sense of being suspended before the immense spectacle of the irrational.
>
> (Krauss 1986: 256)

Krauss concludes: 'To get inside the systems of this work, whether LeWitt's or Judd's or Morris's, is precisely to enter a world without a center, a world of substitutions and transpositions nowhere legitimated by the revelations of a transcendental subject' (ibid.: 258). Craig Owens has suggested that Brown's *Accumulation* pieces share with the work of minimalist visual artists such as LeWitt an externalization of logical procedure and its projection as a spatio-temporal experience that can be seen in terms of allegory (Owens 1992: 56). Owens cites Joel Fineman's discussion of the way mathematical progression can be seen as a paradigm for artistic allegory.

> If the mathematician sees the numbers 1, 3, 6, 11, 20, he would recognize that the 'meaning' of this progression can be recast into the algebraic language of the formula: X plus 2^X, with certain restrictions on X. What would be a random sequence to an inexperienced person appears to the mathematician a meaningful sequence. Notice that the progression can go on ad infinitum. This parallels the situation in almost all allegories. They have no inherent 'organic' limit of magnitude. Many are unfinished like *The Castle* and *The Trial* of Kafka.
>
> (Fineman 1980: 51)

This decentred world with substitutions and transpositions can be found in the insistently and obsessively completed iterative systems of abstract, minimalist choreographies by Brown and Childs. It also seems an appropriate description of pieces from the 1970s that Banes calls metaphorical and metaphysical.

The two indeterminate, immigrant-like figures in Meredith Monk's dance theatre piece *Paris* (1971) or the immigrants in her film *Ellis Island* (1979) seem to inhabit private worlds that have lost their centres and in which the meanings of things have been transposed or subjected to confusing substitutions.[4] The consequent disorientation of these characters is not so different from that of the characters in Bausch's *Café Müller*. These works evoke worlds in which metonymy is in operation. I have argued in previous chapters that the shift from expressive modern dance to the kind of avant-garde dance that began to be performed at Judson Memorial Church in the 1960s is a shift from metaphor and direct expression towards metonymy and allegory. In metaphor, a connection is established between two things that are not literally applicable to one another – for example, 'smouldering eyes' are metaphorically but not literally burning. A direct, transparent relationship is thus established between signifier and signified. Metonymy, however, is a trope that proposes a contiguous or sequential link or substitution. If one hears on the news that the Vatican made an announcement yesterday, one knows that the very buildings and streets of part of the city of Rome were not actually heard speaking, but that the Pope, or someone on his behalf, made a statement. The Vatican, The White House, and 10 Downing Street are metonyms for the world leaders who live in them. These are common, widely recognized metonyms, but others can be more private, and only understood by those who know the particular code through which meaning is shifted and displaced. The structural linguist Roman Jakobson called metonymy the knight's move, referring to the way that in a game of chess the knight can simultaneously jump forwards and sideways. Jakobson was particularly interested in the language difficulties experienced by patients suffering from aphasia. Some aphasics have difficulty making direct associations between words and objects, for example, difficulties with names. However, Jakobson observed that such patients employed metonymy widely: they would substitute fork for knife, table for lamp, smoke for fire (Jakobson 1971: 83). It is this indirect, disorienting quality of Jakobson's knight's move that, at the end of this chapter, I shall identify in the three dances I am discussing.

Craig Owens, Hal Foster, Rosalind Krauss, and like-minded art critics and scholars, who began articulating a postmodern account of the visual arts in the 1970s, have argued that the postmodern turn in the visual arts enacted a shift from signifying structures based on metaphor towards structures that used metonymy and allegory.[5] The three works discussed in this chapter used repetition as part of an exploration of systems whose workings were not self-evident and whose consequences and effects were decentred and displaced in ways that were metonymic. As Craig Owens observed, allegory concerns itself with the projection – either spatial or temporal – of structure as sequence; the result, however, is not dynamic, but static, ritualistic, repetitive (Owens 1992: 57). The three dances discussed in this chapter could also be described as static, ritualistic, and repetitive. What is disturbing about repetition is the way it brings into play qualities that exceed the explicit meaning of the repeated image. In analysing *Accumulation with Talking plus Watermotor, Café*

Müller, and *Rosas Danst Rosas*, I am concerned with the way that, in each piece, serial repetition produces levels of meaning that exceed the explicit content of the material repeated. These, I propose, function as symptoms of unresolved tensions within each of these pieces. In *Accumulation with Talking plus Watermotor*, there is a tension between a redundantly systematic structuring device and a seemingly uncontrolled and unrepeatable flow. In *Café Müller* the tension is between seemingly blind, internally focused performers and the social structures and physical obstacles that threaten to harm them. In *Rosas Danst Rosas* the tension drives the severe abstraction that turns trivial social behaviour into obsessive ritual.

Formal repetition in *Accumulation with Talking plus Watermotor*

By superimposing two older and very different pieces, *Accumulation* and *Watermotor* in *Accumulation with Talking plus Watermotor*, Brown created a piece which, from her own account, created a very different affect from that produced by performances of either on its own. As she told Ann Livet, *Accumulation* was a reductively simple piece:

> Both the dance and its structure were visible and bare-bone simple. None of the movements had any significance beyond what they were. And I never felt more alive, more expressive or more exposed in performance. The result of performance that goes beyond what the audience is familiar with is that you find out what you can do, what your own personal limitation edges are . . . There is also a question of tension in the relationships between an audience and a performer. In dances of this sort it seems that you are stretching or pushing or rather raising the level of tension considerably.
>
> (Brown in Livet 1978: 45–6)

Placing this together with *Watermotor* and the two stories she narrated had a very different affect:

> One of the reasons that I often put my solo *Accumulation with Talking plus Watermotor* first on the programme is to let the audience know that I'm alive and awake, I can see them, they can hear my breathing – just to let them know that I am a human, feeling being. I am trying to maintain my artistic rigor and at the same time express the side of me that is witty and caring and fast as a whip. Those are qualities that people relate to.
>
> (in Goldberg 1986: 160)

Accumulation with Talking plus Watermotor thus presented to the audience personal qualities to which they could relate, whereas *Accumulation* on its own had made Brown feel exposed and aware of the tensions it generated in spectators. Clearly, the fact that Brown talked to the audience, telling two amusing stories about previous performances of the piece and sometimes adding an aside about the present one, contributed to the popularity of *Accumulation with Talking plus Watermotor* – this perhaps being why 'talking' occupies the central place in the title.[6]

The second piece, *Watermotor*, had its origins in Brown's frustration with her improvisational work. Writing in 1975 she described some improvisations she had done in 1972 which had a quality of unpredictable, explosive flow. Considering the space around her body as a sphere, she had given herself the task of filling 'every portion of the interior of that space with randomly explosive parts of my anatomy in a way in which I did not know what was coming next or when it was coming, although I was in control' (Brown 1975: 28). This seems to describe the movement qualities in *Watermotor*. Brown, however, viewing videotapes of her improvisations, concluded that the result was 'awful' and a 'failure', and that: 'In the end the random explosive method was eliminated because I could not do it at will or repeat it' (ibid.: 29). She added: 'There are barrel-fulls of delicious movements to seduce the choreographer who moves to find movement, but the more important issue is how any movement is organized into dance' (ibid.). Faced with the apparent impossibility of improvising this sort of fluid movement material in performance, Brown at that time seemed to have been unable to find a way of avoiding being influenced by subjective responses when choosing among apparently limitless possibilities of deliciously seductive movement. She therefore chose to concentrate on rigorously minimalist systems for organizing repetitive sequences of abstract gestures, devising for *Accumulation* and other related pieces what she called 'dance machines that take care of certain aspects of dance making' (Goldberg 1986: 166). These 'machines' were, in effect, formal, conceptual structures that took care of otherwise imponderable subjective choices but in the process created work whose performance made her feel extremely exposed and made spectators extremely tense.

Brown's dance 'machines' nevertheless failed to eliminate the dancer's subjectivity altogether. As Brown told Effie Stephano:

> It's very frustrating to deal with the human body as material for making art. You don't have the feeling of having 360 degrees in choosing what you'll do. You're just stuck with your humanness and your feet on the ground.
>
> (Stephano 1974: 19)

She later observed:

> The body doesn't move with the clarity of line or mechanics that I wish for. Dancing is like scribbling, you know, because of the inconsistencies of human anatomy . . . It's the human failure factor in the exposition of form that makes for this marvelous thing called dance, which is highly imperfect from the beginning.
>
> (in Goldberg 1991: 6)

Brown's use in the 1970s of formal, repetitive structures was not intended to produce 'pure dance' in a high modernist way but to frame the humanness and lack of physical precision that the dancing body revealed in performance. She told Stephano that while she tried to make the movement in *Accumulation* the same each time, she knew it never was: 'Sometimes I go a bit faster, sometimes I slow down and those changes I don't consciously make. It happens' (Stephano 1974: 21). Brown's execution, therefore, always exceeded the systematically formal shape of the choreography. Traces of her embodied experience emerged as an excess or supplement that Brown recognized as 'this marvelous thing called dance' (Goldberg 1991: 6). Aesthetic and affective qualities seem, therefore, to have resurfaced as an inescapable consequence of the process of performing work created using a 'dance machine'; the qualities were therefore unconnected with any subjective choice or expression of psychological interiority. Recognition of this allowed Brown to return to some of the movement qualities she had earlier rejected in her experiments with random, explosive improvisation and find a way of setting these. This resulted in Brown's *Locus* (1975) and *Watermotor*.

Watermotor, therefore, presented a kind of movement whose deliberate elimination had resulted in the piece *Accumulation*. Each piece in a different way was a machine that took care of certain forms of decision making. In *Watermotor*, successive movements seemed to cancel out one another so that, like *Accumulation*, it too had overall distribution of energy. As Brown told Rainer in 1979:

> I'm always trying to deflect your focus. When 99% of the body is moving to the right, I will stick something out to the left to balance and deflect it, or to set up some sort of reverberation between the two.
>
> (in Rainer 1979: 33)

One of the features of a hologram printed on glass is that, if it is broken, each glass fragment still seems to contain the whole of the object whose image has been imprinted on it. Because of the overall, minimalist distribution of energy, when Brown cut from the 'accumulation' material to the 'watermotor' material in *Accumulation with Talking plus Watermotor*, each section, like a glass fragment of a broken hologram, seemed to allow the spectator a glimpse of the whole of the 'watermotor' or 'accumulation' material. This had the further effect of making it seem that the value of the dance pieces, *Accumulation* and *Watermotor*, lay not in their complete execution but in the conceptual process they performed. Thus repetition of the 'watermotor' or 'accumulation' material in *Accumulation with Talking plus Watermotor* was a repetition of the conceptual processes that generated the piece rather than being a presentation of parts of a whole or copy of an authentic original.

This is also true of the stories that Brown told. These were not, in fact, set but improvised from a stock of stories. Brown told Rainer that she never rehearsed the piece but in one performance she found herself saying:

> 'My father died in between the making of this move and this move.'
> Which knocked me out. I was amazed that my body had stored this memory in the movement pattern ... I became silent and composed myself. I was devastated that I had said that.
>
> (ibid.)

The section about her father's death during the piece's making therefore became part of the stock of stories told during the piece. This demonstrates the way that the piece related together apparently unconnectable aspects of lived experience. In Chapter 3 I cited the art historian Fred Orton's observation about the use of allegory in late twentieth-century art:

> Realizing that the modern world is a space wherein things and meanings disengage – that the world is a thing that designates not a single, total, universal meaning but a plurality of distinct and isolated meanings – the allegorist works to restore some semblance of connection between them whilst hanging on to and asserting the distinction between experience and the representation of experience, between signifier and referent.
>
> (Orton 1994: 126)

The story of Brown's father's death in *Accumulation with Talking plus Watermotor* exemplifies the way the piece's allegorical structure allowed an opening up of experimental dance performance to encompass previously inconceivable connections between memories stored in the dancer's body.

Interpellation and complicity in *Café Müller*

The dancers in *Café Müller* moved in a reactive rather than an active way. Just as the chairs and tables blocked their way as they tried to dance, the dancers seemed unable to act positively but were always blocked by unspecified forces. The way they moved during the piece was always in response to physical obstacles or to events in which they played a passive or detached role. When Bausch came on stage at the beginning with her eyes closed and hands stretched out in front of her, she moved upstage, cautiously and hesitantly along the side wall, knowing that there were unseen tables and chairs around and that a collision could be painful. And she moved on tip toe, her weight forward and knees slightly bent so that she appeared to bob loosely up and down. This bobbing motion was her leitmotif. It exemplified the use of what Laban called 'shadow movements': 'those which [the dancer] does unconsciously and which precede or shadow his [*sic*] deliberate actions' (Laban 1988: 104). The bobbing movement, in Laban's terms, signified a disturbance of effort balance which 'can be observed in the exaggerated use of pure shadow movements which, in personal behavior, are discharges of inner tensions' (ibid.: 187). Most of Bausch's dancing took place upstage in space that was clear of tables and chairs in front of a set of glass doors. Through these a lobby could be seen and beyond them glass revolving doors in which she later ran like a rat in a treadmill. The chair mover, when he came on stage, never moved chairs for her but only for Airaudo and Mercy. As I said earlier, this was his only function – he never interacted with the other dancers, nor did any of them seem aware that he was there. If Bausch's hesitancy was her reaction to the unseen chairs and tables, all of his movements were reactions determined by the need to make space among these for Airaudo and Mercy, and to surreptitiously put the furniture straight again if there was an opportunity to do so without distracting the audience's attention. And yet on one level the audience probably identified with the chair mover if, like him, they became tense each time they could see that Airaudo or Mercy were in danger of hurting themselves. The chair mover's dramatic, last-minute dives to clear obstacles from their path released the audience's tension and were perhaps a fulfilment of their wishes. Bausch used these reactive rather than active situations to make her dancers feel exposed and her audiences tense.

When the music started, it was a cue for Bausch, Airaudo or Mercy to perform sequences of reaching, stretching, and circling movements which, in Laban's terms, gather unseen forces from space around their bodies and bring them towards their centre. Even here, though, the movement seemed to be a reaction to the music, shadow movement rather than a positive expression of feeling. The first Purcell aria played while Airaudo and Bausch were alone on stage, and Airaudo seemed to join in and pick up Bausch's movements. As both had their eyes closed, their erratic doubling had an uncanny affect. The movement phrases that Bausch initiated here and throughout *Café Müller* were beautifully lyrical but short and perfunctory. All too soon they tailed off and ended with her relapsing into the characteristic bobbing walk, only to break once more into an expressive reaching out, arching her back, then rotating her long, delicate arms in an exquisitely restrained flourish. Bausch's version of this material had a precise lyricism that hinted at ballet tempered by Laban-based dance training. Airaudo and Mercy were more forceful and athletic in their execution of these short movement phrases which they broke from to make impulsive, perilous dashes across the cluttered stage. These, in turn, compelled the chair mover to sprint with them to try to clear their path. The beauty of Bausch's movements and Dido's wistful, Baroque lament – 'When I am laid in earth my wrongs create no trouble in thy breast. Remember me but, ah! forget my fate' – seemed lost in the noises of crashing furniture and the dancers' footfalls and panting. Later, towards the end of *Café Müller*, there was a duet variation of this lyrical, reaching dance material as Airaudo held Mercy from behind with an arm firmly grasping around his abdomen and he reached out to the side, then folded forwards and round to the other side. He was using the kind of diagonal pathways around the body that Laban-based training emphasizes. Almost straight away they had exchanged positions and he lifted her off the ground as she did the same sequence. It is when they reached the side wall that their duet degenerated into holding one another from behind in the same way and turning round to propel their partner violently into the wall.

Reaction, uncanny doubling, and degeneration into either incoherence or violence (or both) were therefore the main constituents of *Café Müller*. Repetition in *Café Müller* created different affects to those in *Accumulation with Talking plus Watermotor*. Whereas the movement in the latter was structured in a minimalist, overall way, *Café Müller* was dramatic, in so far as it had identifiable characters and the events that happened to them in the latter part of the piece appeared to the audience to be a result of what the dancers had experienced earlier. Yet there was no straightforward narrative development as the comparatively prolonged interactions between characters in the earlier part of *Café Müller* gave way to shorter, more fragmented and disorienting encounters as the piece drew towards its diffuse, inconclusive conclusion.[7] Repetition in *Accumulation with Talking plus Watermotor* functioned in a formal, abstract way. In *Café Müller*, repetition troubled and disturbed ideas about the autonomy and coherence of the characters as subjects, thus evoking social and psychological experiences. *Accumulation with Talking plus Watermotor* used an allegorical structure to make connections between formal abstract movement and autobiographical experience. *Café Müller* used reactive situations and shadow movements to offer viewers new insights into sublimated and hidden social processes. Bausch's best-known remark is probably that she is not interested in how people move but in what moves them (Servos 1984: 227). The question that probably troubled spectators of *Café Müller* was what made its characters behave as they did.

There is one section in particular that seemed to typify what was most disturbing about the way these characters behaved and to exemplify Bausch's use of repetition. This was the often described sequence in which Minarik intervened in the way Airaudo and Mercy were embracing, making them learn a different way of kissing. It began as Mercy and Airaudo fell into one another's arms and kissed. Minarik walked on, wearing a suit but barefoot, and slowly, without any particular force, shifted their arms around, made Mercy lift Airaudo and kiss her while holding her awkwardly in mid-air in front of him. As soon as he had done this he turned his face away as if not wanting to be unnecessarily intrusive and walked away to leave the stage. The instability of the new embrace led Mercy to drop Airaudo, who picked herself up off the ground and fiercely embraced Mercy again the way they had kissed before Minarik's intervention. Minarik paused when he heard the fall, came back, and rearranged the couple the way he had left them before, in an unhurried, matter-of-fact way. He left them again, the new embrace collapsed and the whole cycle was run through again. This continued a number of times, gradually becoming faster, until a point when Airaudo picked herself up off the floor and embraced Mercy directly but then the two of them, unaided, went on to embrace in the way Minarik had directed them to do, and Minarik left the stage. Airaudo and Mercy repeated this now hectic cycle until they were audibly out of breath and exhausted. They had learned to perform the action without Minarik and no longer needed his presence. Three times, later in the piece, Airaudo and Mercy embraced each other and then seemed compelled to reprise the dysfunctional lifting sequence that Minarik had taught them; but, now, it ended in each instance after one repetition when both collapsed on the floor curled up together in a foetal embrace. Here repetition suggested a staging of something repressed: what returns are symptoms of something that could not be remembered but was nevertheless relived through a performative substitute for the psychologically violating event.

The easy explanation here was that Minarik's role was repressive – that he was a fascistic policeman who frustrated this couple's natural expression of desire. However, the fact that there was nothing forceful in the way he carried out his role, doing it with calm detachment, makes this repressive hypothesis less plausible. If he had been an archetypal, castrating authority-figure then he would have presented an easy target for the audience's loathing. However, he was more like a bureaucrat. Like a clerk issuing a tax demand rather than the government minister who sets the taxes, he was not the originator of the violating imposition of power and not its controller but someone whose role was to teach the couple to behave in a way that acknowledged their subordination. Because of the manner in which Minarik performed his role, the audience focused not on him but on the couple. In some ways his role was not unlike that played by Meryl Tankard. Towards the end of the evening she cleverly positioned herself in front of Mercy so that he bumped into her, seemed to sense her femininity and almost involuntarily allowed his lips to make contact with hers in a kiss, before wandering off in a different direction. She, however, pursued him and stole another kiss, and did the same a third time. Tankard, of course, was reacting towards a potential she had observed in Mercy. What was so disturbing was that Minarik and Tankard seemed to be reminding Mercy and Airaudo of potentials they already had within them. This is a potential that feminist philosopher Judith Butler's account of performativity offers to explain.

Butler has considered the way that individuals are forced to act in ways that conform to normative social and ideological discourses. She cites Althusser's proposal of the way in which ideologies hail or interpellate individuals as subjects. Althusser's well-known example of this is the situation where a policeman shouts out to someone in the street 'Hey! You!' and the individual replies 'Who? Me?'. By acknowledging the call, the individual recognizes her or himself as subject to the law (Althusser 1984). Butler argues that the reply 'Who? Me?' is an act of repetition that is a performative confirmation of the subject's compliance to ideological norms. Performative here refers to J.L. Austin's notion of performative speech acts. Butler does not argue that individuals as subjects are entirely formed by internalizing interventions from outside forces. She proposes instead that the performative act of acknowledging subjection to ideological norms can never fully comply with normative demands. There is always a supplement that has the potential to trouble or resist such demands. If Minarik was not a straightforwardly castrating authority-figure, his role was therefore more complex than that of Althusser's policeman. Airaudo and Mercy, in the scene described above, became complicit with the violating demands that Minarik represented.

Individuals, Butler points out, are complicit with the call to comply with ideological norms:

> We sometimes cling to the terms that pain us because, at a minimum, they offer us some form of social and discursive existence. The address that inaugurates the possibility of agency, in a single stroke, forecloses the possibility of radical autonomy.
>
> (Butler 1997a: 26)

Complicity with violating demands, she argues, 'at once conditions and limits the viability of a critical interrogation of the law. One cannot criticize too far the terms by which one's existence is secured' (Butler 1997b: 129). Through Minarik's intervention, Airaudo and Mercy enacted a repetition of a performative act that acknowledged their subjection to normative ideologies in an excessive way. The encounter between Airaudo, Mercy, and Minarik was one in which the couple, despite their complicity, manifestly completely failed to respond to the interpellating call. *Café Müller* as a whole was full of similar failures. As I have pointed out, the roles played by Airaudo, Bausch, Mercy, and Tankard were all characters who could only react to events, and seemed incapable of achieving the autonomy and coherence of rational subjects. In Butler's terms, the exemplary value of such failures may lie in their potential to expose the unsatisfactory nature of present conditions and evoke possibilities for new, more open kinds of subjectivities. Butler suggests that the failure of interpellation 'may well undermine the capacity of the subject to "be" in a self-identical sense, but it may also mark the path towards a more open, even more ethical, kind of being, one of or for the future' (ibid.: 131). But the terms of Bausch's project seem to have meant that they could only criticize present conditions by repeating their violence. If violence was denounced in Bausch's *tanztheater*, it was nevertheless through violent strategies that this denunciation was made.

I referred in the first chapter to a symposium held at the Goethe Institute in New York in 1985 on German *tanztheater*. During this Anna Kisselgoff observed that:

> Some say Bausch may be condemning violence but that she revels in depicting it; they say she works up the audience so they are thrilled, and it's the thrill of the lynch mob in watching people bang their heads against the wall or hit each other.
>
> (Kisselgoff in Daly 1986: 52)

To this Jochem Schmidt replied that Bausch

is not attracted by violence. I'm sure she's not. She hates it, but she shows it and she shows it in a very comic form. You really have to see the pieces more than one time, and you will find them more comical every time.

(ibid.)

While this may be true of the way Bausch has dealt with violence in some of her work, there are invariably one or two incidents in most of her pieces that are extremely disturbing because of their physical or psychological violence. Despite what Schmidt argues, these could never be seen as comic, but there is no sense of sadism in the infliction of violence during her work. Minarik, in the episode described above, mini-mized his presence as much as possible, going about rearranging Airaudo and Mercy's embrace in a low-key way. Lutz Forster, who danced in Bausch's company for many years, observed: 'In all Pina's pieces people are tender to each other' (ibid.). Perhaps there was a tenderness in the way Minarik carried out his role.

The degree of concentration, commitment, and honesty with which the dancers in *Café Müller* performed the sequences that involved pain and failure – the hard, physical work going on onstage – qualified the violence of these actions. As performers acting out their roles, Airaudo and Mercy seem to have tried not to admit to themselves that the posi-tion that Minarik (and Bausch) directed them to perform was impossible. They tried their best to carry it out, and went through the actions as quickly as they could. They tried not to fail. In doing so, they too, like Brown in her Accumulation pieces, framed the humanness and lack of physical precision that the dancing body reveals in performance. Butler has argued that individuals can never fully comply with the demand to enact the performative act of acknowledging subjection to ideological norms. There is always, she argues, a supplement that exceeds this demand. Airaudo and Mercy's failure revealed that the body was the dangerous and uncontrollable supplement within their danced perform-ance. Through the dancers' concentration, commitment, and honesty they posited their bodies as a site of resistance to impositions of norma-tive ideologies.

Complicity and resistance in *Rosas Danst Rosas*

The title *Rosas Danst Rosas* translates 'Roses dances Roses', Rosas (Roses) being the name of De Keersmaeker's company whose first piece this was. The title, therefore, implies that Rosas dance themselves. What the piece raised were the semantic difficulties surrounding the idea of dancing oneself, particularly if one was female, in the early 1980s. *Rosas Danst Rosas* was a long, intense, demanding work characterized by serial repetition of gestural movement material largely performed in unison by four similarly dressed young women.[8] In the first section, the dancers performed while lying on the floor, in the second while sitting on chairs, while the last three sections were performed standing and walking. I proposed earlier in this chapter that *Rosas Danst Rosas* occupies a place somewhere on a continuum between dramaturgy and formal abstraction. On the one hand it explored, through a complicated and at times mesmerizing structure, a number of formal permutations of slowly developing movement sequences. At the same time the movement vocabulary of these sequences was largely made up of what appeared to be trivial, everyday, feminine movements. I say largely, but these were perhaps more in evidence in the first half of the piece. There was more and more 'dance' movement in its last three sections. As the gestural material became increasingly familiar through repetition, abstract and referential movement became increasingly blurred. While the first section was almost entirely performed in unison and in silence, in the next three sections De Keersmaeker created a subtle interplay between dance and music, and a play within dance material choreographed in unison and in counterpoint. Often phrases of material were introduced as a unison sequence; then one dancer broke from the group to perform different material in counterpoint, a second joined her, the second and third dancers performed the new material together while the first and fourth performed the old; then first and second were in counterpoint with third and fourth, then all but the fourth were together, and finally all came together in unison again. The pattern of this is: 4 together, 1 with 3, 1 with 2 and 1, 2 with 2, 3 with 1, 4 together. Using these kinds of logical, symmetrical methods of composition together with modular units and cumulative repetitive structures allowed each section of *Rosas Danst Rosas* to develop gradually.

In the seated section, the dancers set out rows of chairs directly facing the audience; two rows were placed side by side with a gap between, one behind them in the gap, and another row forward and to one side. When seated, turning their heads around to make eye contact with one another and share a little, complicitous smile and a brief nod, they signalled readiness to begin. Their dance used a severely limited movement vocabulary that was recycled with changing speeds, dynamics, and accentuation, accompanied by a minimalist soundtrack of light, syncopated drum beats. Their movements suggested adolescent women's behaviour: running a hand through their hair; jerking the head upwards to toss their hair out of their eyes; getting up and sitting down again, and forcefully swinging both their arms together, fingers interlinked, to one side. These mannerisms were observed and executed with almost realistic precision. As hands were suddenly wedged between the thighs of tightly crossed legs, or a clenched fist seems to relax unwillingly, these seemed to be very personal, private, idiosyncratic, habitual actions. When a dancer slumped tersely back in her chair, it was as if she was momentarily giving up and stepping out of her role for a rest, to rejoin the group in a moment when the sequence cycled back round to the top. It was all, of course, carefully choreographed and, a few moments after the solo dancer rejoined the other three, two more dancers 'gave up' in unison.

When a gesture was first performed by one dancer on her own, this might have suggested a psychological interiority – an individual who is slightly self-conscious and uneasy; or it might have reminded the viewer of other cultural forms in which this kind of 'acting' perhaps appears natural. Although De Keersmaeker referenced a young, feminine self-consciousness in her choreography, these mannerisms were incorporated through repetition and unison into the logic of the choreography. This made it impossible to forget that each performer was merely mirroring the others and suggested that their femininity was no more than masquerade. It was all choreographed to make layers within layers of referential meaning, just as the minimalist choreographic structure eschewed classical sonata form and nested logical, symmetrical sequences within sequences. Like Rosalind Krauss's postmodern interpretation of minimalist sculpture quoted earlier, to get inside the systems of De Keersmaeker's work was 'to enter a world without a center, a world of substitutions and transpositions nowhere legitimated by the revelations of a transcendental subject' (Krauss 1986: 258). I am not arguing that there is such a thing as a self but that the idea of gendered subjectivity informing De Keersmaeker's piece is much more complex than normative accounts allow.

The brief smiles and complicitous looks, the passing of gestures from one to another – all these suggested shifting alliances or identifications between the dancers. These troubled the seemingly intimate qualities of the gestural material. This was a play of surfaces rather than an expression of depth. Rather than suggesting individuality and psychological interiority, the minimalist monotony of the repetition of mundane gestures suggested compulsion to repeat and conform to pre-scripted behaviour. If Bausch presented, through Minarik's role, a personification of the ideological processes that interpellate individuals into normative modes of behaviour, De Keersmaeker and her fellow dancers had already learned the movement script to which authority required them to conform. For Mercy and Airaudo, the demand made on them was impossible and the gap between what they did and what they were trying to achieve constituted their failure. For De Keersmaeker and her fellow dancers there seemed to be no failure because, on one level at least, the uniformity and clarity of their performance seemed to fulfil their obligation. Judith Butler's notion of the performativity of gender is useful here. Butler proposes that the demand to repeat performative acts that signify compliance with gender norms cannot be refused but neither can it be followed in strict obedience. Butler points to a possibility of not repeating faithfully. There were signs that there might be a gap between what was demanded of the dancers in *Rosas Danst Rosas* and their performance of these demands. Their complicitous looks suggested the possibility that, although the dancers were conforming to their script, there might have been some unfaithfulness in the way they were doing it, compliance, on one level, creating, on another, an ideological space for subversion. To be clear, I am not arguing here that De Keersmaeker intentionally set out to disrupt codes of gender representation through her use of repetition in *Rosas Danst Rosas*. She has always resisted being drawn by interviewers into conversation about such issues.[9] Nevertheless, I suggest that Butler's notion of gender offers an analogy to the way De Keersmaeker used repetition to confound normative representations of femininity and create a space, albeit a problematic one, that in some ways allowed a provisional and contingent freedom from interpellating demands. I am therefore arguing that *Rosas Danst Rosas* exemplified what the feminist philosopher Adriana Cavarero has called 'the clear refusal by women – which has exploded in the contemporary era – to recognize themselves in the images of women thought for millennia by Man' (Cavarero 2000: 52–3).

The longest sequences of gestures which, in Butler's terms, performed compliance with norms of feminine behaviour, came as long solos in the long third section of *Rosas Danst Rosas*. Here, the four dancers performed rhythmical sequences based on stepping to the side, turning, leaning off balance to one side and swaying, that made them travel from side to side of the stage. A dancer would break out of line and approach the audience directly while the other three carried on this stepping sequence behind. One hand tugged the shoulder of her T-shirt so that its loose neck revealed a bare shoulder and perhaps the strap of a bra, and then the other hand lifted the T-shirt back to hide it. Whereas the danced stepping sequence behind used the syncopated rhythm of the music to accentuate moments of suspension or flow, the actions accompanying showing a shoulder didn't fit the rhythm of the music although the cues for each movement within it seemed to be counted. Each dancer took her turn in this, before running back, in an impulsive, adolescent way, to join her companions. As the section continued, the dancers shifted between three or four variations of the danced stepping sequence and there were also different 'solos', including variations on the shoulder-revealing sequence, complicit looks at companions, and revealing two shoulders rather than one. There was an awkward vulnerability about most of these actions as the dancers revealed themselves to the spectator's gaze, drawing attention to the power relationship between performer and spectator. Although the sequence was identical, each dancer brought a different nuance or intensity to the way they interpreted the actions, either shy, vulnerable, cold, or almost imperceptibly seductive. The more convinced the spectator was that this was what the dancer was 'really' like, the more troubling their vulnerable self-revelation became. If in *Café Müller* Minarik personified the process of interpellation, in *Rosas Danst Rosas* the spectator had taken on his role, as if the dancers one by one were responding to the audience's call to perform their femininity correctly. Yet at the same time and paradoxically, all the spectator seemed to be watching was choreographed movement. The more precise the material and the more familiar it became through repetition, the more the spectator became aware of fine distinctions between the way each different dancer performed it. Paradoxically, while on one level repetition seemed to generate a sense of sameness, on another level it produced a heightened sensitivity to irreducible difference.

This tension or oscillation in *Rosas Danst Rosas* between abstract choreography and dramatic, theatrical performance has manifested itself throughout De Keersmaeker's career. She has used text in her choreography, including excerpts from Peter Handke, Peter Weiss, and Tennessee Williams. She has often oscillated between making 'theatrical' dance pieces that include spoken text and ones that deal purely with abstract movement. Thus, *Bartok/Aatekeningen* (1986) included text while *Microcosmos* (1987) also used Bartok's music but was an abstract dance. As a graduate student at New York University, where one of her teachers was Valda Setterfield, De Keersmaeker wrote an essay on the dancer, actor, and cabaret performer Valeska Gert (1892–1978) that was published in *TDR*. Interestingly, in this she said that Gert's dances were often 'neither really acting nor pure dancing' but what Gert herself called 'danced acting figures' (De Keersmaeker 1981: 62). The same description can be applied to *Rosas Danst Rosas*. In its first two sections, referential gestures and actions were incorporated into repetitive movement sequences, so that by the third section the audience had become used to seeing these actions as material for abstract choreographic manipulation, albeit dance material that generated dramatic affects. De Keersmaeker seems to have been trying to keep the spectator confused as to whether they were watching abstract movement or dance theatre that referenced social experience. Her programme statement about *Rosas Danst Rosas* seems almost to have avoided commenting on any of the associations of the movement material and discussed, instead, the fact that formal dance and social reference became blurred. I quote her statement in full.

> Underlying the concept as well as the choreographic composition of this performance is the exploration of two seemingly opposite data: to work with mathematical and repetitive patterns often seems to exclude emotional depth. Yet, through the use of purely choreographical elements only (the choice of movements, spatial ordering, rhythm, connections between dance and music, the quality and energy of the movements, the structure of the sentences) this work tries to create a well considered dramatic intensity. These elements, which are not to be separated, are absorbed in a rigorous structure. It is exactly this strictness that shows to full advantage the intrinsic value of the individual elements. In this way some movements and positions borrowed from daily life, rather than from the traditional language of dance, are given choreographic import.
>
> (De Keersmaeker 1983)

If in *Rosas Danst Rosas*, De Keersmaeker set danced acting figures to work within her choreographic text, it was as if she were denying the binary distinction I discussed in the first chapter between US notions of abstract 'pure' dance and the kind of dramaturgical dance that was more typical of European dance theatre. These danced action figures inhabited the opposition between social reference and abstraction, resisting and disorganizing them. De Keersmaeker did not produce a dialectical, transcendent fusion of the two but allowed the dance to be read as formal, abstract choreography while at the same time luring the spectator by performances of feminine social behaviour. She was trying to keep both working in tension with one another so as to open up new possibilities for dramatic and affective intensity. Serial repetitions of De Keersmaeker's danced acting figures in *Rosas Danst Rosas* opened up a discursive space in which De Keersmaeker's company *Rosas* could dance themselves (as the title of the piece suggested). Within this space, they were free, in a limited and circumscribed way, from some of the power of the interpellating demands of normative ideologies. By dancing *as* women, De Keersmaeker and her dancers invited spectators to appreciate difference as something that should be valued and not feared.

Knights' moves

So far I have compared and contrasted the effects of serial repetition in these three works. I have referred to Judith Butler's work in order to identify what I believe were the innovative characteristics of these pieces, arguing that they troubled and problematized the sorts of aesthetic values and representational codes that characterized mainstream modernist dance, and that were valorized within high modernist dance criticism. All three works, I have suggested, asserted in different ways and with differing affects the physicality of the dancing body; this is a characteristic that in previous chapters I have identified with the new American dance of the 1960s. This chapter, in moving on from the 1960s to the late 1970s and early 1980s, has considered the materiality of dancing bodies from a later period of what I contend is a common tradition of innovative and experimental dance. What had changed were the historical and cultural contexts of this dance practice. In Chapter 5 I discussed the failures of left-wing and libertarian politics in 1968, and in its aftermath the new, more pessimistic awareness of the role of radical, critical art under the shadow of political disappointment. I proposed that ambitiously innovative dancers began to see the body as a site of resistance against a constraining conformity to conservative ideologies.

Taking a historical perspective from 1968 to the early 1980s, if there was continuity within the way advanced theatre dance asserted the materiality of the dancing body, there was also a gradual change in the way this was articulated. This emerges within these three works. In the face of the turbulent events of 1968, Rainer asserted that, in relation to her own practice as an artist, her body remained the enduring reality. For Brown in the 1970s, the body, through its failure to move with the clarity of line or mechanics that she wished for, nevertheless 'makes this wonderful thing called dance' (Goldberg 1991: 6). Bausch's work, through its unflinchingly honest engagements with pain and failure, could (and still can) provoke an acknowledgement of the extent to which the material body is a site of contestation between the individual and interpellating ideologies. However, in De Keersmaeker's early work the body was no longer an enduring reality but a discursive construction within which experimental dance made deconstructive interventions. All three choreographers intervened within hegemonic discourses in order to create a space in which to imagine new ways of embodying subjectivity. It was De Keersmaeker, however, and the younger generation of choreographers to which she belonged, most of whom lived and worked in continental Europe, who built on the achievements of Bausch and Brown's generation to shift the terms of radical, experimental dance practice away from the existential reality of embodied experience and towards the discursive construction of embodiment. Yet this radical turn, as this chapter has shown, is implicit in the way Bausch and Brown resisted metaphorical modes of expressive dance and made works that I have argued signified meanings in allegorical and metonymic ways.

What was at stake within these three pieces was not what 'content' might have been signified allegorically but how the structure of allegory as a signifying practice offers a way of analysing the formal structures within the pieces. Art historian and critic Craig Owens has argued that the artist who devises allegorical imagery does not invent images but appropriates them. The artist does not change the original meaning of this imagery with which the allegory is created. 'Rather he [*sic*] adds another meaning to the image. If he adds, however, he does not only replace: the allegorical meaning supplants an antecedent one; it is a supplement' (Owens 1992: 54). So if *Rosas Danst Rosas* worked as an allegory, it did not then invent the imagery of self-conscious adolescent femininity but appropriated it, and it did not add to the meaning of femininity but replaced it. It supplanted the notion that feminine movement expressed feminine identity, and that pure dance expressed pure essence. Like the other two works I have discussed, *Rosas Danst Rosas* supplanted the idea of an absolute, instantaneous equivalence between a unique signifier and a unique signified with a deconstructive chain of metonymic shifts and displacements.

Each of the pieces I have discussed in this chapter performed a knight's move as Bausch, Brown, and De Keersmaeker each seem to have become aware of their reluctance or inability to use metaphorical, expressive modernist modes of choreography. In *Accumulation with Talking plus Watermotor*, Brown didn't directly tell her audience that the experience of live performance made her feel alive and awake, and as sharp as a rake. What she did was to tell them stories that hinted at the strong feelings and memory traces she experienced while dancing. Like Jakobson's aphasics, she didn't directly name the experience itself but referred to it through displacement and substitution. Repetition of the break from one dance to another and from one story to another created radical juxtapositions and discontinuities that allowed Brown to hint at her unique and particular qualities as an individual: repetition thus creating difference. Bausch's *Café Müller* also seems to have explored experiences that could not be named directly. Its honest, unflinching performance of pain and failure was disturbing because its cause and its dancers' motivation remained mysterious. Its metonymic displacement seemed to form an allegory of something that could not be stated openly, traumatic experiences too terrible to be allowed into conscious memory, but which nevertheless returned as repressed symptoms. Bausch's use of repetition allegorized progress as the eternal return of catastrophe. The café, by a knight's move, emerges as a late twentieth-century equivalent to the baroque emblem of a ruined landscape which allegorized the irreversible process of dissolution, decay, and mortality. If Rosas were dancing Rosas, then the discursive step that connected the young De Keersmaeker and her fellow dancers yet again was surely a knight's move but this time onto a different level of discourse and one in which allegory was yet again at work. The kind of physical and emotional intimacy, suggested by De Keersmaeker's use of gestural material, was derived from everyday behaviour. This surfaced, however, through a knight's move, as an allegory of femininity at a moment when there was no uncontaminated space available in theatre dance practice for any direct feminine self-representation. Repetition thus created the difference between the dancers as individuals and normative feminine roles.

All three pieces used failure in ambiguous ways. For Brown the body's failure to execute perfectly geometric shapes produced the wonderful thing called dance. In *Café Müller* the dancers' failure proved the possibility of resistance. In *Rosas Danst Rosas* the women's subversive complicity signified their failure to comply faithfully with gender norms. Judith Butler has argued that: 'By establishing the ambivalence of embodying and failing to embody that which one feels then a distance will be opened up between that hegemonic call to normativizing gender and its critical approbation' (1993: 137). It was by keeping open such spaces within the discourse of innovative dance that dancers, despite political disappointment, revealed the extent to which the body had become a site of resistance against normative ideologies. If innovative choreographers in the late 1970s and 1980s no longer saw their work as avant-garde, they nevertheless continued embodying radical alternatives. Rather than giving in to the idea that it was now impossible to work in a radical, critical way, they continued the project of undoing dance for the sake of the possible.

7 Traces of intimacy and relationless relations

In May 1994, Trisha Brown first performed a new solo she had created for herself which she danced entirely while facing away from her audience. *If You Couldn't See Me* was a piece in which the performer therefore controlled what the audience was looking at in an unusually restrictive way. Brown herself found that the challenges and difficulties which this created were stimulating, and hoped that spectators would also appreciate them. As she told Christy Adair, she respected the audience and didn't want them to think that she was turning her back on them (Adair 1996: 51). The result was a curiously intimate yet at the same time paradoxically distant performance that staged a kind of relationless relation. Not only had Brown transgressed normative conventions surrounding the ways in which a dancer presents material to their audience; in doing so she put her viewers into a position in which they were unable to establish their normal, habitual relationship to the dance (and dancer) that they were watching. Both dancer and spectator, therefore, occupied disturbingly mobile and fluid positions in relation to one another. Brown's dancing was informed by the sorts of clear, fluid, visceral ways of moving whose development through movement research I have discussed in earlier chapters. In this solo, Brown wore a dress, designed for her by Robert Rauschenberg, whose back was cut extremely low so as to allow the spectator to see as much as possible of the workings of her muscles and bones as she danced. What made performances of this solo seem so intimate was the way the powerfully physical quality of Brown's dancing, revealed through the workings of her back, lured and took over the spectator's attention; this had the effect of entangling dancer and spectator together in the unfamiliar, mobile positions they found themselves occupying in relation to one another.

If You Couldn't See Me was the first solo that Brown had made for herself since *Accumulation with Talking plus Watermotor* in 1979, which I discussed in Chapter 6.[1] In May 1995, one year after Brown, Pina Bausch also gave the first performance of a new solo that was part of the evening-length group work *Danzon*. This was the first role she had made for her-self since *Café Müller* in 1978, which I also discussed in Chapter 6. Bausch's solo, like Brown's, was also curiously intimate yet at the same time strangely distant, because of the way Bausch severely limited both her visibility and the range of movement she performed. She was dressed all in black so that only her neck, face, and her arms below the elbows were visible against a dark background. She danced on the spot, only moving her arms, upper body, and head in a curiously fluid yet unpredictable sequence of bending and reaching movements. Although her dancing itself was very different from Brown's, the effect of its unfixable flow and of Bausch's half-hidden appearance was also to entangle dancer and spec-tator together in the unfamiliar, mobile positions they found themselves occupying in relation to one another.

Both these solos by Bausch and Brown exemplify the way that a number of other pieces during the mid-1990s and 2000s, some of which I will discuss in this chapter, have radically reformulated the performer–spectator relationship. In doing so, they have revisited concerns that, during the 1960s, Brown and others explored. But whereas in 1965 Yvonne Rainer had said no to seduction of the spectator by the wiles of the performer (Rainer 1974: 51), in 1996 Brown didn't want the audi-ence, whom she respected, to think that she was turning her back on them. When performing works such as *Word Words* (1963) and *Inside* (1965), which I discussed in Chapter 3, Brown, Paxton, and Rainer had been part of a fringe, avant-garde movement that aimed to open up and imagine alternative values. In the 1990s, Bausch and Brown were, in many ways, leaders in the international dance world. The disturbingly fluid and rela-tionless relations between dancer and spectator in *If You Couldn't See Me* and the solo in *Danzon* no longer expressed the naive idealism of an anarchic, underground. They nevertheless still addressed a sensibility that was overshadowed by the problem of political disappointment. Con-sequently, the solos resonated with radical, philosophical discussions about ethics. As feminist philosopher Adriana Cavarero observed: 'The fact is that human beings live together. Whether artificial or natural, their com-munity is involved with a problem of acting and living together that cannot refrain from taking the other into consideration' (Cavarero 2000: 88). This chapter discusses a number of dances from this relatively recent period which challenged and disrupted normative relations between dancer and spectator in ways that asserted the problematic necessity of, as Cavarero put it, taking the other into consideration. But these pieces have done so through what I have been calling a relationless relation. This term for an aesthetic of neutrality that is paradoxically not impersonal was proposed by the French author and theorist Maurice Blanchot. He developed the idea of an alternative kind of friendship which he called 'le rapport du troisième genre' or 'un rapport neutre'. As Simon Critchley explains, this is a relationless relation that 'no longer takes place at the level of you or me, but rather at the level of the neutral il, an anonymous neutrality' (Critchley 1999: 265). Such a concept of friendship, he goes on, 'cuts across or deconstructs the distinctions between the private and the public, between the personal (the pre-political) and the political' (ibid.). Where the dance pieces I have discussed cut across the distinction between private and public, this idea of friendship enables a consideration of the ethical and political issues they thereby raised. This is not to argue that these works were political, but to point out that they explored, through cultural and aesthetic means, the implications of these issues.

Taking the other into consideration, as Cavarero put it, entails respecting and valuing difference rather than fearing it. I argued in Chapter 5 that one of the shortcomings of the 1960s avant-garde was its members' lack of awareness of issues relating to difference. This was evident in instances where dancers appeared to be largely oblivious of the power relations that they brought into play when they discussed black and Asian cultural traditions. In Chapter 6, I argued that *Café Müller*, *Accumulation with Talking plus Watermotor*, and *Rosas Danst Rosas* exemplified an increasing recognition of the way that the dancing body was situated in relation to dominant discourses. While these dances used serial repetition to disrupt notions of interiority, I showed that repetition nevertheless produced difference. The increasing recognition that dancing bodies could be a site of resistance to dominant ideologies was, I argued, accompanied by a shift towards the signifying structures of allegory. The latter provided a way of recognizing ambiguities and associations between kinds of material that seemed fragmentary and disconnected. Allegories challenge normative, supposedly universal points of view. To read something in an allegorical way requires taking up a point of view that is provisional and contingent. It is this characteristic of allegory that helps to explain how the relationless relations embodied in solos such as *If You Couldn't See Me* and *Danzon*, and in other pieces discussed in this chapter, operated. Through an aesthetic of neutrality that was not impersonal, these pieces opened up the possibility of an ethical relationship – a relationless relation – to the embodiment of alterity and difference. I ended Chapter 6 with the idea of going on embodying radical, new possibilities in the knowledge that the possibility of doing so had come to an end. This chapter is about works that tried to create new kinds of relationships between dancer and spectator despite the shadow that the problem of political disappointment cast over radical, critical artistic practice.

Point of view

The intimate yet distant relationship that entangled performer and spectator in the works discussed in this chapter exemplified what the art historian Mieke Bal has called a baroque point of view (Bal 1999). Bal has identified this both in the work of historical baroque painters such as Caravaggio and within recent paintings, installations, and photographically based conceptual works that exemplify what she calls a contemporary baroque aesthetic. This, I suggest, offers a useful way of looking at similar contemporary baroque concerns within recent dance performance. On a theoretical level, Bal has derived her concept of a baroque point of view from the philosopher Gilles Deleuze's 1980 book *Le Pli* (*The Fold: Leibniz and the Baroque*, 1993). The unfixed relationship between dancer and spectator that I identified in Bausch and Brown's solos at the beginning of this chapter corresponds with the relational qualities that Deleuze attributed to philosophy in the baroque period. Bal finds in Deleuze a concern with: 'the movement back and forth between the subject and the object of point of view, thus emphasizing the mobility that characterizes it' (Bal 1999: 29). Bal's concern is with visual art but her definition of object could equally apply to performance:

> Objects, seen as thus enfolded with the subject in a shared entanglement are considered events rather than things – events of becoming rather than being. What is specifically baroque about this view is the point of view of two mobile positions.
>
> (ibid.: 30)

What Bal proposes entangles the spectator and the work of art, and I suggest in the case of performance entangles the spectator and the dance (and dancer), is an odd but fascinating detail. This lures the spectator and traps their attention. Where visual art is concerned, the spectator becomes vulnerable to the impact of the object (ibid.: 31). Where performance is concerned, the viewer becomes vulnerable to an unusual but fascinating aspect of the performance. This ambivalent and sometimes contradictory point of view, in Bal's account, entails 'something that is not simply relativism, or universalism, objectivism, or absolutism' but a quality of entanglement and co-dependency (ibid.: 30). On a social and political level, these properties of entanglement and co-dependency within performance imply the ethical necessity that Cavarero mentioned of taking the other into consideration. I shall return at the end of this chapter to the ways in which progressive choreographers, in their exploration of the shifting boundaries between the public space of performance and the intimate spaces created by this baroque point of view, have had to consider ethical issues. The complication of this baroque point of view thus correlates with the complications and difficulties, during the 1990s and 2000s, of responding in an ethical and non-discriminatory way towards those whose values and culture seemed so different as to be threatening.

The difference between the allegorical structures of the works discussed in Chapter 6 and the baroque point of view staged by *If You Couldn't See Me* and the solo in *Danzon* lies in the way the former required a specific mode of interpretation while the latter trapped the viewer and spectator in an involvement that could be both fascinating and de-stabilizing. A comparison between two short solos by Tim Etchells and Meg Stuart is useful for further clarifying what is at stake here. Etchells' *Down Time* (2001) and Stuart's *private room* (2000), which both use video projections, were performed together in a shared programme that the two artists put together in 2001.[2] Etchells is founder, artistic director, and writer for the British Live Art group *Forced Entertainment*.[3] In *Down Time*, he sat casually on a wooden chair on one side of the stage half turned towards a large screen at the back onto which an unedited video of a single shot of his head and shoulders was projected. As he watched himself, he talked to the audience about what had been going through his mind while the video was recorded. He spoke in a casually confidential way using a microphone which he held in his left hand while occasionally using his right to emphasize points. At the time, he told us, he was thinking about goodbyes: he began with his son's anxieties about saying goodbyes around the time that: 'his mum and I were breaking up', and went on to other goodbyes including ones to a lover in a hotel room and at an airport. As his narrative commentary unfolded, he seemed to be using minimal changes in his recorded facial expressions as cues to remember what he had been thinking about at that moment. One anecdote concerned a funeral for his brother's girlfriend; he said he'd felt a fraud at this because he'd never met her. Every anecdote was sad but neither his expression in the video nor the way he spoke about it conveyed any real feelings. When in the video he closed his eyes he said he had done so while thinking about being in a public place and crying. But he then remembered thinking as soon as he had shut them: 'Oh that's melodramatic and ridiculous and I should stop immediately from going in that direction'. Part of what was ironic about Etchells' performance was that, regardless of its melancholy content, he sat on stage in a seemingly casual, neutral way, hardly moving at all and delivering his monologue in an even, unexcited voice. *Down Time* did not deny the existence of an emotional and psychological interiority;

it merely suggested that, if this existed, there was no verifiable way of identifying it solely by watching an individual's appearance.

At another moment, Etchells said: 'I don't know what I'm thinking here' but then remembered looking at the camera and thinking about the gadgets that we have for recording 'all these things so we don't have to say good bye to them'. The fact that Etchells seemed to remember in such depth and detail these ordinary, trivial, ephemeral thoughts suggested a reluctance to let go. It was almost as if he wanted to be able to mirror the past exactly and not change or grow old since the (unspecified) time in the past when the video was shot. Etchells' role in *Down Time* mediated between spectator and projected image, talking to the audience in a public, direct address. But the fact that the audience laughed when he said he didn't know what he'd been thinking showed that we had already decided that it was all made up. The discontinuities between video and commentary, and Etchells' failed attempt to mirror the past became a source of fascination. The performance, therefore, invited an ironic complicity between performer and spectator with both recognizing the unfaithful way that the performance undermined the apparent content of the commentary. *Down Time*, therefore, depended upon the kind of ironic, allegorical mode of interpretation discussed in Chapter 6. To look at it in this way is to concentrate exclusively on the video and the words of Etchells' commentary. However, to focus on the way the inventiveness and implicit humour of his monologue contradicted his lack of physical expressiveness is to shift from the allegorical aspects of the piece to its elaborate manipulation and destabilization of both the performer and the spectator's points of view. *Down Time* generated a complex, fictitious play between three different events: the effort of remembering in the present moment while watching the video; the affects supposedly present while the video was being shot; and the past experiences that were supposedly their source. Etchells' point of view was fluid and mobile, somewhere between these three positions, while the spectator was pleasurably torn between irony and suspension of misbelief.

Meg Stuart is an American dancer and choreographer who, having trained in New York and danced in Randy Warshaw's company, moved to Europe in the early 1990s where she founded her company *Damaged Goods*. Created in collaboration with dancer Rachid Ouramdane, theatre director Stefan Pucher, and video artist Jorge Leon, *private room* was part of her project *Highway 101*. As well as the projection screen, the dimly lit stage contained a large, square, brown armchair turned almost completely away from the audience. Stuart sat in this for the entire ten minutes of the piece, watching a video of a domestic room in which a young man, Ouramdane, was initially revealed sitting in the same armchair. Whereas the video in *Down Time* was silent, Stuart's piece was accompanied by an atmospheric soundtrack of dreamy music. Its black and white video appeared to be recorded with a security-type camera attached to the apartment's ceiling. The young man sat uncomfortably, fiddling restlessly with the cushions. When he started to get up, Stuart said sharply, 'Don't stand up!', and he sank back disconsolately. Ouramdane's apparent uncertainty about himself, suggested by his movements, contrasted with Stuart's calm, knowing maturity. She gave him instructions and then commented on what he was doing in a critical, knowing way. 'You're not in the right position', she said, and then thanked him when he moved. It was unclear whether she was a choreographer working with her dancer or a friend or former lover who knew him intimately. The normative power relation between the sexes was thus reversed: the high view point of the camera looking down made Ouramdane appear vulnerably exposed. Stuart, however, sitting in shadow, largely escaped the audience's gaze; the projected video on the screen providing the focus of both her own and the audience's attention.

Stuart's role, like Etchells' in *Down Time*, mediated between spectator and projected image, but whereas he spoke about himself in the first person, she apparently addressed the man in the video in an intimate second-person narrative. I say 'apparently' because some of her comments were clearly for the audience's benefit. After she admonished him not to be ashamed, he began to take off his clothes until he was only wearing white underpants. As if to defuse the seductive power of seeing his young male body, she told us: 'He remembers until he was fifteen, adults always thought he was a girl.' Later she told us equally intimate details about his relationship with his girlfriend. There was something voyeuristically fascinating about witnessing someone cruelly breaking a confidence by revealing in public someone else's intimate secrets. Etchells had also touched on revealing in public things that were embarrassing. Both pieces thus cut across the distinction between public and private.

Whereas *Down Time* lured the audience's attention by inviting them to appreciate discontinuities between commentary and video in an ironic way, *private room* did so by involving the audience and drawing them inside, complicit with the unfolding narrative. Stuart's piece, therefore, complicated a number of intersecting gazes: that of the spectator at the video; the video camera looking down on Ouramdane; Stuart's gaze at him in the video; his sullen gaze back at the camera; the spectator, through identification, looking at Ouramdane from Stuart's point of view. There is a further level that drew the spectator into the piece. I found the cumulative effect of listening to Stuart's calm, even tone of voice was to lull me into a state of receptivity. Second-person narrative invites its listeners to respond. As both Stuart and the audience were physically present while Ouramdane was apparently absent, I as a spectator felt uneasy at my own passivity in response to Stuart's apparent direct address to me. Both pieces, therefore, staged what Bal called a baroque point of view, though in different ways. In *private room*, the vicarious way that spectators experienced the piece provided a lure that entangled their gaze with Stuart's, while leaving open and ambiguous the audience's and Stuart's relationship to the video and to one another. In *Down Time*, discontinuities between video and commentary rendered Etchells' point of view unfixed and ambiguous, and because this mediated the way in which the viewer interpreted the video, this too was destabilized. Nevertheless, the irony and humour within the piece was a source of fascination which entangled spectator and performer. At the beginning of the chapter, I identified a similar entanglement of unfixed and ambiguous points of view within performances of Brown's *If You Couldn't See Me* and Bausch's solo in *Danzon*. Before returning to look in more detail at the way these two works articulated a problematic, relationless relation, I shall follow up two further aspects of the baroque point of view which Etchells and Stuart's pieces have raised; these are mirroring, and the intimacy of the one-to-one relationship initiated through second-person narrative.

One-to-one

Down Time and *private room* are particularly useful examples of the unconventional ways in which some recent performances position spectators. Nevertheless, they depended to a considerable extent, but not entirely, on using the spoken word to develop narratives. As I noted in the first chapter, since Diderot and Lessing in the eighteenth century, philosophers have argued that dance is a visual rather than a discursive art and therefore deals with space and the visual aspects of movement but not the spoken word. Narrative, in this view, is the prerogative of the literary arts which use words to develop meanings through time. The fact that theatre dance tells conventional stories badly seems to confirm this view. Audiences often depended upon printed synopses and mime scenes to follow the plots of nineteenth-century ballets. Influential twentieth-century dance writers such as André Levinson argued that theatre dance was not a narrative form at all. Only the formal qualities of dance movement itself were, in Levinson's view, of aesthetic value. There are, however, other non-verbal ways in which dance movement can develop kinds of narratives. I have argued throughout this book that critical methods based on a formalist view of dance fail to account for what was different and innovative about the new dance of the 1960s. I have focused, instead, in earlier chapters, on the signifying structures in some of the new dances of the 1960s, including some by artists whose work has received little attention from other scholars. It is these structures, I suggest, which have enabled the fresh kinds of meanings generated within progressive dance work of the 1980s and 1990s.

private room created a narrative by exploiting a tension between a black and white visual image of the mute but expressive male body and the physical, live presence of a speaking female performer. Stuart exerted power over Ouramdane not just because she had access to verbal language but also because her second-person narrative revealed her intimate understanding of embodied experience. One of the legacies of Judson Dance Theater has been a rejection of the idea that a dancer is someone whose specialized training and rarefied artistic sensibilities separate them from ordinary life. Stuart's piece drew on the resulting, more democratic idea that dance articulates properties and qualities of embodied knowledge and experience to which everyone has access. The use in this piece of a second-person narrative appealed to individual spectators directly in a one-to-one way to recognize this common experience. As a form of address, a second-person narrative binds a speaker and the person to whom she or he is speaking in a particular way that is pertinent to live performance. As I have pointed out, this form demands a response from the listener. But it also binds the speaker to the person they are addressing. As Mieke Bal has pointed out, 'this second person [the listener] is crucial for it is that subject which confirms the I as a speaker' (1999: 178). A second-person form of address involves 'you' and 'me', people who are actually present. The fact that, in *private room*, Ouramdane was not physically present in the theatre but only appeared on video further entangled the listener with the performer. This is a characteristic of what, following Bal, I see as the baroque point of view within the pieces discussed in this chapter. In *private room*, this second-person narrative largely depended upon the use of verbal discourse, but there are other examples where the dance movement itself constituted a form of second-person narrative that entangled the spectator and dancer in an intimate relationship.

Felix Ruckert's piece *Hautnah* (1995–9), in which the spectator saw a solo performed by the dancer of their choice in an intimate one-to-one situation, exemplifies some of the ways in which second-person narratives have been used in recent, progressive dance performance. Ruckert is a German choreographer who, having studied at the Folkwangschule in Essen, danced for two years in Tanztheater Wuppertal and in France for Mathilde Monnier, Charles Cré-Ange, and others before starting to present his own choreography in the mid-1990s. Much of his work has involved spectators as participants, *Hautnah* being an early example of this. My entry ticket gives me two free drinks at the bar and I have to choose which of ten solos I want to see, and obtain a badge to see it. Fixed to a wall in the bar are ten large pieces of black card, one for each solo, and each has a small nail on which the badge for the solo can hang. Each card has one image or object, each different. One has a bent bit of wire, another a dashed chalk line across one corner, another a mysterious photograph of blurred hands. Below each card, sometimes in an L-shape around a corner, is the dancer's name. I have to wait a while but, having finally got a badge, I go upstairs and sit and wait in the negotiating room. This is a small, half-lit room, close with the atmosphere of half-clad, sweaty bodies – dancers taking a breather after performing or quietly negotiating with the person who has their badge. I have chosen to see Ann Rudelbach, who finally introduces herself; she is tall, with straight blonde hair and is German, possibly in her late twenties, and I have the feeling she has been observing me. I offer her $15 and she says 'Okay' and when I give it to her she says: 'You're very direct.' Then she asks me to take off my shoes. Picking up a piece of chalk on the way out of the room, she leads me – no physical contact, but with intent glances – up another flight of stairs to the top floor.

We enter a large, hot dance studio that is divided into little cells with screens – twelve-foot squares of unbleached cotton stretched over thin aluminium frames. Ann leads me slowly through a gap between screens that open into a narrow, zigzagging corridor between different cubicles. Her space is at the far end. On the floor is a school exercise book and, in a corner, a red velvet dining chair on which I sit. With the chalk Ann draws a quick line marking off this corner from the rest of the room, recalling the chalk line across the corner of the card downstairs from which I had taken her badge. She makes eye contact with me, smiling intently so that I make a choice and smile back – a second-person narrative that demands a response. Hers is an innocent, friendly smile, not a frank, sexual one. But then, with a quick change of mood, she stands to one side, turned away from me and lifts up her vest to reveal her naked back. I'm shocked. She pulls her vest back down again and then does a sequence of movements with her hands and arms outstretched, miming pulling invisible things, twitching her hands and fingers around her neck. Her eyes are shut. She rubs her stomach and whispers dates (from the last twenty years), finishing by folding her arms, hands free, open. At the end of the sequence, she quickly steps over the chalk line right up close to me and whispers: 'Do you want to know what I just did?' I say yes, and she explains that she has been pulling threads out of her neck with one hand, and catching them with the other. 'Why', I ask, 'did you rub your stomach?' 'To raise energy.' She hasn't really explained much, though.

She doesn't offer any more explanations, but goes back over the line and carries on dancing, some of which is abstract and seems improvisatory, some of it mimetic. At one point she dances with her eyes shut and her hand cupped over her ears like headphones. At another she takes off her vest completely, and, when she is facing me, hides her breasts behind her hands. At another time she holds one hand over her crotch while her other hand seems to be miming pulling a thread out from the base of her spine. As she does this she smiles at me and, as before, I smile back. Later she performs a sequence of crouching movements with her face screwed up and makes a low growl. She whispers more numbers and dates, says 'United Kingdom' and smiles at me (I'm probably the only English person in the building). Then she picks up the exercise book and once more crosses the chalk line to stand right up close to me to read from it 'a list of places I have never been', and a 'list of things I have never eaten'. Her solo ends with her standing at the corner through which we entered. This is my memory of a performance of Felix Ruckert's *Hautnah* at the Joyce Soho, New York in October 1999.

Usually a box office has a fixed tariff, and seems entirely separate from the dancer. By making me wait for a badge, then negotiate a price for the performance with the dancer and hand her the money, *Hautnah* made me uncomfortably aware of how my desire as a consumer is always already implicated in the dance world economy. The piece systematically robbed me of the safe distance between auditorium and stage. Going upstairs was already going inside, and going up a second floor was going in even deeper. Then, in the cubicle itself, while the chalk line Rudelbach drew might have promised a clear distinction between dancer and watcher, this was almost immediately disrupted as she crossed the line. The dancers, as I realized from later discussions with Felix Ruckert,[4] knew that, by doing certain things, the spectator participant would almost certainly react in particular ways. Each dancer had her or his own template for a solo but each performance was unique. This was not only because each spectator reacted differently when invited to participate but also because the dancer used their observation of the spectator as a basis for their improvisation. In Bal's terms, this entangled spectator and dancer in the particular and unusually unfixed positions they found themselves taking up in relation to one another.

Four days later I come back a second time. Being Saturday at the end of the run, it is much busier. There are hostile, competitive queues for dancers' badges right from the start. After a very long wait I get the badge of a young French Canadian dancer, Catherine Jodoin. Her solo is quite different. Unlike the bare wooden floor of Ann Rudelbach's cell, Jodoin's room has a carpet which continues up the wall on one side. There are two spotlights at floor level, a similar red velvet chair, and on the carpet a pair of heavy, stack-heeled boots and a thick, baggy cardigan. Jodoin has long, straight, hennaed hair and wears velvet trousers and a long-sleeved red and purple T-shirt. Her solo starts with sharp, precise gestures as she crouches on the carpet stretching her hands out and staring at them. Then she gets up and comes to me. I am sitting with legs crossed and hands folded in my lap. Moving my leg and putting my hands by my side, she hugs my leg and places my arm round her shoulder. Then she gets me to my feet and we dance together for a while, another second-person narrative to which I respond rather woodenly, unsure exactly what I am supposed to do. At one point she places my hands on either side of her head and makes me press it hard. At another she parts my legs and crawls through them from behind me, squatting in front of me on all fours. Our 'duet' ends when she does some movements that are much faster and more precise – a standing version of the opening sequence crouching on the floor. She dances on her own, ending with a more gestural, mimetic sequence, covering her eye then her mouth, then one hand closing over the fingers of her other hand. She puts on her boots and cardigan, hiding her face inside its high, zipped collar, and lies down very still. I think it is as if she is dead. Then she sits up, looks expectantly at me, says 'Adieu' and smiles.

Both solos were erotically charged. While Rudelbach had undressed during her solo, she had avoided physical contact with me. But, as Jodoin embraced me and drew me into the dance, I could detect garlic and nicotine on her breath and worried about how I myself might smell to her. Following on from paying the dancer directly, this aspect of the piece provocatively alluded to relations between a prostitute and client. Sexual hints were a fascinating lure, used strategically to unsettle the spectator participant and stop her or him viewing the piece in the kind of habitual manner usually adopted when attending dance performances. It thus had the potential to create a heightened sense of physical aware-ness towards the movement material performed. It would be a mistake, however, to interpret this intimacy literally and see it as no more than a re-enactment of prostitution. The experience of watching and partici-pating in *Hautnah* was the destabilizing one of entering an unknown situation where rules and conventions were transgressed and where one both witnessed and helped create an intimate performance. *Hautnah*'s solos were second-person narratives of largely non-verbal utterances addressed by the dancer directly to the spectator without whose responses this particular performance would not have existed. More directly than Stuart in *private room*, Jodoin and Rudelbach used their intimate understanding of their spectator participants' embodied experience to provide a mirror that reflected back to them their own individuality and gave them an opportunity, through participation, for self-awareness.

Mirroring

In the preface to his 1891 novel, *The Picture of Dorian Gray*, Oscar Wilde wrote: 'It is the spectator, and not life, that art really mirrors' (1962: 18). Mirrors have accumulated rich, symbolic meanings in western culture, on the one hand mirroring nature and truth,[5] while on the other reminding the one who looks into them of their own mortality. In the Greek myth to which both Dorian Gray and the narrator in Wilde's novel refer more than once, the beautiful young Narcissus, having spurned all his suitors, fell in love with his own image reflected in a remote woodland pool. Misrecognizing this reflection for another, he became so obsessed with it that he wasted away and died. Iconographically, mirrors are traditionally associated with vanity and mortality, for example in paintings of Venus and Narcissus. In Wilde's novel, the handsome young Dorian Gray was given an uncannily beautiful portrait of himself. While he himself appeared to be blessed with eternal youth and beauty, the portrait provided a true reflection of the way his personality gradually became distorted and vicious as a result of his crimes and immoral actions. Thus, while Gray's appearance in the mirror remained unchanged, his appearance in the portrait became increasingly and horrifyingly ugly. Time, for Gray, as for Etchells in *Down Time*, appeared to be standing still. Only the portrait intimated Gray's death. If, as Wilde proposed, it is the spectator that art mirrors, then mirroring is a baroque device that can put melancholy spectators in touch with absence and death. In an important essay on the Baroque, the art historian Erwin Panofsky commented on criticisms about the sentimental theatricality of Baroque art. He wrote:

> The feeling of Baroque people is (or at least can be in the works of great masters) perfectly genuine, only it does not fill the whole of their souls. They not only feel, but are also aware of their own feelings. While their hearts are quivering with emotion, their consciousness stands aloof and 'knows'.
>
> (Panofsky 1995: 75)

But there are also instances where a melancholy inability to register emotion signifies that what the actor 'knows' is that his or her own mortality is reflected in the mirror.

In 1998, British choreographer Lea Anderson made a sixty-minute live performance with her all-male dance company the Featherstone-haughs, called *The Featherstonehaughs Draw on the Sketchbooks of Egon Schiele*.[6] In 2000, Anderson and the six Featherstonehaughs worked with director Kevin McKiernan to make a ten-minute dance film for BBC television called *The Lost Dances of Egon Schiele*. This was not a filmed record of the stage work but a reinterpretation of some of its themes through rearranged and newly choreographed movement material that took advantage of aesthetic possibilities offered by film. Both works referred to Schiele's drawings and paintings. The Featherstonehaughs wore costumes and heavy make-up, which created the illusion that they were animated versions of works by Schiele. Their faces, the suits that they wore at the beginning and end of the pieces, and the tight, all-in-one body suits that they wore during the central sections were hand dyed with short, acrid, coloured marks that resembled Schiele's harsh, dry brush strokes in oil paint or gouache.

Internationally, Schiele is probably the best-known Austrian painter, and his images circulate widely in books, postcards, posters, and repro-ductions. Anderson's Schiele pieces depend upon the familiarity that the market has produced. Initially, Anderson wanted to call the dance film *Mirrorman* because of a 1914 photograph of Schiele taking up a char-acteristic pose in front of a mirror. Mirrors were a recurring subject in Schiele's works, particularly where he depicted himself with others. In a 1910 pencil drawing, *Schiele Drawing a Nude Model in Front of a Mirror*, the artist, clothed, sits on a chair with a sketch-pad across his knees while a nude, boyish, female model stands boldly in front of him. Both of them face the mirror, he in order to draw what he sees; she, obliv-ious of the artist's close proximity, seems excessively fascinated by her own appearance. As the viewer looks at the drawing, it is as if they do so from the other side of the mirror. Anderson involved spectators of these two dance pieces in complicated ways that directly cited such pictures. At one moment in both the dance film and live performance, the Featherstonehaughs posed as life models in positions that resembled Schiele's drawings of his own nude, male body. Drosten Madden's musical score at this point included the scratchy sound of a stick of char-coal drawing on a large sheet of drawing paper. During this section, two men in suits walked on at the back to sit down and gaze at these models, mirroring back to the audience their own gazes in a way that replicated the complex chains of gazes and identifications brought into play in Schiele's 1910 pencil drawing.

There is a highly idiosyncratic and recognizable way in which people seem to pose within Schiele's self-portraits, double portraits, and drawings of female nudes and couples. Anderson and the dancers investigated and analysed the kinds of gestures and postures that Schiele and his models take up in these works, using this as a basis for creating embodied animations of the drawings. The choreography developed out of these exercises. The resulting movement style brought to life the distinctive distortions in Schiele's work which themselves arise from the way his drawings and paintings compress bodily posture within a narrow, frieze-like, pictorial space. Bodies in Schiele's work are often foreshortened through close observation, or looked down upon so that the picture plane is severely flattened. In putting this space on stage, the choreography was full of hunched shoulders, craned necks, awkwardly twisted arms, and hands displaying curiously separated fingers. Hampered by the need to maintain these awkward details, the dancers seemed clumsy and precariously unstable as they picked their way along their carefully defined pathways (Figure 7.1). Anderson's two works drew attention to the artificiality of the scenes Schiele depicted. As spectators, it was through our own knowledge and experience of embodiment that we appreciated the difficulties that the performance of such movements must entail, but in doing so we recognized their dissimilarity from our ordinary, everyday experience. These difficulties were central to the way in which the film and live performance distanced the viewer.

In both the film and the live performance there are moments when two dancers move together in a physically intimate yet emotionally absent way, drawing on imagery from Schiele's double portraits. Through the use of close-up shots in the film, this sequence makes the viewer aware that while they look at the screen, the dancers are looking intently back at them as if they are looking at their own mirror images reflected in the camera's lens or the audience's eyes. But they seem either unable to recognize themselves beneath their grotesque masks of heavy make-up; or, like the Baroque people Panofsky discussed, they seem to stand aloof and 'know'. The Schieles in Anderson's two pieces, like Etchells in *Down Time*, show no verifiable evidence of any psychological interiority, but whereas *Down Time* treated sadness in a lightly ironic way, Anderson's pieces were dark and melancholy.

The dance film starts and finishes with sequences based not on Schiele's drawings but on the 1914 photograph of him before a mirror. First, two parallel hands, their backs facing each other, their fingers tautly extended, enter the frame on the left, as if the farther hand is a reflection of the nearer one. The arms and then heads and upper bodies follow these onto the screen, and it is as if one were looking over the shoulder of the nearer dancer at his reflection in a mirror. Both dancers raise their arms in unison to join above the head. Then both turn their heads as if looking towards

Figure 7.1 Lea Anderson's *The Lost Dances of Egon Schiele* (dir. Kevin
  McKiernan). Steven Kirkham and Rcm Lee's waltz: trying to
  become like each other being Schiele.

Photo: Lea Anderson.

one another in the mirror but break the illusion by both turning to stare,
somewhat complicitously, at the camera and viewer. From being mirror
reflections they become doppelgangers or clones. At the end of the film
the same sequence takes place in reverse. The uncanny clones turn back
into their slightly less disturbing mirror images and retreat out of the frame
leaving their hands till last. One understands the Featherstonehaughs'
mirrored bodies through mapping the body of the nearer dancer onto
the farther one, noting their reflected symmetry in a way that repeats
the process through which one uses one's own embodied experience to
understand that of another. Or one tries to understand it, because the more
the two dancers try to become like each other being Schiele, the more one
becomes aware of elements and qualities, both visible and invisible, that
aren't quite right but remain irreducibly different. When another and
yet another Featherstonehaugh is introduced, each performing the same
role, their individual differences become increasingly disturbing and
uncanny. Anderson's two Schiele pieces engaged one in what seemed to

be a straightforward, familiar succession of images from a popular, recognizable source, only to make one aware that it was not quite so simple. Throughout both the film and live performance, each of the six Featherstonehaughs took the same role, 'were' Egon Schiele and yet failed to be identical. What the mirror reflected back was, therefore, not a perfect image of the self but one that was fragmented and distorted. Each Featherstonehaugh, therefore, stood aloof from one another and 'knew' that the illusion had failed, and accepted the melancholy fact that they were all irreducibly different from each other. What made them, nevertheless, a group, was not therefore their similarity but their mutual acceptance of each others' differences, a recognition that provided the basis for their relationless relation.

Bausch's melancholia

In psychoanalytic theory, melancholia is a state where the individual is so traumatized by loss that she or he is unable even to accept that there has been a loss and therefore unable to grieve and forget. Instead, the loss is internalized and the individual reproaches him or herself for something that cannot be consciously acknowledged.[7] The sensibility surrounding someone who has turned in on him or herself in this way is often a melancholy one. In Anderson's two Schiele pieces, a complete absence of affect through the dancers' turning in on themselves in this way suggests a melancholy recognition of what they 'know' but cannot consciously accept. But if what art mirrors, according to Wilde, is the spectator, the lack of individuality or transcendence in Anderson's two pieces turned them into blank screens or fragmented mirrors which reflected back to the spectator aspects of their own fragmented experience. This melancholy, baroque mirroring also occurred in Bausch's work. Bausch was in her mid- to late fifties when she first danced her solo in *Danzon*, while Trisha Brown was even older when she first performed *If You Couldn't See Me*. Many of those who have seen *Danzon* must have been following Bausch's career for many years, and will surely have found in this solo traces that remind them of her younger self. Such memories of a younger Bausch surely provoked intimations of loss and mortality.

As with other works Bausch made in the 1990s, the tone of *Danzon* was relatively wistful and humorous in comparison with the dark pieces that made her reputation in the 1970s, and there was more undisguised dancing in it than in the earlier work. But, like Anderson's two Schiele pieces, Bausch's solo itself was deeply melancholic. *Danzon* had, for Bausch, a small cast of twelve dancers and, at an hour and forty-five minutes, it was a relatively short piece when compared with most of her work. Nevertheless, as in many of her pieces, men wore smart suits while women wore dresses with high heels. The music was a pot-pourri of popular classics and raw-sounding folk music, popular songs, and jazz, a 'danzon' being a Cuban dance. Dancers told stories about themselves and undressed on stage. The piece as a whole was a collage of overlapping sketches, incidents, and running gags; almost, in fact, an avant-garde revue. Peter Pabst's design for *Danzon* used, for the first time in Bausch's work, digital photographic images that were projected onto scrims, and Bausch's solo was danced in front of a video projection of tropical fish enlarged to gigantic proportions.[8] It followed a scene where the dancers appeared to be camping in a wood, sitting around their tents by lamp-light, telling stories and jokes. While the audience were laughing at the last joke, the stage suddenly went dark, a scrim was lowered at the front and a still image of a tropical fish projected onto it.[9] Up until this moment, all the projections had been still images, but suddenly this fish came to life and started to swim. Pina Bausch walked quickly but lightly in front of the scrim to take up a position slightly to the right of centre stage below the fish, and began to move. Her hair was drawn tightly back and she was dressed all in black – trousers, shoes, a top with a deep v-neck and tight sleeves to just below her elbows. She danced with her feet as a still point above which the rest of her body, particularly the upper torso, neck, and arms twisted and curled in an almost disturbingly smooth and continual flow.

Bausch's movements in *Danzon* were substantially different from the more energetic and protracted material she had danced in *Café Müller* (which I discussed in Chapter 6). In both pieces Bausch delineated gathering and scattering gestures with her long, thin arms, but in *Danzon* their clarity and spareness were accompanied by a greater angularity and extension. It was as if she had designed her material to project linear shapes into the much larger spaces of the theatres in which her company was now performing. I have suggested that in *Café Müller* the staging seemed to do everything it could to stop the viewer concentrating on Bausch's dancing. As she swayed and bent over to the haunting words and melody of 'Dido's Lament' from Purcell's *Dido and Aeneas*, her lyricism had to compete against the sounds of crashing chairs and tables. Whereas her focus in *Café Müller* had been inwards, eyes seemingly closed, upper torso either arching back or forwards so that her head never directly faced the audience, in *Danzon* she was alone right at the front of the stage, dancing material that rendered her almost vulnerably open to the audience. In *Down Time*, Etchells' decision that it was a bad idea to close his eyes resulted in performance that demonstrated that neither open nor closed eyes revealed any emotional experience. Similarly, in *Danzon*, Bausch dancing with her eyes open seemed just as distant as she had been while dancing with them closed in *Café Müller*.

When I saw this solo in 1999, I found that without any key movement images or motifs on which to fasten, it was difficult to concentrate on Bausch herself. Her head seemed to be responding to her arms and spine rather than leading them. Indeed, now and then a hand gently pushed her head to the side. Like *Café Müller*, the 1995 solo enacted a refusal that left an absence, a vacancy that resonated with a sense of loss, which included the older dancer's loss of her younger self. In *Danzon*, although she seemed to be offering herself in an exceptionally open way to the audience, addressing them in a non-verbal, second-person narrative, at the same time she was not actually offering anything. She provided nothing to look at, or focus on, or save within her beautifully seamless folding and unfolding movements that seemed to turn things inside out and back again. Like Anderson's two Schiele pieces, Bausch's interpretation of this choreography showed no verifiable evidence of any psychological interiority, and, as in *Down Time*, any movements that might betray signs of this were minimized. Bausch, however, appeared open and vulnerable where Etchells had perhaps seemed guarded. Bausch's deliberate, melancholy emptiness, together with the melancholy sense of loss, made her into a kind of mirror in which the audience could see reflected back their own experience of fragmentation. What was deliberate about this aesthetic of emptiness was the way that Bausch stood aloof from her role and 'knew' that by doing so she was creating this space for reflection, despite the knowledge that such spaces are no longer imagined to exist.

The politics of friendship

By using Mieke Bal's concept of a baroque point of view, I have identified issues and concerns within progressive, experimental dance created in the mid-1990s and early 2000s. In this final section I return to my earlier discussion of friendship and ethics. What is important about these works is the way they resonate with contemporary discussions about the politics of friendship. *The Politics of Friendship* (1997) is the title of one of the philosopher Jacques Derrida's later books in which he used a critique of traditional ideas about friendship within western culture to pose questions about the nature of politics. 'The figure of the friend,' he pointed out, 'seems spontaneously to belong to a familial, fraternalist and thus androcentric configuration of politics' (Derrida 1997: viii). The problem with this kind of politics is that it excludes those who are different, or can only include them if their otherness is identifiable and the threat this poses to a constraining normality can be neutralized. Derrida thus raises questions about our ethical and political responsibilities towards minorities in general, including those as yet unknown. Traditional philosophical discussions by Aristotle, Cicero, Montaigne, and others describe friendship as a discovery that another is like oneself and shares identical ideas and feelings. Through a critique of these texts, and an examination of works by Nietzsche and Blanchot, Derrida posited an alternative account of friendships which do not just depend on sameness and reciprocity but acknowledge difference. These ideas, I suggest, illuminate the space of interaction between dancer and audience in works that, following Blanchot, rehearse what I have been describing as a relationless relation. The baroque point of view enacted within the pieces discussed in this chapter, thus, raised questions about shifts in the nature of the space which theatre dance performatively creates. By cutting across the division between public and private, these pieces introduce, in aesthetic rather than political terms, the same issues as those that Derrida, Blanchot, Laclau, Cavarero, Critchley, and others have examined in their attempts to find, as a solution to the problem of political disappointment, a new, more ethical basis for a radical, critical politics.

In her nine-minute solo, *If You Couldn't See Me*, as with most of her choreography since the late 1970s, Brown seemed to be continuously and surprisingly changing the direction and spatial dynamics of her movement. What was distinctive about this solo was its slow, considered pace as Brown seemed to pick her way from one state to another. It was as if she was multitasking between an even greater number of different movement tasks than usual while she herself stood aloof and 'knew' that her dancing was taking her off in directions that continually fascinated the spectator. As I have already pointed out, a refusal to face the audience, and therefore an imperative to use her back as a means of expression was the choreography's initial premise. The underlying ethics of Brown's relation with her audience correlates with what the French philosopher Emmanuel Levinas called the face. Much of Levinas's work is concerned with the phenomenology of the encounter between the self and other. Dance scholars may know Maxine Sheets-Johnstone's work on the phenomenology of dance in which she bracketed off the initial, pre-reflective experience of dance from the intellectual processes that follow this initial encounter. Levinas was similarly concerned with trying to identify the initial, pre-reflective experience of encountering the other. He believed that an awareness of the other's vulnerability, passivity, and openness to wounding derives from a face-to-face encounter. Ethics, in his account, is refraining from exploiting the other's vulnerability and thus obeying the biblical commandment 'thou shalt not kill'. For Levinas, the other makes an intense, almost religious claim on one, so that one is unable to hold back anything in responding to the other's needs. This claim, in Levinas's terminology, comes from the face. By this, Levinas did not mean the physical features of the face or the personality or character of the person, but referred to their humanity. This intimately anonymous humanity was signified by the expressive potential of the body itself.

Levinas gave as an example a situation within a story by Vassili Grossman where the qualities that he termed the face were actually expressed by the human back, a proposal with obvious pertinence to Brown's solo. In this story, which is set in Soviet Russia, wives, relatives, and friends of political prisoners congregate at the Secret Police head-quarters in Moscow to ask for news of their loved ones.

> A line is formed at the counter, a line where one can see only the backs of others. A woman awaits her turn: [She] had never thought that the human back could be so expressive, and could convey states of mind in such a penetrating way. Persons approaching the counter had a particular way of craning their neck and their back, their raised shoulders with shoulder blades like springs, which seemed to cry, sob, scream.
>
> (Levinas 1996: 167)

Like the waiting woman, I found, when watching Brown perform her solo, that I had never thought the human back could be so expressive. But it was also, as I have argued, intimately anonymous, just as the face for Levinas signified an anonymous humanity. Following Levinas, Brown's back, therefore, made a claim on the audience to recognize and respect her vulnerability and openness.

A significant factor in the piece was Brown's gender. At one moment near the beginning of her solo Brown twisted right round towards her left and would actually have been facing the audience were it not that her head was so bowed that it faced the floor. This move bears an unexpected similarity to a moment near the beginning of Yvonne Rainer's 1985 film *The Man Who Envies Women* in which Trisha Brown plays the role of Trisha, the film's principal narrator.[10] In an early scene she visits her ex-husband Jack's apartment finding him working out on his exercise bicycle while listening to the radio news. Trisha steps across between the camera and the table on which the radio sits, to turn it off so that she can speak to Jack, and as she does so the camera/spectator can almost but not quite see her face. For the rest of the film only her voice can be heard as if she is present but off screen. In this scene, as in her later solo, Brown seems to turn through as much of the space around her body as she can without allowing the audience actually to see her face.

In her 1985 film, Rainer was referring ironically to ideas about the male gaze in feminist film theory through the device of the invisible female protagonist.[11] These feminist ideas coincided with her own long-term concerns. As I pointed out in Chapter 3, issues about how performers meet the audience's gaze had been a shared concern of Brown, Rainer, and Steve Paxton during the 1960s. (It also informed Rainer's new duet in 1999 which I discuss in Chapter 8.) This concern about the dancer–spectator relation led Rainer, in the 1970s, to abandon live dance performance for film making. As she observed in a letter to Nan Piene, she had become dissatisfied with theatre dance because: 'Dance ipso facto is about *me* (the so-called kinaesthetic response of the spectator notwithstanding, it only rarely transcends the narcissistic-voyeuristic duality of doer and looker); whereas the area of the emotions must necessarily concern both of us' (Rainer 1974: 238, emphasis in the original). As I noted earlier, while Narcissus had eyes only for himself, art mirrors the spectator. The pieces discussed in this chapter have done this in a fragmented way, thus exploring aspects that concern both performer and spectator, entangling them together. Their relationless relation was one that did not deny emotional experience or psychological interiority; instead, by finding ways of leaving this private, and thus avoiding Rainer's problem that dance ipso facto is only about the performer, these pieces allowed what is public to be revealed.

In the 1990s Brown herself revealed to Christy Adair that she was aware of the issues raised by feminists. An incident where an admirer had kept presenting roses for her at the stage door made her realize how sexy her piece *Set and Reset* (1983) was, which was performed wearing a semi-transparent costume with no underwear and, as Brown put it, danced 'in a froth of joy' (Adair 1996: 51). But Brown maintained that there wasn't any eroticism in *If You Couldn't See Me*: 'This is the ambient outcome of my task because the body is erotic. It depends on your focus and perception' (ibid.). Dealing with the audience's perceptions, she said, can be 'a source of friction and frustration that I have to overcome. They center on a stereotype of what a dancer is and what a woman is, specifically when dancing before an audience' (ibid.). As I noted earlier, while Brown didn't want the audience, whom she respected, to think that she was turning her back on them, this was a way of dealing with their expectations. I have described the anonymous way she therefore related to her audience as a relationless relation. Brown's respect for the audience was a form of friendship based on mutual recognition of (gendered) difference.

In his open 'Letter to Trisha' about *If You Couldn't See Me* published in 1995 in *Contact Quarterly*, Steve Paxton brought together ideas about vulnerability and spectatorship:

> Facing upstage, you aren't blinking uncomfortably in the light of our avid eye. You know you cannot know or concern yourself with how you may look to us, and so try to deflect us. With that issue aside and privacy assured, you seem to relax and really put out. Lordy, how you dance. Pure, assured, full-bodied, wild and fully self-knowing. We are not watchers but onlookers. You are not our focus exactly but a medium mediating between us and something, some unknowable or unthinkable vision in the upstage volume or, something beyond.
>
> (Paxton 1995: 94)

Paxton thus acknowledged Brown's vulnerability when he suggested that the spectators' avid eyes try to invade her privacy. In his account, her device of not facing the audience allows her to redirect energy that she would otherwise have had to divert into a reactive process of deflecting avid eyes, and thus to focus instead on infinity. Paxton and Brown are old friends who first met and performed in each other's dance pieces in the early 1960s. Unusually in the professional dance world, both have continued to perform in their fifties and sixties.[12] Brown's dancing provided Paxton with the pretext to write for the community of dancers who read *Contact Quarterly*[13] as an old friend of hers, and he therefore used a second-person narrative, calling Brown 'you'. Blanchot has suggested that friendship: 'does not allow us to speak *of* our friends, but only to speak *to* them' (Blanchot 1971: 328, translated Critchley 1999: 268, emphasis in original). In a letter that was private but made public, Paxton spoke *to* Brown although he in effect wrote *about* her. Just as for Levinas the face demands that one respond to the other's needs, for Blanchot, friendship obliges one to speak to one's friend; Paxton implies that Brown's solo thus spoke to him in a second-person narrative that demanded a response. Yet what he wrote *about* and made public in his letter was that her solo was unknowable. While he said that Brown herself was fully self-knowing, she herself stood aloof and 'knew'. Much of what she knew, therefore, remained private, allowing what was public to emerge more clearly.

Paxton's letter enacts the same linguistic procedures as the other second-person narratives I have discussed. In *private room*, Stuart spoke to Ouramdane in order to speak about him to others, while in *Hautnah*, Jodoin and Rudelbach spoke through movement and gesture to the spectator participant in order to incite their responses. Each of these pieces generated what I have called a baroque point of view that entangled spectators and performers together within provocative and unusual relationships. While *Down Time* problematized the idea that performance communicates ideas about psychological interiority, the performers in Anderson's two Schiele pieces, and Bausch's solo in *Danzon* provided the spectator with a neutral, fragmented mirror that invited the audience to perceive their own vulnerability and difference. By cutting across the distinctions between public and private, these pieces presented material that focused in challenging and critical ways on the embodiment of experience. They, therefore, responded to Rainer's desire for dance that was not, ipso facto, about the performer but addressed an area of experience that must necessarily concern both performer and spectator. Whereas much of the work presented at Judson Dance Theater consisted of short pieces stripped down to minimal forms and simple concepts, the new dance of the 1990s and 2000s has been more extended and has dealt with more complicated and fragmented forms and concepts. The difference between Rainer's 'no' in her 1965 statement 'NO to spectacle' and Brown's use of the word 'respect' in 1996 to characterize her relation to her audience is the difference between naive idealism and the shadow of the problem of political disappointment. Where radical experimental dance artists in the 1990s and 2000s have embodied an aesthetic that is neutral without being impersonal, they have kept open possibilities for respecting others through their rehearsal of the sometimes melancholy emptiness of relationless relations.

8 The Judson tradition at the start of a new century

This book about Judson Dance Theater and its legacy has been written during a period in which there has been a revival of interest in the art of the 1960s and early 1970s. A few examples from the visual arts include the many recent books and exhibitions about Andy Warhol's paintings and films, a revival of interest in conceptual art, and meetings, exhibitions, and publications to celebrate the anniversary of the founding of the Fluxus movement. Concurrent with these has been a similar interest in the new dance of the 1960s. Quattuor Albrecht Knust, a French-based group, which included Christophe Wavelet, Jérôme Bel, Boris Charmatz, Emanuelle Huyn, and Xavier Le Roy, performed 're-readings' of Steve Paxton's *Satisfyin' Lover* (1967) and Yvonne Rainer's *Continuous Process Altered Daily* (1970) in 1996 at festivals in Avignon, Montréal, and Stockholm.[1] When I began to research this book in 1999, I just missed seeing Clarinda MacLow's revival, in April that year, of the *Judson Flag Show* version of *Trio A* (discussed in Chapter 5). In October, however, I was lucky enough to see Rainer's return to active involvement in dance with her programme *Trio A Pressured* at Judson Memorial Church. There, in the audience, was Mikhail Baryshnikov with Trisha Brown and David Gordon. Baryshnikov had already commissioned Rainer to make a piece for his White Oak Dance Project *After Many a Summer Dies a Swan* (2000). Apparently as a result of discussing *Trio A Pressured* with Brown and Gordon, Baryshnikov had the idea of performing a number of works from the Judson period and its aftermath. This, in 2000, became the programme *PASTForward* which I saw at MC93 Theater in Paris that December as part of the Festival d'Automne. In 2002 Rainer used a video of her piece for White Oak Dance Company as a basis for a new video installation, *After Many a Summer Dies a Swan: Hybrid*.

This chapter looks at these developments in the US together with related work in Europe in order to evaluate the legacy of Judson Dance Theater at the start of the twenty-first century. Whether these recent performances are reconstructions, or new interpretations, or citations of the 1960s, they raise three related questions. First, what, if anything, does it mean, at the start of the twenty-first century, to repeat avant-garde gestures that had only had a strategic and contingent meaning in the context of the 1960s? Or, to put this another way, if the failure of the 1960s counterculture indicated that the time of the avant-garde was past, what relevance could it have at the start of a new century? How is it possible to go on? Second, if the dance work of the 1960s and 1970s that Sally Banes called post-modern was exclusively an American (US) phenomenon, what relevance does it have for Europeans, and on what basis do we Europeans understand it?[2] Finally, what does all this say about the way these dancers, as they refer back to the new dance of the 1960s (and earlier periods), view dance history? What sort of history is it, and what sort of historical methodologies have supported these performances?

Noël Carroll explicitly addressed the question of dance historiography from the point of view of a philosopher, in an essay 'Art history, dance, and the 1960s' that also deals with the problem of the end of the avant-garde and the place of the US in relation to European cultural traditions. His essay was developed from a talk he gave in 1996 at the festival *Talking Dancing* at the *House of Dance* in Stockholm, where Quattuor Albrecht Knust were also performing their 're-readings' of *Satisfyin' Lover* and *Continuous Process Altered Daily*. Carroll took the Greenbergian modernist view of dance history, which I discussed in Chapters 1 and 3, and developed it in line with Arthur Danto's argument about the end of art (1997). Where Danto had argued that Andy Warhol's 1964 sculpture, *Brillo Box*, represented the end of art, Carroll applied the same argument to the work of Judson Dance Theater. In his view the latter constituted the end of dance because it represented the conclusion of an evolutionary process whereby a representational theory of dance collapsed in favour of an expressionist and a formalist theory which, in turn, were superseded by a modernist project. This is a dialectical account where the modernism of Judson Dance Theater was the new synthesis that not only transcended expressionism and formalism but, in doing so, brought the whole historical process to a halt, a point beyond which it could go no further. Rainer, Paxton, Gordon, Forti, Dunn, and others have, according to Carroll:

> demonstrated that anything could become dance no matter how it looked ... they have extended the range of possibilities for contemporary dance momentously. They have opened a new world of dance: not an end to dance, but perhaps a new beginning.
>
> (Carroll 2003: 96)

The ideas that history and art have come to an end were first formulated by the philosopher G.W.F. Hegel (1770–1831), who viewed the end of history in a positive light as an absolute moment of victorious, spiritual importance.[3] A key term in Hegel's philosophy is *aufhebung*, a German word with no equivalent in English. Hegel used it to mean transcendence or sublation, where the original synthesis is raised to a higher level which, nevertheless, negates it. Carroll eschewed Hegel's Christian metaphysics but nevertheless tried to put a positive spin on the notion of the end of dance. He thus played down negative aspects which, I suggest, have been central to the way dancers such as Rainer in the US and Bel in Europe have used their work directly to interrogate the problem of how to go on.

In the 1990s Carroll and Danto were not alone in citing Hegel. As John Rajchman has observed, 'Hegel's depressive idea that we are the End of History gained new currency in one way through Arthur C. Danto, in another through Francis Fukuyama, along with variations on the old theme of "the death of art"' (Rajchman 1993: 166). For Fukuyama (1992), the collapse of Soviet Communism announced the end of history in so far as it proved the superiority of a model of liberal democracy over all other ideologies such as hereditary monarchy, socialism, and fascism. To put this in crudely historical terms, the US was founded through revolution against colonial rule in the name of a hereditary British monarch, helped defeat Hitler in the 1939–45 war, and won the cold war. In cultural terms, many in the US view the European artistic tradition as decadent and exhausted, and believe that their own country has taken it on and brought it to completion. Although Carroll doesn't explicitly say so, his account implies that the achievements of Judson Dance Theater demonstrate the superiority of an American tradition of modernist dance over European ballet and an expressionist modern dance tradition that flourished in both Europe and the US. This is a selective view of dance history that only takes into account those figures whose work has been legitimated as part of the dance history canon, one which Carroll suggests is now complete. Some recent reconstructions or revivals of works from the 1960s, I suggest, are informed by ideas about the canon. Other works created in Europe around the beginning of the twenty-first century have cited earlier dances, including the new American dance of the 1960s, in ways that treat dance history not as a canon but as an archive. Rainer's recent dance works and her video installation are exercises that suggest a desire to put her archive in order.[4]

Reconstructions

Susan Manning, in part of her contribution to the Terpsichore in Combat Boots debate (discussed in Chapter 1) proposed that postmodern dance marked the end of the division between ballet and modern dance (Manning 1988: 36–7). By the 1960s in the New York dance world, ballet and mainstream modern dance found themselves on the same side of a new divide between 'uptown' and 'downtown', between the mainstream theatres and the fringe venues of the underground. This was originally established by John Martin of the *New York Times* and Walter Terry of the *Herald Tribune* in their unwritten gentlemen's agreement in the 1950s to remain silent about anything performed below 30th Street. Although Clive Barnes did review performances by members of Judson Dance Theater in the *New York Times*, he retained this binary distinction by rubbishing anything downtown and thus maintaining an economy of geographically defined artistic value. Baryshnikov's career has been marked by a number of projects that exemplify the gradual erosion of the distinction between ballet and modern dance and between uptown and downtown. Twyla Tharp was perhaps the first downtown choreographer to go uptown, choreographing *Deuce Coupe* for the Joffrey Ballet in 1973 and *Push Comes to Shove* for American Ballet Theater in 1976, a piece that was a star vehicle for Baryshnikov, who had defected from what was then the Soviet Union two years earlier. Writing in 1980, Banes argued that Tharp's 'aspirations have changed, or so her recent work seems to say, and rather than using popular forms in an avant-garde context, she works seriously in mainstream forms: ballet and movie musicals' (Banes 1980: 19). Arguably, however, her work in the 1970s and 1980s was ambiguously both popular and in some ways innovative, belonging to the postmodern dance milieu, yet within the ballet mainstream.[5]

Shortly before abandoning dance for film in the early 1970s, Rainer too was exploring an ambiguous space between ballet and the avant-garde in *Solo with a Red Ball*. This was a solo that she created in 1971 for Valda Setterfield as part of *Grand Union Dreams*,[6] and which Baryshnikov subsequently danced in *After Many a Summer Dies a Swan*. Unlike Rainer's work from the early 1960s, which had largely explored task-based, everyday movement qualities, this solo was tightly choreographed and made use of Setterfield's knowledge of ballet and her experience of dancing Cunningham's work. With a small, red ball (about the size of a tennis ball) in her hand, Setterfield proceeded through a number of statuesque positions and slow, graceful transitions between these with her gaze fixed either on the ball or travelling from where the ball had been to where the hand holding it would next come to rest. She wore a full-length, black dress with bare shoulders that allowed the delicacy and precision of her arm movements to be clearly seen. The opening of the solo was almost a direct quotation from *Trio A* when first Setterfield's left hand and then the right (holding the ball) circled round her trunk to touch her back and then return to the front, movements repeated five times. Further resemblances between the two pieces included the slow, unemphatic pace, and the choreographed gaze. Where the two differed was in the solo's employment of classical 'line', in particular in the arms and shoulders (port de bras, épaulement). In *After Many a Summer Dies a Swan*, Baryshnikov danced this bare-chested with trousers, and with a long black dress that resembled Setterfield's tied around his torso.

Baryshnikov's desire to create a space for performance that includes both ballet and modern dance dates back to the time of *Push Comes to Shove* if not earlier, and found what is perhaps its most significant manifestation with the formation of the White Oak Dance Project in 1990. As Susan Foster has observed:

> Co-founded with choreographer Mark Morris, the White Oak Dance Project has served as a major vehicle for presenting new work by choreographers of modernist descent, purveying modern dance aesthetics and a modern dance sensibility to audiences primarily oriented towards ballet.
>
> (Foster 2001: 22)

The *PASTForward* programme was, of course, an extreme test of this commitment. But, in Foster's opinion:

> One of the remarkable features of *PASTForward* is the company's traverse of the distance between standard notions of virtuosity, which they can easily demonstrate, and Judson's quest for an alternative virtuosity grounded in the discard of anything extraneous to the performance of simple action.
>
> (ibid.: 23)

Baryshnikov himself has explained that his wish to do the show that became *PASTForward* came from his appreciation of the difference between the manner of performing traditional ballet roles and the ways of performing he had observed in dancers associated with Judson Dance Theater. 'In Russia,' he wrote, 'dancers are trained as theater artists, almost as dancing actors' (Baryshnikov 2003: ix). Thus, performing the role of Bathilde or Giselle in the ballet *Giselle* is to perform a role:

Even though the role was not created with them in mind, [Russian ballet dancers] managed to put themselves inside it in a personal way. Still it was them, in a role, in a metaphor. With the Judson dancer, on the other hand, what you saw was not a metaphor. It was *them*, and when it worked, it was you too.

(ibid.)

The staging of *PASTForward* was historical in its approach with a documentary video, narrated by Baryshnikov himself, projected on stage as a link and introduction to pieces. Made by Charles Atlas, this showed photographs, old film, and contemporary interviews with choreographers. If people didn't already see Judson Dance Theater as part of the canon, *PASTForward* suggested that they should. Baryshnikov and members of his regular company danced works that had first been performed in the 1960s – including *Flat*, *Trio A*, and Lucinda Child's *Carnation* – and more recent work – including Trisha Brown's *Foray Forêt* (1990), Child's *Concerto* (1993), and Deborah Hay's *Whizz* (2000).[7] Other pieces were danced by a group of 'community' dancers recruited in each city. Nancy Duncan, the director of the company's education programme, taught them Paxton's *Satisfyin' Lover* (1967), Forti's *Huddle* (1961) and *Scramble* (1970), and Gordon's *Overture to the Matter* (1979).[8] *Huddle* was danced in the middle of the crowd in the theatre foyer before the programme started, and later repeated on stage. During the tour of the US, a number of the choreographers took part in post-performance discussions, and Deborah Hay toured with the company, dancing *Single Duet* (2000) with Baryshnikov. At the theatre MC93 in Bobigny, Paris, Steve Paxton appeared as a guest artist dancing a new solo, *Earlyman. Deadlines* (2000). He was, at the time, also touring his own programme of solo pieces including *Flat*. When he saw Baryshnikov dance *Flat* in Paris, this was the first time he had seen anyone else dance it. On the Saturday of their season in Paris there was a matinée as well as an evening performance. At the matinée Baryshnikov danced *Flat* and invited Paxton to perform it in the evening.

I discussed *Flat* in some detail in Chapter 4. In this piece the dancer walked a circular path around an area containing a chair; he gradually, item by item, took off his shoes and socks, then jacket, shirt, and trousers and hung each on a hook that had been taped to his skin; between taking off these items, he continued walking around the space, occasionally freezing in a sports pose; then he progressively redressed and exited. The act of sitting down, and the actions of taking off shoes and clothes were mostly interrupted as the dancer unexpectedly froze half way through, often pausing long enough to unsettle his audience. It is a piece that radically disrupts any expectation of organic flow. Its pauses and freezes are frustrating, seeming to present the body in a very instrumental and unlyrical way. Baryshnikov danced *Flat* roughly the way I remember Paxton dancing it in the early 1980s, and his performance of it usually took about eleven minutes.[9] In the evening Paxton took twenty-five minutes. This was roughly the length of time he took to dance it in his own solo programme, which he had performed in both the US and England earlier that year. Its slow pace was typical of the extraordinary focus and concentration that has characterized Paxton's dancing since the late 1980s. For Paxton, this was not a historical reconstruction of a canonical work, but a performance of a piece that allowed him to focus on physical and aesthetic concerns that he had begun to investigate in the 1960s and which continued to preoccupy him.[10]

The change of cast for *Flat* on Saturday night had not been announced, so that the first I knew of it was when Paxton came on in his suit – his walk was different from Baryshnikov's, less bouncy. Compared with Baryshnikov, Paxton seemed to make the solo seem simpler, although he divided the actions of taking off his shoes and clothes into much smaller fragments, analysing each and performing it with meticulous detail. His sudden, sharp freezes seemed to be more unexpected and were more prolonged than Baryshnikov's had been. Apparently the two pieces that Parisian audiences had liked least were Paxton's *Flat* and Child's *Carnation* – both had been booed earlier in the week.[11] In the afternoon people had walked out when Baryshnikov danced *Flat*. In the evening when Paxton danced it, a lot of the audience, particularly around where I was sitting at the back of the auditorium, became extremely restless. Some people stopped concentrating on the piece altogether, some started barracking and heckling, while others began chatting to one another. *Flat* was, of course, made with a comparatively intimate performance space in mind, not a thousand-seat auditorium like MC93. A friend who had a seat at the front said she had the impression that the riot was going on behind her. From where I was, I could see a continual stream of people walking out, which was ironic as in the section of video introducing *Flat* Paxton had mentioned audiences walking out of concerts at Judson Memorial Church in the 1960s. Meanwhile Paxton subdivided the actions of undoing a lace or taking off a sock into minute sections between uncomfortably long pauses. When finally the sock came off there were cheers. Clearly the audience was sharply divided. Some people appreciated the piece, and there were 'ssshs!', while others barracked and slow hand-clapped. In the midst of this, it was extraordinary to see Paxton not losing any concentration, but just carrying on going so slowly, so calmly at the centre of the storm he had unintentionally provoked.

Parisian audiences have a history of forthrightness. In the theatre at Bobigny I heard people actually referring to Victor Hugo's *Les Hernani*. During the first two performances of this play at the Comédie Française in 1830 a famous battle broke out between those for and against romanticism. The riot during the first night of Nijinsky's *Sacre du printemps* at the Theatre des Champs Elysée in 1913 is equally celebrated. The premier of Jérôme Bel's *The Show Must Go On* at Paris's Théâtre de la Ville, a few weeks later in January 2001, also split its audience between supporters and noisy detractors who jeered and barracked for the last half of the piece in a very similar manner to *PASTForward*'s audience. Paxton subsequently observed that audiences in the US and in England had been quite happy to sit through performances of *Flat* that were as long or longer than his performance at MC93. Admittedly these were in smaller venues. More people saw *Flat* in his one performance at MC93 than all those who saw it in the 1960s.[12] Baryshnikov's admittedly shorter performances of *Flat* had been comparatively well received in the US and subsequently at the Edinburgh Festival in Scotland. Audiences in France, one might therefore conclude, are more volatile than audiences in Britain and the US. There seems to be a connection between the high level of State subsidy for the arts in France and the fact that French audiences feel that they have a right to express their opinions about questions of aesthetic value. In *The Rights of Man*, the eighteenth-century revolutionary Tom Paine argued that American revolutionary democracy was the future, and hailed the French Revolution as the beginning of a new Europe inspired by the example of the US. Similarities between the reception of *Flat* and Bel's *The Show Must Go On* suggest that Judson Dance Theater was an American dance revolution that has inspired a new, revolutionary European dance.

Judson in Europe

As well as the French group Quattuor Albrecht Knust, other European choreographers have also taken a recent interest in the more radical aspects of the new American dance of the 1960s and 1970s. While the new European work has explored parameters that Bausch and De Keersmaeker were largely responsible for identifying, the younger dance makers have taken these ideas in radical directions that are implicit in the older generation's work but which the latter had not directly explored. André Lepecki has summed up their concerns as:

> a distrust of representation, a suspicion of virtuosity as an end, the
> reduction of unessential props and scenic elements, an insistence on

the dancer's presence, a deep dialogue with the visual arts and with performance art, a politics informed by a critique of visuality, and a deep dialogue with performance theory.

(Lepecki 2004a: 173)[13]

As I have shown in the first half of this book, much of this could also be said about members of Judson Dance Theater during the 1960s. Many of the generation of European dancers who began making work in the 1990s had gained experience dancing for older European choreographers as well as taking classes in New York in the studios and schools of older American modern dance choreographers. With benefit of a deeper knowledge and understanding of dance history and theory, these younger dancers questioned their elders' cults of newness by deliberately engaging with older models of contemporary dance.

As a result of Quattuor Albrecht Knust's performances, Bel, Le Roy, and Charmatz all subsequently formed personal relationships with Paxton and Rainer. For example, in 2000, Le Roy collaborated on two events, *Meetings*, with Yvonne Rainer during the *Internationales Tanzfest* in Berlin. Their interest in Judson Dance Theater preceded the group's Judson revivals. For example, *A bras le corps* (1994), a collaboratively choreographed duet by Charmatz and Dimitri Chamblas, recalled the early years of contact improvisation. In this piece the audience sat on benches facing inwards around a small square performance area, and the two dancers sat with them while not performing. Just as the setting recalled a contact jam, some of what the dancers performed looked like rough, inexperienced contact improvisation – falling and rolling on the floor, awkward, heavy holds and lifts. But there were also bravura jumps and turns. The audience were too close to see these balletic moves properly, and too close not to be aware of the dancers' effort and perspiration. The result looked rough, and was reminiscent of the roughness one sees, for example, in videos of the first duets between Steve Paxton and Nancy Stark Smith.[14] When we look back at these now with the benefit of hindsight, we know what contact improvisation will become, but at the time Paxton and Smith were looking for something new and unknown. Similarly, Charmatz and Chamblas in 1994, with the awkward, impulsive, irrepressible energy of teenagers,[15] were looking for something new and unknown, but doing so by deliberately referencing the informal staging and ways of moving of an older generation. They were seeking something new by working through rather than rejecting older ideas.

Charmatz subsequently got to know Paxton well. They first came in contact with one another when Charmatz was invited, as someone who was not particularly involved with the improvisation scene, to be what he calls a 'UFO' in improvised performances. Having danced with Paxton in Amsterdam, Brussels, and Lisbon, Charmatz invited him in 2000 to join a group of artists for a summer project in the French Alps at Annency, *Ouvrée – artistes en alpage* ('Opened up – artists in high mountain pasture').[16] The group included choreographers, artists, and the veteran sound poet Bernard Heidsieck. During a ten-day period they experimented with a variety of approaches to making and presenting work outdoors. They examined the way dances made for black box theatres in densely populated metropolitan centres were destroyed when presented in the wide open spaces of the Alps. They also considered their relationship with early German modern dance, both with the open air festivals that Laban had organized at Monte Verita, and the later *bewegungschor* (movement choirs) of the Nazi period. Using labanotation scores, they were able to perform *Feierlicher Kanon* (Solemn Canon, 1933) by Grete and Harry Pierenkämper and *Die Welle* (The Wave, undated, *c.*1932–5) by Albrecht Knust. When asked about the experience of dancing in *Die Welle*, Steve Paxton told me that:

> there was something in the structure of the cube dance which would have been at home and welcome at Judson. The funny thing is, I have long known vaguely about these dances from another age, which thought it interesting to employ 'non-dancers' and had to build a structure apparent enough to contain them. Perhaps I would have gained time if I had known them more, or had known more of them; perhaps on the other hand I would have been pre-empted and had no exploration to make.[17]

The work of Judson Dance Theater was not particularly well known in Europe in the mid-1990s. Rather than being part of the canon, this new generation saw it as marginal and subversive, and thus useful in their own project of troubling and subverting what they saw as the complacency and conventional modernism of contemporary European dance during the 1970s and 1980s. Several recent European pieces have cited twentieth-century dances from a wide range of different periods. In Jérôme Bel's *Le dernier spectacle* (The Last Performance, 1998) dancers each performed a solo by Susanne Linke that they had learnt from watching a video tape, introducing themselves by saying 'Ich bin Susanne Linke' (I am Susanne Linke). Tino Sehgal's piece *20 minutes for the 20th century* (2001) was full of quotations from twentieth-century dances that involved nudity, including works by Isadora Duncan, William Forsythe, and John Jasperse. Mårten Spångberg's *Powered by Emotion* (2004) whose first half is titled 'Goldberg Variations by J.S. Bach, played by Glenn

Gould, improvised by Steve Paxton, filmed by Walter Verdin, and recon-structed by Mårten Spångberg' apparently does just that.[18] *Affects/Rework* (2000) by B.D.C included reconstructions of some of Dora Hoyer's cycle *Affectos Humanos* (1962–4).

Many of the earlier pieces that these recent European dances have explicitly cited were not well known. Rather than learning from dances considered to be the masterworks from the canon, these dance artists have engaged in well-informed investigations of the archive of dance history. Whereas, in Carroll's view, the canon is whole and transcendentally com-plete, these dancers experienced the archive as collections of fragments that resist closure. The works they have cited are largely ones that have been negated through the historical process of canon formation. For example, neither Hoyer nor her *Affectos Humanos* cycle, part of which Martin Nachbar reconstructed in *Affects/Rework*, are particularly well known. Hoyer committed suicide because she believed there was no future for modern dance in Germany. *Affects/Rework* did not advocate her inclusion within the canon in the way that *PASTForward* did for Judson Dance Theater. Nachbar danced three solos by Hoyer during a per-formance that also included a solo by Plischke and the projection of a dig-ital film of the latter shaving, all announced by Alice Chauchat. Nachbar tried to perform the movement content of *Affectos Humanos* as faithfully as possible. Hoyer's piece is conventionally seen as a direct development of the new German dance of the 1920s and 1930s, part of the lineage of Hoyer's teacher, Mary Wigman. *Affects/Rework* drew attention to the dif-ficulties of transmission of the embodied memories of dancers who worked outside institutional structures. Nachbar had come across an old film of Hoyer dancing, and went through an arduous process of getting permis-sion to dance the cycle from Waltrand Luley, an old retired dancer in her eighties who had been close to Hoyer and held the performing rights to her work. Having eventually given permission, Luley worked with Nachbar closely to ensure that he got the dances right. Nachbar has said that in order 'to find out the differences, you have to try to be the same' (in Cook 2001: 73). Rather than pretending it is only possible to find something new and contemporary by rejecting the past, Nachbar found what was different about the present through recognizing his own failures and observing what he couldn't do. Faced with the problem of how to go on, after what Carroll called the end of dance, Nachbar along with Bel, Sehgal, Spångberg and, as I shall show, Rainer, created works that embodied a refusal of meaning which, in effect, reflected the kinds of explanations of historical process that Carroll and others put forward.

Gerald Siegmund has given a useful summary of how Jérôme Bel has addressed this:

Le dernier spectacle, in 1998, was supposed to have marked his farewell to the world of dance after just three personal creations. It was meant to have been his last piece, but no such doing. Yet how is one to continue, when one has chosen to pull out, programmatically speaking, as the theme of the show . . . Nevertheless, Jérôme Bel came up with a device to keep on going. He asked his colleague Xavier Le Roy to develop a choreography in his vein and with his dancers, which he then signed, the way an artist signs a painting.

(Siegmund 2001, n.p.)

In programmes, the resulting piece *Xavier Le Roy* was credited as follows: 'by Jérôme Bel. Conception and realization: Xavier Le Roy'. Bel subsequently, with his 2001 piece *The Show Must Go On*, acknowledged through this title his return to choreography, showing that it is not as easy as one might think to make an end of dance. In many ways Bel's self-consciously mythologized investigation of the problem of going on working paralleled Yvonne Rainer's departure from dance making in the early 1970s. While rehearsing her piece *Grand Union Dreams*, Rainer encouraged the dancers to take the initiative and devise their own material which could, in some cases, replace hers. She encouraged them to improvise during performance rather than perform her set material. She then invited Trisha Brown to join the piece, not only because of her long experience of improvisation but also because she hadn't learnt and therefore couldn't perform Rainer's choreography. Rainer then changed the name of the company to The Grand Union and announced that she was no longer its director but that it was a collective. And then she resigned from it and turned to film making. Her return to performance in 1999 could therefore have also been given the title 'the show must go on', while her two *Swan* pieces were her 'dernier spectacles'.[19]

Going on, the American way

The audience who had crammed themselves into Judson Memorial Church on October 4 1999 for the programme *Trio A Pressured* were, of course, highly reverential about the occasion of Rainer's return to dance after over twenty-five years as a film director, and excited about the opportunity to see her most famous piece in the same venue in which it had first been performed. This was very different from the atmosphere of its first performance in January 1966. Then, as I pointed out in Chapter 3, the audience were highly unsympathetic and some even walked out. *Trio A Pressured* included Pat Catterson dancing *Trio A* as a solo in retrograde while Rainer read out a long description by Vladimir Nabokov of a butterfly, and Catterson and Rainer performing a duet *Trio A* to the Chambers Brothers' 1960s hit *At the midnight hour*. A trio version in silence by Paxton, Rainer, and Douglas Dunn, who the programme suggested was taking the position that David Gordon had filled in 1966, was followed by a silent duet version by Paxton and Dunn. Paxton's performance was significantly slower and more internally motivated than that of Rainer or Dunn.

Rather than showing one fixed, canonical *Trio A*, the programme demonstrated some of the many differing ways in which it has been performed over the years. A new duet version for Rainer and Colin Beatty suggested its possibilities had still not been exhausted (Figure 8.1). Rainer was a rather gaunt, bespectacled figure having survived breast cancer – she reveals her mastectomy scar in her film *MURDER and murder* (1996) – and who had already been on stage for about half-an-hour at this point. Those who had not previously seen the piece – either performed live or on video – were by now becoming familiar with her deliberately flattened presence on stage and with the piece's minimalist vocabulary and style. This new duet gave a twist to the way the dancer's gaze is choreographed so as to avoid making eye contact with the audience. Beatty was not a trained dancer but a film maker. His task was to move around Rainer so that he was always making eye contact with her wherever the twists and turns of *Trio A* directed her gaze. With a fine sense of comic timing he would lie down and look up with nerdish intensity from just the spot on which she was about to look down. Then, picking himself up and circling rapidly round her in one direction while she herself turned in the other, he would again stop and once more meet her gaze. Even when she stared up at the ceiling, he was there, jumping up in front of her. His role thus put pressure on and drew the audience's attention towards her attempts to minimize her presence. By doing so, this duet created a knowing, complicitous relationship between audience and performer about the particular rules of this game. As we watched Rainer discover Beatty again and again looking back at her from all the previously empty spaces towards which she directed her gaze, Beatty was like an intermediary, entangling us in the audience with Rainer in the contemporary baroque way that I discussed in Chapter 7. Whereas Rainer in the 1960s had said no to seduction of the spectator by the wiles of the performer, in this new duet it was as if we were acknowledging the extent to which we cannot escape being seduced by Rainer's presence, however much she tries to avoid seducing us. This is because dancers and audiences are always already implicated in the power they may seek to oppose. In the 1970s she had complained, in her letter to Nan Piene (discussed in Chapters 5 and 7) that dance was ipso facto only about 'me' whereas she wanted to make work that 'must necessarily concern both of us' (Rainer 1974: 238). This new duet found this common ground in shared recognition of the problem of what, in previous chapters, I have been calling political disappointment. By confronting this in a more explicit way in *After Many a Summer Dies a Swan: Hybrid*, Rainer provided an artistic response to the discussion of the end of art and history developed by Carroll, Danto, and Fukuyama.

After Many a Summer Dies a Swan: Hybrid combined a video documentation of a studio performance of the dance piece Rainer made for The White Oak Dance Project with material about *fin-de-siècle* Vienna. With the gorgeously romantic chromaticism of Schoenberg's early *Verklärte*

Figure 8.1 Facing from *Trio A Pressured*. Yvonne Rainer and Colin Beatty.
Photo Christian Uhl.

Nacht (1899) as a musical background, the installation juxtaposed visual images of art and architecture from the Vienna Secession against Rainer's choreography – the latter initially only occupying small areas of the screen but gradually expanding to fill the whole frame by the end. On top of these visual images were printed a fragmentary selection of texts from and about the Vienna Secession. These included extracts from Robert Musil's unfinished novel *The Man Without Qualities*, Carl Schorske's book *Fin-de-siècle Vienna: Politics and Culture* (1981) and, in red, words by Schoenberg, Kokoschka, Loos, and Wittgenstein.[20] As an installation, this was projected on the inside of a small cubicle, around whose circular wall the image slowly rotated so that periodically the spectators had to adjust their positions to follow it.

The implications of Rainer's focus on the problem of the Viennese avant-garde are provocative. Schorske's much-admired study showed how the Emperor Frances Joseph's government used patronage of modernist art and architecture for public projects in Vienna in order to present a progressive image despite the fact that, politically, the Austro-Hungarian Empire was undemocratic, chaotically dysfunctional, and a breeding ground for fascism and anti-Semitism. Furthermore, the Viennese middle classes, denied any role at all in political life, turned their backs on the deteriorating public situation and sought refuge instead in patronage of modern art. Schorske then showed that, in the early 1900s, Loos's attacks on ornament in architecture, Schoenberg's abandonment of tonality in music, and Kokoschka's subversion of the moral and aesthetic pieties of Secession-style painting, each represented a refusal to allow a dysfunctional bourgeoisie to use their art as a panacea and thus avoid social realities.

The printed text in Rainer's installation, drawing on Schorske and others, summarized this argument. This, in itself, is not particularly controversial. The Austro-Hungarian state exemplified precisely the kind of hereditary monarchy whose political impotence, in Fukuyama's view, proves that the American model of liberal democracy is the only viable political system. For American cultural commentators, the failure of the Viennese avant-garde exemplified the exhaustion of the European cultural tradition which had been rescued and brought to a redemptive conclusion in the work of artists living in the US. However, this is not, I suggest, the reading that Rainer's work invites. The text of the video installation ends as follows:

> With the emergence of cultural modernism, history had lost its power as a source for meaning and action. / *Emmanuèle Phuon speaks* [a dancer in The White Oak Dance Project – R.B.] / In 1980 US executives made 43 times more than factory workers. / In 1988

US executives made 419 times more than factory workers. / [in red] Redeem us from our isolation!

(Rainer 2002: 128)

Rainer was, therefore, not only inviting the viewer to read the argument about *fin-de-siècle* Viennese art in relation to a performance by a contemporary US dance company; she was also drawing a parallel between Viennese politics at the end of the nineteenth century and social injustice in the US a hundred years later. Where Fukuyama argued that liberal democracy was the end of history, Rainer still found social and political inequalities a source of disappointment.

Ann Daly found her experience of viewing Rainer's installation a dispiriting one:

> If the installation suggests despair, or just her usual doubts, the avant-garde still remains an enabling ideology for Rainer. True, the avant-garde did not prevent the rise of Nazism in early 20th-century Vienna, nor did it produce the egalitarian America envisioned by the '60s counterculture. But Rainer disavows any romantic expectations of success. What matters, she reassures us in her programme note, quoting the playwright and director Richard Foreman, is to 'resist the present'.

(Daly 2002)

I began this chapter with three questions: about the shape of dance history, the end of dance, and the nature of American cultural identity. Rainer, along with some of a younger generation of dancers, has resisted the idea of a closed, concluded canon, seeing dances of the past, instead, as an unfinished archive that is still open to addition, modification, and citation. The works I have discussed in this chapter have demonstrated the difficulty of ending dance, particularly when it is used as a refuge from facing up to urgent issues of social inequality. As a European I am uncomfortable with the American question as it is one that I am least qualified to answer. Rainer's installation, I suggest, criticizes the idea of American exceptionalism in order to re-imagine how the US might otherwise be. Stanley Cavell, in an essay on *King Lear*, written in 1969 against a background of protests against the Vietnam war, argued: 'The hatred of America by its intellectuals is only their own version of patriotism' (Cavell 1976: 345). *After Many a Summer Dies a Swan: Hybrid* rehearses the same patriotic gesture as *The Judson Flag Show* version of *Trio A*. Both reminded viewers that the US was founded through a revolution which has, indeed, inspired the rest of the world. The legacy of Judson Dance Theater in Europe and the US is part of that inspiration.

Notes

1 Introduction: transatlantic crossings

1 I myself was in Montréal for the first Festival International de Nouvelle Danse. To my surprise and pleasure, I found myself staying in the same hotel as not only the other dance critics and dance scholars (attending the festival and an accompanying conference) but also most of the foreign dance companies appearing in the festival. I was in the coffee shop that evening and subsequently wrote about it in my review of the festival in *New Dance* magazine (Burt 1986). Asked in 2000, Brown did not remember meeting Bausch (Brown 2000).

2 I am grateful to Deborah Jowitt for this description: personal communication 1999.

3 For American critics on Bausch in the mid-1980s, see Langer and Sikes 1984, Tobias 1984, 1985a,b, Aloff 1984, Croce 1984, Rose 1985, and Acocella 1986.

4 For a discussion of Bausch's involvement with Feuer and Sanasardo and their piece 'Laughter After All', see Franko 2005.

5 American scholars in the fields of theatre and performance studies have been more appreciative of her work. To be fair, Kisselgoff has articulated a much more ambiguous and complex response to Bausch's work. Writing about *Kontakthof* in 1984, she observed:

> Some will object to the length of Miss Bausch's piece (it might well have ended at intermission) or to the pessimism (or realism) of her observation. Those who won't will find her rigor and devices admirable, her dancers – especially Josephine Ann Endicot – equally so.
>
> (Kisselgoff: 1984: 14)

6 Yvonne Rainer is credited with coining the phrase 'postmodern dance'. Don McDonagh uses the term in the chapter on Rainer in his 1970 book *The Rise and Fall and Rise of Modern Dance*. Michael Kirby was the first to define it in 1975 in his introduction to the 'Post modern dance issue' of *The Drama Review*. The term 'postmodern' became much more widely used in the dance world after the publication of *Terpsichore in Sneakers: Post-Modern Dance*. Although Banes used the spelling 'post-modern', I am using 'postmodern' except in quotations where Banes spelt it with a hyphen.

7 See Barthes's essay 'The death of the author' (1977: 142–8), Foucault's 'What is an author?' (1977: 113–38), Baudrillard's *Simulations* (1983). On Derrida's notion of undecidables, see *Positions* (1981), and for his notion of spectrality, *Specters of Marx* (1994).

8 See, for example, André Lepecki's edited collection *Of the Presence of the Body* (2004b) and Isabelle Ginot's discussion of Vera Mantero's work (Ginot 2003).

9 See Manning 1993, 2004.

10 See also Bürger 1984, Buchloh 1984, Huyssen 1988.

11 One possible exception to this is Carolee Schneemann, who read Simone de Beauvoir's work during her Master's degree. I discuss this further in Chapter 4.

12 Susan Foster (1986: 236) also used literary tropes including metaphor and metonymy but made different associations between choreographers and tropes.

13 Trisha Brown, Lucinda Childs, and Steve Paxton all wrote articles for *TDR* between 1973 and 1975, most of them contributing essays or interviews in Livet 1978.

14 Bausch in Hoghe 1980: 73, Brown in Stephano 1974: 21, Rainer 1999: 141–64.

15 For different sides of this argument, see Karina and Kant (2003), Guilbert (2000), Launay (1996), Preston-Dunlop (1998).

2 Cunningham, Judson, and the historical avant-garde

1 *Entr'acte* is French for interval or intermission – literally meaning between acts.

2 In his early twenties while living in Los Angeles, Cage became acquainted with Louise and Walter Arensberg, then living in Hollywood. The Arensbergs had been Duchamp's chief patrons when he first arrived in New York in 1915, and the first owners of the *Large Glass*. So Cage, who was at the time undecided as to whether to become a painter or a composer, would have seen works by Duchamp in their collection. Cage may even have met Duchamp at this time, since the latter visited the Arensbergs (see Retallack 1996: 88).

3 Simone Forti was for a time married to Morris and then to the multimedia performance artist Robert Whitman. Rainer had been married to the painter Al Held, and then lived with Morris after he separated with Forti. Deborah Hay was for a time married to the painter Alex Hay.

4 Michael Nyman has pointed out that Cage and Satie did not have identical views of furniture/furnishing music.

> For Satie, furniture music would be 'part of the noises of the environ-ment', whereas for Cage the noises of the environment are parts of his music; for Satie 'it would fill up those heavy silences that sometimes fall between friends dining together', while for Cage ambient music filled those empty silences that regularly fell between the notes of his music until about 1960.
>
> (Nyman 1973: 1229)

5 There is a short piece by Cage on Robert Rauschenberg's 'White paint-ings' written in 1953 that Rainer probably wouldn't have known in the

early 1960s, but which is nevertheless suggestively similar to her polemic in its repeated Noes:

> To whom / No subject / No image / No taste / No object / No beauty / No message / No talent / No technique (no why) / No idea / No intention / No art / No feeling / No black / No white (no *and*).
>
> (Kostelanetz 1970: 111)

6 *Cinésketch* was directed by René Clair from Picabia's idea of imitating the vitality and instantaneity of the silent cinema. The tableau vivant was based on Lucas Cranach's diptych, *Adam and Eve*. In this, Marcel Duchamp in a false beard represented Adam, naked but for a fig leaf, while Brogna Perlmutter, also naked with a fig leaf, was Eve. This work by Cranach had inspired Duchamp in 1912 when he was starting his painting of *The Bride*, whose image he used again for the bride in the upper glass panel of *The Large Glass*. Duchamp later made a sculpture called *Female Fig Leaf* (*Feuille de vigne femelle*, 1950, cast 1961). Cranach's *Adam and Eve* is one of the works that Jasper Johns used in his tracing drawings and paintings of the early 1980s, one of innumerable, usually private, references to Duchamp and his work which Johns has made throughout his career. Johns owned a cast of *Female Fig Leaf*, which he used to make an almost undetectable mark on his painting *No* (1961).

7 The progamme for the Buffalo and New York performances of *Walkaround Time* in 1968 lists 'décor: After Marcel Duchamp's *The Large Glass* in the Philadelphia Museum of Art, supervised by Jasper Johns'. There is no further information than that about the piece's links with Duchamp, and the New York Program includes a paragraph by Cunningham which, in effect, discourages any speculation about possible connections:

> Dancing has a continuity of its own that need not be dependent upon either the rise and fall of sound (music) or the pitch and cry of words (literary ideas). Its force of feeling lies in the physical image, fleeting or static. It can and does evoke all sorts of individual responses in the single spectator. These dances may be seen in this light.
>
> (Merce Cunningham Dance Company 1968b: 4)

I am grateful to David Vaughan for giving me copies of company programmes from 1968 and 1969.

8 See Crow 1996: 159 and Kotz 1990: 127.

9 Deborah Rothschild (1991) has argued that one of the most shocking things about the earlier *Parade*, for which Satie also composed the music, was this blurring of high and popular within a ballet. In their highly critical reviews, the composers George Auric and Roland Manuel (both of whom were involved in a long-running, acrimonious feud with Satie) denigrated Satie's use of well-known melodies – obscene soldiers' songs from the trenches, and songs from the nursery and from the music hall: see Harding 1972: 167 and Gillmor 1988: 251–2.

10 I am grateful to David Behrman for information about ... *for nearly an hour* .... Interview, 9 February 2000, New York. I am also grateful to David Vaughan for discussing *Walkaround Time* with me.

11 Made in 1918, it includes a magnifying glass and a pyramid, and is related to the 'oculist witness' in *The Large Glass*.

12 For a full discussion of the various performances of *Vexations*, see Bryars 1983.

13 For an account of Duchamp's reactions when Johns showed him the set for *Walkaround Time* and the circumstances through which he came to take the stage in Buffalo, see Johnston 1996: 211–12.

14 'L'homme nu' is named as Marcel Duchamp. 'La femme nue' is listed as Francisque Picabia out of concern for Perlmutter's reputation. Programme in the press book of the Ballets Suedois held in the archives of the Dansmuseet, Stockholm. I am grateful to Erik Näslundt and the staff and the Dansmuseet for their generous help.

15 The score is marked '"Danse sans musique" de la Femme' (Satie 1926: 9). For a very interesting, detailed discussion of *Relâche*, see Batson 2005.

16 See D'Emilio 1983: 40–57.

17   The idea that works of art could be created with the minimum of 'human' intervention is one of the central passions of Duchamp's career; and it is this haunting sense of human detachment ... that characterizes the work of Cunningham and company as well.

                                        (Copeland 2004: 94)

18 *498, 3rd Ave.*, made for the television station, Norddeutscher Rundfunk, Hamburg, and directed by Klaus Wildenhahn, eighty-one minutes long. I saw a video copy at the archives of the Merce Cunningham Dance Company. There is also a copy in the Dance Collection at the New York Public Library.

19 For more information about these classes, see McDonagh 1990: 46–59, Dunn 1989, and Banes 1995: 1–34. The Dunns ran these courses three times. In Autumn 1960–1 and Autumn 1961–2, in Cunningham's studio, and in Summer 1964, in Judith Dunn's studio in East Broadway, Chinatown.

20 These were Fred Herko's *Once or Twice a Week I Put on Sneakers to Go Uptown* and David Gordon's *Helen's Dance*. Rainer subsequently performed her solo *Three Satie Spoons* and a duet with Trisha Brown entitled *Satie for Two*.

21 William Davies was a member of the company 1963–4, Judith Dunn 1959–63, Barbara Dilley 1963–8, Deborah Hay 1964, Steve Paxton 1961–4, Albert Reid 1964–8, and Valda Setterfield 1961, and 1965–75.

22 Deborah Hay only joined the Merce Cunningham Company for one year, 1964, for their world tour. This was after she had made *Would They or Wouldn't They?*.

23 This agreement was between John Martin and Walter Terry. When Allen Roberston succeeded Martin at the *Times*, he didn't know about the agreement, hence his positive reviews of early concerts at Judson. However, he was soon replaced by Clive Barnes who wrote with a scathing lack of comprehension about the work at Judson. I am grateful to Don McDonagh for this information.

3   Minimalism, theory, and the dancing body

1 In this published interview, Rainer states that this concert was in January or February 1965. There was, however, a concert the three shared in January 1966 at which Rainer first presented *Trio A*. At this concert, as I will discuss in the next chapter, David Gordon received such bad press reviews that he gave up choreography for some years.

2 Fried himself subsequently acknowledged this during a panel discussion in 1987, commenting: 'Boy, was I right about art moving towards theatre! There's a sense in which everything new in art since then has happened in the space between the arts which I characterized as theatre' (Fried in Foster 1987: 84).

3 See Batchelor 1997: 71–2.

4 For Halprin's views on Todd and H'Doubler, see Halprin 1995, especially the interview with Nancy Stark Smith pp. 5–24. For a discussion of dance education in the US, see Janice Ross's *Moving Lessons* (2000).

5 Susan Foster is surely correct to point out that the connections between African-American improvised music and dance traditions and the use of improvisation by dancers associated with Judson Dance Theater have been largely overlooked (Foster 2002).

6 Rainer and Marianne Goldberg call her June Eckman (Rainer 1999: 54; Goldberg 2002: 30).

7 Forti gives the text of the song in her *Handbook in Motion* and in her 1991 interview with Ann Kilcoyne. I have identified it as *Desert Blues*, recorded by Jimmy Rodgers in 1929.

8 Rainer recalled this during a lecture she gave at the Fales Library, New York University in October 1999. Dunn himself told Don McDonagh:

> Simone was the first person I'd heard of who would say, I've brought a dance and I will *read* it to you. And it was an action not performed, it was an action that was a natural action outside the human being, it was a situation and that was her dance.
>
> (McDonagh 1990: 57)

9 Schneemann only appeared in New York performances of *Site*, which Morris also presented in Europe in the mid-1960s.

10 Hans Namuth's photographs of *Site* are not from a live performance but from a photo shoot staged at Robert Rauschenberg's studio. In these pictures she is entirely nude whereas when *Site* was performed at Judson Church, Schneemann wore paper pasted over her nipples in accordance with the church's wishes to stay within the law concerning nudity in public performance.

11 Brown attended Robert Dunn's second composition class in 1961–2 along with Yvonne Rainer, Steve Paxton, Ruth Emerson, Alex Hay, Deborah Hay, Fred Herko, Al Kurchin, Dick Levine, Gretchen MacLane, John Herbert MacDowell, Joseph Schlichter, Carol Scothorn, Elaine Summers, and occasionally David Gordon and Valda Setterfield. See Banes 1995: 19–22.

12 Brown has spoken of how important attending John Cage's lecture on 'Indeterminacy' in 1961 had been for her (Teicher 2002: 290). She also mentioned her excitement reading Alain Robbe-Grillet's essays (Goldberg 1991: 6): Susan Sontag, Barbara Rose, and Rainer herself all cited Robbe-Grillet in published essays during the 1960s.

13 When Brown remounted this solo for Mikhail Baryshnikov in 2000 for his White Oak Dance Company PASTforward show, she wrote that she gave him 'identical instructions "to enact important memories" and his material was integrated into the original dance' with a new film of him dancing his material made by Babette Mangolte (Brown 2003: 194).

14 Rainer was presumably remembering *Three Satie Spoons* and *The Bells* which she performed at the Living Theater, 31 July 1961.

15 Rainer spoke of her conversations with Steve Paxton when I interviewed her in January 2000.
16 Rainer has listed many of these in an essay about her decision to have a labanotation score made of the piece (Rainer 2005: 3–7).
17 See Judd 1975, Morris 1993, and Rose 1969.
18 Raskin has pointed out the difference between behaviourism and phenomenology: 'The behaviorist holds that the real world exists in a meaningful manner outside of our engagement with it, but as Merleau-Ponty himself wrote, "The perceived world is the always presupposed foundation of all rationality, all value and existence"' (Raskin 2004: 84, fn. 30). I am speaking of an American gestalt tradition because, although this theoretical approach was initiated in Germany in the early 1900s, the three founders, Max Wertheimer, Kurt Koffka, and Wolfgang Köhler all emigrated to the US in the 1930s and their ideas were widely taught in American universities in the 1950s.

4 Allegories of the ordinary and particular

1 This was what in the US is called a non-profit organization and in Britain a charity.
2 For a fuller discussion of Waring's work and his involvement with Judson Dance Theater, see Satin 2003.
3 Paxton told me he remembered the two of them auditioning together for work in Broadway musicals: personal interview, London, 24 February 2001.
4 There is probably more information about Herko scattered through Diane di Prima's autobiography (di Prima 2001), but she writes more about Herko as a person and little about his choreography as such.
5 Warhol may have been trying to make amends as he is reported to have said, when first informed of Herko's death that he would have filmed it if only he'd known it was going to happen: see Bockris 1989: 208.
6 As well as *Haircut* (1963), Herko was in two other Warhol films: *Thirteen Most Beautiful Boys* (1963–4) and *Roller Skate* (1963).
7 This is how di Prima remembered the piece:

> Almost everyone we'd worked with in the theater world was there that night, either dancing or in the audience. The place was full. Then the dance began and I could tell at once that almost nobody was getting it. A full-out work – I thought it was extraordinary. Oh, I could see as well as anyone the flaws, the places that needed to be cut, the technical mistakes. Or the places where it got corny: too much emotion and you had to say no in self defense. I could see all this, 'cause these were the kinds of things I'd come to recognize as necessary risks ... I saw the dance as extraordinarily brave. Mapping internal journeys no one else was looking at. But the audience didn't know what to make of it.
>
> (di Prima 2001: 392–3)

8 See Butt 1999: 115. See also Bruce Boone 1979 on O'Hara's poetry.
9 *Freddie Poems* (1966), consisting of poems dating from between 1957 and 1966. Di Prima also carried out a forty-nine-day cycle of ceremonies for Herko from the *Tibetan Book of the Dead* (di Prima 2001: 400–1).
10 Herko's review of Paul Taylor was in *Floating Bear* no. 17, and Edwin Denby's response in issue no. 19.

11 Waring, himself, choreographed a *Poet's Vaudeville*, and the many dedications to his pieces include several to old Hollywood stars.

12 The concert was early in January but the review, which was a long one and published in two parts, didn't appear until the beginning of February. Jill Johnston, who normally covered dance for the *Village Voice*, may have been out of town and missed the performance.

13 David Vaughan has printed Cunningham's plan for the dance, which he divided into ten scenes (Vaughan 1997: 105–6).

14 *Site* was first performed at a concert organized under the umbrella of the *Surplus Dance Co.* at *Stage 73*, 731 East 73rd Street, 2 and 9 March 1964. It was then performed at Judson Memorial Church in Concert #16 on 29 April 1964. Jill Johnston gave her review of *Site* and *Carnation* the title 'The object' (Johnston 1964).

15 Dunn offered his first class in autumn 1961, and his second in autumn 1962, both at the Cunningham Studio. He then had a break for a year, offering it a third time in summer 1964 in Judith Dunn's studio on East Broadway in Chinatown. His decision not to offer his class in autumn 1963 was the catalyst for the formation of the Judson Workshop.

16 Childs's shoulder was the subject of Warhol's film *Shoulder*, and she was also one of the *Thirteen Most Beautiful Women*, both 1964.

17 Paxton had previously used photo scores for *English* (1963): performers were given these and told to develop movements from the photographs, which they then showed to Paxton. He, himself, recalls that the scores 'had to do with me not being the person to transmit the material . . . so that I didn't become the model for their performance or dictator' (cited in Bear 1975: 28).

18 It was under the name Judson Dance Theater that a group of artists, musicians, and dancers, who formed a cooperative workshop in the autumn of 1962, presented concerts at the Judson Memorial Church (see Banes 1993: xiii). After the very successful first concert of dance at the church, Robert Dunn decided that he would no longer offer his composition class, and the dancers formed the workshop to continue meeting and working together. Initially meeting in James Waring's studio, they were offered the use of the gym at the church.

19 Schneemann suggested this in an interview with the author, New Paltz, summer 2000.

20 Schneemann told Rebecca Schneider that she had shown *Eye Body* in her own loft. When Alan Soloman, director of the Jewish Museum (where 'Primary Structures', the first major exhibition of minimal art was shown), saw them, he said: 'If you want to paint, paint. If you want to run around naked, you don't belong in the art world' (Schneider 1997: 37–8).

21 See Lippard 1976: 121–38, Parker and Pollock 1981: 114–33.

5 Before and after 1968

1 Writing about Anna Halprin's work during the 1960s, Janice Ross states:

> While the New Left was aggressively seeking massive social change (the withdrawal of the American armed forces from Vietnam and an end to the draft), cultural activists like Halprin dreamed of effecting more modest cultural changes in the frontiers of the performing arts rather than in American society at large.
>
> (Ross 2003: 28)

I am arguing that for Rainer and other dancers in New York, pushing back the frontiers of the performing arts was connected with a dream of social and political regeneration (albeit a naive one). Ross does go on to cite a few correspondences between Halprin's practice and radical politics.

2 For example, Foucault wrote about Raymond Roussel, Magritte, and Manet; Derrida wrote about Mallarmé and Artaud; Kristeva wrote about avant-garde poetry; Deleuze wrote about Francis Bacon.

3 See Johnston 1983: 129, 146–7.

4 As well as Rainer's many writings to which I have already referred which in previous chapters, Trisha Brown, Lucinda Childs, David Gordon, and Steve Paxton all wrote articles for *TDR* between 1973 and 1975, most of them contributing essays or interviews in Livet 1978.

5 I'm grateful to Susan Manning for first drawing this passage to my attention.

6 Francis Frascina discusses 'Angry Arts Week' in some detail in his book *Art Politics and Dissent* but doesn't mention any of the dancers involved in it. See Frascina 1999.

7 Phoebe Neville implied to me that there was a certain resistance to new-comers among the original group. Personal communication May 1999.

8 This connection was the starting point for Dusan Makavejev's scandalously popular 1971 film *WR Mysteries of the Organism*. For a discussion of radical, countercultural politics in the US during the 1960s, see James Miller's *Democracy in the Streets* (Miller 1987).

9 Solomons is not mentioned at all in Sally Banes's account of Dunn's classes in *Democracy's Body*. He was a member of *Studio 9*, formed by members and ex-members of the Tamiris-Nagrin modern dance company which Monk, Neville, and King subsequently joined (see McDonagh 1990: 102). He may have gone along with them to Dunn's class in 1964.

10 Baraka reviewed a concert by James Waring at the Henry Street Playhouse in the 19th issue of *The Floating Bear* (di Prima 1974: 215–16).

11 Diane di Prima, reviewing the concert in *The Floating Bear*, noted 'It was some of Cecil's very exciting playing, and after a while the dance started to work with it, and the whole thing turned into something marvelous and unexpected' (di Prima 1974: 239).

12 Norman Mailer coined this title in an essay 'The white negro: superficial reflections on the hipster', originally published in *Dissent* in 1956.

13 She had just returned from Italy where, being bilingual in Italian and English, she had been a central figure in planning the Rome Festival of Music, Dance, Explosion and Flight. During this the artist David Bradshaw had organized a performance that involved killing fish in a pond with dynamite. Hardly surprisingly, this seems to have particularly shocked her (Forti 1974: 100–2). It was immediately on her return from Italy that she took the drug LSD for the first time, went to the Woodstock Festival and then spent a year in a psychedelic commune.

14 I discussed this in Burt 1998.

15 Ringgold and Wallace both appeared in Rainer's 1990 film *Privilege*. (I referred to this panel in Chapter 2).

6 Repetition

1 Strictly speaking, Goldberg is wrong here. The phrase 'the house that Jack built' always comes at the end of each sentence. Each line of the nursery

rhyme accumulates in reverse order: (0) This is (8) the man all tattered and torn that kissed (7) the maiden all forlorn that milked (6) the cow with the crumpled horn that tossed (5) the dog that worried (4) the cat that killed (3) the rat that ate (2) the malt that lay in (1) the house that Jack built.

2 Banes wrote in 1987: 'But if we were to call sixties and seventies postmodern dance *postmodern* and dub eighties new dance *post-modernist*, the confusion would not be worth the scrupulous accuracy' (1987: xv).

3 Brown told Marianne Goldberg about her strong feelings of recognition when she first read Robbe-Grillet's essay 'Towards a new novel': see Goldberg 1991: 6. Rainer discussed the same essay in her 1967 essay on Morris and Warhol: see Rainer 1967.

4 See Valerie Briginshaw's (2001) discussion of Ellis Island.

5 For example: Krauss, 'Notes on the index' (Krauss 1986: 196–220); Owens, 'The allegorical impulse' (Owens 1992: 52–87); and Fineman (1980) – all of which were initially published in *October*. For further discussions of allegory or metonymy at the time, see Baudrillard 'Metamorphosis, metaphor, metastasis' (Baudrillard 1988: 45–56); and Orton (1994) *Figuring Jasper Johns*. Paul De Man's essay 'The rhetoric of temporality' (De Man 1983: 187–228) also influenced thinking about the difference between allegory and symbolism, metaphor and metonymy.

6 The talking also functions as music in that it gives the audience something relatively easy to listen to while they watch, whereas silent dances or dances with 'difficult' modern music tend to make audiences uncomfortable. The first two composers with whom Brown chose to work – Robert Ashley and Laurie Anderson – both used words as music.

7 Norbert Servos records that the original version of *Café Müller* was only thirty minutes long, part of an evening of the same name with three other parts made by guest choreographers Gerhard Bohner, Gigi-Gheorge Caciuléanu and Hans Pop (then a member of Bausch's company). He says that the present version is not substantially different, only longer. See Servos 1984: 107 and 243.

8 I saw this piece at the first F.I.N.D in Montréal in 1985, but my memory of it has been helped by viewing the recent video version of the piece. My description, however, refers to the live version.

9 For example, De Keersmaeker told Jill Johnston in 1988 that she was bored with feminist questions about her work. Johnston recorded that 'she says she's definitely not a feminist, but that she cannot deny being a woman, therefore (she implies) her gestures will naturally be feminine ones' (Johnston 1994b: 134). This comes in a long review of De Keersmaeker's work that Johnston wrote for *Art In America*, having recently returned to art and dance criticism after a decade of deep involvement in radical feminist politics.

7 Traces of intimacy and relationless relations

1 Brown did, however, dance in group works during the 1980s.

2 I saw this shared programme at The Place Theatre, London in April 2002. It consisted of *private room* (Stuart), *Starfucker* (Etchells), *Down Time* (Etchells), *I'm all yours* (Stuart), and *soft wear* (Stuart).

3 Etchells is someone who, while not primarily concerned with dance as such, has nevertheless worked with dancers, and written about this. In some ways,

therefore, his position in relation to the dance of the 1990s and 2000s is comparable to that occupied by Robert Morris and Carolee Schneemann in relation to the new dance of the 1960s, discussed in Chapters 3 and 4.

4 I interviewed Ruckert about his work in May 2001, and then subsequently took part in his research project *Love University* during the 2002 Nottdance Festival in Nottingham.

5 See, however, Richard Rorty's critique of this tradition in his 1980 book *Philosophy and the Mirror of Nature.*

6 Anderson, who has been making work for over twenty years, has two companies, the Cholmondeleys who are all women and the all-male Featherstonehaughs, but sometimes makes pieces for both companies together.

7 In his 1917 essay, 'Mourning and melancholia', Freud wrote: 'So we perceive that the self-reproaches are reproaches against a loved object which have been shifted away from it on to the patient's own ego' (Freud 1984: 257).

8 Deborah Jowitt, writing in the *Village Voice,* says Bausch was behind the scrim, not in front of it. The two times I saw the performance at the Brooklyn Academy of Music in November 1999, I was too far away to tell.

9 A large tank of goldfish is part of the set of *Two Cigarettes in the Dark* (1985) into which one of the dancers duly dives for a swim. In *Nelken* (Carnations) (1982) a man tells a story about training his pet fish to live on land, but it dies when he returns it to the water. Norbert Servos used this story as a symbol for *tanztheater* in his 1984 book on Bausch, whose subtitle is 'The art of training a goldfish'. Fish out of water, he points out, are a recurring motif in Bausch's work. The process of civilization, he suggests, is like this, leaving people high and dry in an alien environment (Servos 1984: 25). Anna Kisselgoff has suggested that, in *Danzon,* dancing with the giant projected fish is an acknowledgement that the human is only part of the universe, not its centre (Kisselgoff 1999).

10 As Barbara Kruger concisely puts it, 'her no-nonsense but nonsensical voice-over . . . holds court over much of the proceedings' (Kruger 1986: 124).

11 Rainer admits this in her wonderfully titled essay 'Some ruminations around cinematic antidotes to the Oedipal net(tles) while playing with de Lauraedipus Mulvey or, he may be off-screen but . . .' (Rainer 1999: 214–23).

12 Brown danced publicly for what she said was the last time in April 2005.

13 *Contact Quarterly* is an unusual publication in that it started off in the 1970s as a newsletter between people who attended or taught contact improvisation workshops and who therefore nearly all knew its editors, Paxton and Nancy Stark Smith, and many of its contributors and subscribers. Even today it seems as if everyone who writes for it or reads it knows one another.

8 The Judson tradition at the start of a new century

1 The cast for these performances was: Dominique Brun, Anne Collod, Simon Hecquet, Christophe Wavelet, Martha Moore, Alain Buffard, Matthieu Doze, Xavier Le Roy, Emmanuelle Huynh. In 1994 the group performed forgotten pieces by Humphrey and Jooss from labanotation, and in 2000 used the labanotation version of Nijinsky's score to remember three historical versions of *L'Après midi d'un faune* in a piece titled ... *d'un Faune (éclats).*

2 Consider two very different points of view. Sandra Aberkalns, reviewing a performance in 2001 at the Kitchen in New York of the French choreographer Boris Charmatz's 1996 piece *Herses (Une lente introduction)* wrote:

it started nowhere, didn't go anywhere, and the contact work between the dancers was what was in vogue here in the US 20 to 30 years ago (i.e. been there, done that). It was slow, and boring, because there was nothing to stimulate me emotionally, intellectually, or kinetically.

(Aberkalms 2001)

André Lepecki (1999) took the opposite point of view, arguing that radical European choreographers had left their US colleagues far behind.

3 Hegel announced the end of history after Napoleon won the Battle of Jena in 1806. In his *Aesthetics*, he wrote that:

Art, considered in its highest vocation, is and remains for us a thing of the past. Thereby it has lost for us genuine truth and life, and has rather been transferred into our ideas instead of maintaining its earlier necessity in reality and occupying its higher place.

(Hegel 1975: 11)

4 Relevant in this context is her initiation of a project to create a labanotation score of *Trio A*. See Rainer 2005.

5 Susan Foster takes a different view of Tharp's position in relation to the work of Monk and of the Grand Union in her 1985 essay 'The signifying body'.

6 It is also shown in Rainer's film *Lives of the Performers*, 1972.

7 These choreographers' statements from the *PASTForward* programme were reprinted in Banes 2003.

8 *Overture to the Matter* might seem an odd choice, being so much later than the Judson period. Baryshnikov knew it from film footage shown at the end of the PBS television documentary *Beyond the Mainstream* (Brockway 1980).

9 This is how long it took when I saw Paxton dance it at a Dartington International Dance Festival in the early 1980s.

10 Personal communication, Steve Paxton, 2001.

11 Personal communication, Nancy Duncan, 2001.

12 Rainer made a similar statement in her programme note for *PASTForward*: 'More people will see my choreography during this brief tour than ever saw my entire oeuvre from 1960–1975' (Rainer 2003: 208).

13 Lepecki draws attention to a manifesto that Christophe Wavelet together with Bel, Le Roy, and a number of other dancers drew up at a meeting at the *Tanzquartier* in Vienna in 2001 which includes 'We consider dialogue, thinking, research and making as equal constituents of our labour. These activities are not only the search engine for our art and related practices, but also for our societies, for our cultures'. See www.freietheater.at/kulturpoltik/020702.htm.

14 See the video 'Fall after Newton: Contact improvisation 1972–1983' (Paxton: 1987).

15 When they first made the piece, Charmatz was nineteen and Chamblas, seventeen.

16 See Ploebst 2001: 182–3.

17 Email communication, 21 May 2002.

18 At the time of writing I have only heard and read about this work but not seen it myself. Paxton performed his improvised piece to Gould's recordings of Bach's Goldberg Variations between 1986 and 1992. See Burt 2002.

19 At the time of going to press in March 2006, Rainer was working on a new piece which cited Balanchine's *Agon* (1957), fragmenting and reworking it for four female dancers.

20 For the full text and credits see Rainer 2004.

Bibliography

Aberkalms, Sandra. 2001. 'Nada from naked means', *Flash Review* 3, (25 April): www.danceinsider.com/f2001/f425_3.html [accessed 28 March 2002].

Acocella, Joan. 1986. 'Pina Bausch Tanztheater Wuppertal', *Dance Magazine* 60, (March): 20–3.

Adair, Christy. 1996. 'Rebellion against stereotype: Christy Adair talks to Trisha Brown', *Dance Theatre Journal* 13(2) (Autumn/Winter): 50–1.

Albright, Ann Cooper. 1997. *Choreographing Difference: The Body and Identity in Contemporary Dance*. Hanover, NH: Wesleyan/New England Press.

Alexander, Elena. 1998. *Footnotes: Six Choreographers Inscribe the Page*. Amsterdam: G&B Arts International.

Aloff, Mindy. 1984. 'Wuppertaler Tanztheater', *The Nation* 239 (1 Sept.): 156.

Althusser, Louis. 1984. 'Ideology and ideological state apparatuses: notes towards an investigation', in *Essays on Ideology*. London: Verso: 1–60.

Anderson, Jack. 1966. 'Yvonne Rainer, David Gordon, Steve Paxton: Judson Memorial Church January 10, 11, 12, 1966', *Dance Magazine* (March): 30.

Auslander, Philip. 1997. *From Acting to Performance: Essays on Modernism and Postmodernism*. London and New York: Routledge.

Bal, Mieke. 1999. *Quoting Caravaggio: Contemporary Art, Preposterous History*. Chicago, IL and London: Chicago University Press.

Banes, Sally. 1977. 'An interview with David Gordon', *Eddy* 9 (Winter): 17–25.

—— 1980. *Terpsichore in Sneakers: Post-Modern Dance* [First edn]. Boston, MA: Houghton Mifflin.

—— 1987. *Terpsichore in Sneakers: Post-Modern Dance* [Revised second edn]. Middletown: CT: Wesleyan University Press.

—— 1993. *Greenwich Village 1963: Avant-Garde Performance and the Effervescent Body*. Durham, NC and London: Duke University Press.

—— 1994. *Writing Dancing in the Age of Postmodernism*. Hanover, NH and London: Wesleyan University Press.

—— 1995. *Democracy's Body: Judson Dance Theater 1962–1964*. Durham, NC and London: Duke University Press.

—— 1998. *Dancing Women: Female Bodies on Stage*. London and New York: Routledge.

—— 2003. *Reinventing Dance in the 1960s: Everything Was Possible*. Madison, WI: University of Wisconsin Press.

—— with Carroll, Noel. 1994. 'Cunningham and Duchamp', in Sally Banes *Writing Dancing in the Age of Postmodernism*. Hanover, NH and London: Wesleyan University Press: 109–18.

—— 1998. *Dancing Women: Female Bodies on Stage*. London and New York: Routledge.

Baraka, Amiri. 1995. *Blues People*. Edinburgh: Payback Press.

—— 1997. *The Autobiography of LeRoi Jones*. Chicago, IL: Lawrence Hill Books.

Barnes, Clive. 1967. 'Dance: recital used to protest war', *New York Times*, 31 January.

Barthes, Roland. 1977. *Image-Music-Text*. Glasgow: Fontana.

Baryshnikov, Mikhail. 2003. 'Foreword', in Sally Banes ed. *Reinventing Dance in the 1960s: Everything Was Possible*. Madison, WI: University of Wisconsin Press: ix–xi.

Batchelor, David. 1997. *Minimalism*. London: Tate Gallery Publishing.

Batson, Charles. 2005. *Dance Desire and Anxiety in Early Twentieth-Century French Theater: Playing Identities*. London: Ashgate.

Baudrillard, Jean. 1983. *Simulations*. New York: Semiotext(e).

—— 1988. *The Ecstasy of Communication*. New York: Semiotext(e).

Bear, Liza. 1975. 'Steve Paxton: like the famous tree. . .', *Avalanche* 11 (Summer): 26–30.

—— 1997. 'Meredith Monk: invocation/evocation – a dialogue with Liza Bear', in Deborah Jowitt ed. *Meredith Monk*. Baltimore, MD and London: Johns Hopkins University Press: 79–93.

—— and Sharp, Willoughby. 1972. 'The performer as persona: an interview with Yvonne Rainer', *Avalanche* 5 (Summer): 46–59.

Behrman, David. 1965. 'What indeterminate notation means', *Perspectives of New Music* (Spring–Summer): 58–73.

Benjamin, Walter. 1973. *Illuminations*. Glasgow: Fontana.

Benoit, Agnès. 1997. *On the Edge/Createurs de l'imprevu*. Brussells: Contredanse.

Berger, John. 1980. *About Looking*. London: Writers and Readers.

Birringer, Johannes. 1986. 'Pina Bausch: dancing across borders', *TDR* 30(2) T110 (Summer): 85–97.

Blanchot, Maurice. 1971. *L'amitié*. Paris: Gallimard.

Bockris, Steven. 1989. *The Life and Death of Andy Warhol*. New York: Bantam Books.

Boone, Bruce. 1979. 'Gay language as political praxis: the poetry of Frank O'Hara', *Social Text* 1.

Briginshaw, Valerie A. 2001. *Dance, Space and Subjectivity*. Basingstoke: Palgrave.

Brockway, Merrill. 1980. *Beyond the Mainstream*, video recording/WNET/ Thirteen; directed by Merrill Brockway; produced by Merrill Brockway and Carl Charlson.

Brown, Carolyn, Dunn, Douglas, Farber, Viola, *et al.* 1992. 'Cunningham and his dancers', in Richard Kostelanetz ed. *Merce Cunningham: Dancing in Space and Time*. London: Dance Books.

Brown, Trisha. 1975. 'Three pieces', *TDR* 19 T-65, (March): 26–32.

—— 1978. 'Trisha Brown: an interview', in Anne Livet ed. *Contemporary Dance.* New York: Abbeville: 44–54.

—— 1996. *Interview*, video recording; produced and directed by Douglas Rosenberg. Oregon, WI: ADF.

—— 1998. *Trisha Brown: danse, précis de liberté.* Marseilles: Musée de Marseilles – Réunion des musées nationaux.

—— 2000. Personal interview, Ramsay Burt, London, 2 November.

—— 2003. 'Pastforward statement', in Sally Banes ed. *Reinventing Dance in the 1960s: Everything Was Possible.* Madison, WI: University of Wisconsin Press: 194–6.

Brunel, Lise. 1987. *Trisha Brown.* Paris: Éditions Bougé.

Bryars, Gavin. 1983. '*Vexations* and its performers', *Contact* no. 26 (Spring): 12–20.

Buchloh, Benjamin. 1984. 'Theorizing the avant-garde', *Art in America* (November): 19–21.

Bullivant, Keith and Rice, Jane. 1995. 'Reconstruction and integration: the culture of West German stabilisation 1945–1968', in Rob Burns ed. *German Cultural Studies.* Oxford: Oxford University Press: 209–57.

Bürger, Peter. 1984. *Theory of the Avant-garde.* Minneapolis, MN: University of Minnesota Press.

Burt, Ramsay. 1986. 'New dance in Canada', *New Dance* 35 (January): 14–17.

—— 1998. *Alien Bodies: Representations of Modernity, 'Race', and Nation in Early Modern Dance.* London: Routledge.

—— 2002. 'Steve Paxton's Goldberg Variations and the Angel of History', in *TDR* 46(4) T-176 (Winter): 46–64.

Buskirk, Martha and Nixon, Mignon. 1996. *The Duchamp Effect.* Cambridge, MA and London: MIT Press.

Butler, Judith. 1993. *Bodies That Matter.* New York and London: Routledge.

—— 1997a. *Excitable Speech.* New York and London: Routledge.

—— 1997b. *The Psychic Life of Power.* Stanford, CA: Stanford University Press.

Butt, Gavin. 1999. 'The greatest homosexual? Camp pleasure and the performing body of Larry Rivers', in Amelia Jones and Andrew Stephenson eds *Performing the Body/Performing the Text.* London and New York: Routledge: 107–26.

Cage, John. 1961. *Silence: Lectures and Writings.* Hanover, NH: Wesleyan University Press.

Carmines, Al. 1967. 'In the congregation of art', *Dance Scope* 41: 25–31.

Carroll, Noël. 1981. 'Post-modern dance and expression', in Gordon Fancher and Gerald Myers eds *Philosophical Essays on Dance.* Brooklyn, NY: Dance Horizons: 95–103.

—— 2003. 'Art history, dance, and the 1960s', in Sally Banes ed. *Reinventing Dance in the 1960s: Everything Was Possible.* Madison, WI: University of Wisconsin Press: 81–97.

Cavarero, Adriana. 2000. *Relating Narratives: Storytelling and Selfhood.* London and New York: Routledge.

Cavell, Stanley. 1976. *Must We Mean What We Say?* Cambridge: Cambridge University Press.

Chave, Anna C. 2000. 'Minimalism and biography', *Art Bulletin*, March, LXXXIII: 149–63.

Childs, Lucinda. 2003. 'Pastforward statement', in Sally Banes ed. *Reinventing Dance in the 1960s: Everything Was Possible*. Madison, WI: University of Wisconsin Press: 197–8.

Chipp, Herschell B. 1968. *Theories of Modern Art: A Source Book by Artists and Critics*. Berkeley, CA: University of California Press.

Cohen, Marshall. 1981. 'Primitivism, modernism and dance theory', in Gordon Fancher and Gerald Myers eds *Philosophical Essays on Dance*. Brooklyn, NY: Dance Horizons: 138–54.

Cook, David. 2001. 'Questions of ownership echo in Leipzig', *Dance Magazine*, April: 72–3.

Copeland, Roger. 1983. 'Postmodern dance, postmodern architecture, post-modernism', *Performing Arts Journal* 7(1): 27–43.

—— 1985. 'Theatrical dance: how do we know it when we see it if we can't define it', *Performing Arts Journal* 9(2/3): 174–84.

—— 2004. *Merce Cunningham: The Modernizing of Modern Dance*. New York: Routledge.

Critchley, Simon. 1997. *Very Little . . . Almost Nothing: Death, Philosophy, Literature*. London and New York: Routledge.

—— 1999. *Ethics – Politics – Subjectivity: Essays on Derrida, Leivnas and Contemporary French Thought*. London and New York: Verso.

Croce, Arlene. 1984. 'Dance Theatre of Wuppertal', *The New Yorker*, v60 (16 July): 81–5.

Crow, Thomas. 1996. *The Rise of the Sixties*. London: Weidenfeld & Nicolson.

Cunningham, Merce. 1985. *The Dancer and the Dance/Merce Cunningham in Conversation with Jacqueline Lesschaeve*. New York: M. Boyars.

Dalva, Nancy. 1992. 'The way of Merce', in Richard Kostelanetz ed. *Merce Cunningham: Dancing in Time and Space*. London: Dance Books: 179–86.

Daly, Ann. 1986. 'Tanztheater: the thrill of the lynch mob or the rage of a woman', *The Drama Review* 302, T110, (Summer): 46–56.

—— 2002. 'The hybrid Yvonne Rainer: avant-garde aesthete, utopian activist', *The Chronicle of Higher Education*, (22 November), www.anndaly.com/articles/rainer.html [accessed 24 June 2005].

Danto, Arthur. 1997. *The End of Art: Contemporary Art and the Pale of History*, Princeton, NJ: Princeton University Press.

De Keersmaeker, Anne Theresa. 1981. 'Valeska Gert', *TDR* 25(3) T-91 (Fall): 55–67.

—— 1983. 'Programme statement', from www.rosas.be.

Deleuze, Gilles. 1993. *The Fold: Leibniz and the Baroque*. London: Athlone Press.

—— 1994. *Difference and Repetition*. London: Athlone Press.

D'Emilio, John. 1983. *Sexual Politics, Sexual Communities: The Making of a Homosexual Minority in the United States 1940–1970*. Chicago, IL and London: The University of Chicago Press.

Derrida, Jacques. 1981. *Positions*. London: Athlone Press.

——. 1994. *Specters of Marx*. New York and London: Routledge.

——. 1997. *Politics of Friendship*. London: Verso.

di Prima, Diane. 2001. *Recollections of My Life as a Woman: The New York Years.* New York: Viking.

—— with Jones, LeRoi. 1974. *The Floating Bear.* La Jolla, CA: L. McGilvery Press.

Duchamp, Marcel. 1973. 'The creative act', in Gregory Battcock ed. *The New Art: A Critical Anthology.* New York: E.P. Dutton & Co.: 46–8.

Duncan, Isadora. 1983. 'I see America dancing', in Roger Copeland and Marshall Cohen eds *What Is Dance?* Oxford: Oxford University Press: 264–5.

Dunn, Robert Ellis. 1989. 'Judson days', *Contact Quarterly* 141 (Winter): 9–13.

Duve, Thierry de. 1990. 'The monochrome and the blank canvas', in Serge Guilbaut ed. *Reconstructing Modernism: Art in New York, Paris, and Montreal 1945–64.* Cambridge, MA: MIT Press: 244–310.

Dyer, Richard. 1987. 'Judy Garland and gay men', in *Heavenly Bodies: Film Stars and Society.* Basingstoke: BFI/Macmillan: 141–94.

—— 1992. 'It's being so camp as keeps us going', *Only Entertainment.* London & New York: Routledge.

Endicott, Jo Ann. 1999. *Je suis une femme respectable.* Paris: L'Arché.

Fineman, Joel. 1980. 'The structure of allegorical desire', *October* 8 (Spring): 42–70.

Flam, Jack. 1996. 'Introduction: Reading Robert Smithson', in Jack Flam ed. *Robert Smithson: The Collected Writings.* Berkeley, CA: University of California Press: xiii–xxv.

Forti, Simone. 1974. *Handbook in Motion.* Halifax, NS: The Press of Novia Scotia College of Art and Design.

—— 1993. *Art Archives: Simone Forti.* Exeter: The Arts Documentation Unit, University of Exeter.

Foster, Hal. 1987. *Discussions in Contemporary Culture.* Seattle, WA: Bay Press.

—— 1994. 'What's Neo about the Neo-Avant-Garde?', *October* 70: 5–32.

Foster, Susan Leigh. 1986. *Reading Dancing.* Berkeley, CA: University of California Press.

—— 2001. 'PastFORWARD and rewind', *Dance Theatre Journal* 17(2): 22–4.

—— 2002. *Dances that Describe Themselves: The Improvised Dances of Richard Bull.* Hanover, NH and London: Wesleyan University Press.

Foucault, Michel. 1977. 'What is an author?', in *Language, Countermemory, Practice: Selected Essays and Interviews.* Ithaca, NY: Cornell University Press: 113–68.

Franko, Mark. 1993. *Dance as Text: Ideologies of the Baroque Body*, Cambridge: Cambridge University Press.

—— 2005. *Excursion for Miracles: Paul Sanasardo, Donya Feuer and Studio for Dance (1955–1964).* Hanover, NH: Wesleyan/New England Press.

Frascina, Francis. 1999. *Art, Politics, and Dissent: Aspects of the Art Left in Sixties America.* Manchester: Manchester University Press.

Freud, Sigmund. 1984. *On Metaphysics: The Theory of Psychoanalysis.* Harmondsworth: Penguin.

Fried, Michael. 1969. 'Art and objecthood', in Gregory Battcock ed. *Minimal Art: A Critical Anthology.* London: Studio Vista: 116–47.

Fukuyama, Francis. 1992. *The End of History and the Last Man.* London: Hamish Hamilton.

Gere, David. 2001. '29 effeminate gestures: choreographer Joe Goode and the heroics of effeminacy', in Jane Desmond ed. *Dancing Desires: Choreographing Sexualities On and Off Stage.* Madison, WI: Wisconsin University Press: 349–84.

Gillmor, Alan M. 1988. *Erik Satie.* London: Macmillan.

Ginot, Isabelle. 2003. 'Dis-identifying: dancing bodies and analysing eyes at work. A disussion of Vera Mantero's *a mysterious thing said e.e. cummings*', *Discourses in Dance* 2(1): 23–34.

Goldberg, Marianne. 1986. 'Trisha Brown: all of the person's person', *TDR* 30(1) T-109 (Spring): 149–70.

—— 1991. 'Trisha Brown's Accumulations', *Dance Theatre Journal* 9(2) (Autumn): 4–7, 39.

—— 2002. 'Trisha Brown, US dance, visual arts: composing structure', in Hendel Teicher ed. *Trisha Brown: Dance and Art in Dialogue, 1961–2001.* Cambridge, MA: MIT Press: 29–46.

Goldberg, Roselee. 'Performance: the art of notation', *Studio International* 192, (July 1976): 54–8.

Goodeve, Thyrza. 1997. 'Rainer talking pictures', *Art in America* 857 (July): 56–63.

Gordon, David. 1975. 'It's about time', *TDR* 19(1) T-65 (March): 43–52.

Gottschild, Brenda Dixon. 2005. 'By George! Oh Balanchine!', *Discourses in Dance* 3(1): 12–17.

Graham, Martha. 1991. *Blood Memories: An Autobiography.* London: Sceptre Books.

Greenberg, Clement. 1982. 'Modernist painting' [1960/65], in Francis Frascina and Charles Harrison eds *Modern Art and Modernism: A Critical Anthology.* London: Harper & Row: 5–19.

Guilbaut, Serge. 1985. 'The new adventures of the avant-garde in America', in Francis Frascina ed. *Pollock and After: The Critical Debate.* London: Harper & Row: 153–66.

Guilbert, Laure. 2000. *Danser avec le IIIe Reich: les danseurs modernes sous le nazisme.* Paris: Complexe.

Halprin, Anna. 1995. *Moving Toward Life: Five Decades of Transformational Dance.* Hanover, NH and London: Wesleyan University Press.

Harding, James. 1972. *The Ox on the Roof: Scenes from Musical Life in Paris in the Twenties.* London: Macdonald.

Harrison, Charles and Wood, Paul. 1992. *Art in Theory 1900–1990: An Anthology of Changing Ideas.* Oxford: Blackwell.

Hegel, Georg Wilhelm Friedrich. 1975. *Aesthetics: Lectures on Fine Art.* Oxford: Clarendon Press.

Hoghe, Raimund. 1980. 'The theatre of Pina Bausch', *TDR* 24(1) T-85 (March): 63–74.

Hughes, Alan. 1962. 'Dance program seen at church', *New York Times* (7 July): 42.

Humphrey, Doris. 1959. *The Art of Making Dances.* New York: Grove Press.

Huyssen, Andreas. 1986. *After the Great Divide: Modernism, Mass Culture and Postmodernism.* Basingstoke: Macmillan.

Jackson, Naomi. 2000. *Converging Movements: Modern Dance and Jewish Culture at the 92nd Street Y.* London and Hanover, NH: University Press of New England.